TERRORIST HUNTER

The Extraordinary Story of a Woman Who
Went Undercover to Infiltrate the Radical
Islamic Groups Operating in America

An Imprint of HarperCollins*Publishers*

TERRORIST
HUNTER

Anonymous

HarperCollins books may be purchased for educational, business, or sales promotional use. For information please write: Special Markets Department, HarperCollins Publishers Inc., 10 East 53rd Street, New York, NY 10022.

FIRST EDITION

Designed by Cassandra J. Pappas

Library of Congress Cataloging-in-Publication Data has been applied for.

ISBN 0-06-052819-2

03   04   05   06   07   BVG/RRD   10   9   8   7   6   5   4   3   2   1

To Mama and Baba

This is a true story. It is true as I remember it, and as scores of documents and affidavits and audio- and videotapes reinforce my recollections.

Some identifying details about some of the characters and events have been altered to enhance the participants' safety and to make sure no current investigations will be jeopardized.

When a full name of a person or a place is mentioned, it is the real name. Whenever only a first name is provided, it may not be the actual name of the character.

Otherwise, resemblance to any living persons is purely intentional.

Contents

TERRORIST HUNTER

Escape

THE CHILDREN WALK UP on the stage, one by one, and they seem so cute in their reds, greens, and whites. Looks as if this skit is going to be less menacing than some of the other events at the conference. Maybe it's even going to be entertaining. I need the change. I feel that I can't deal with any more serious stuff, not now, not this evening, and I'm grateful for the levity. It's been a very long day. It's been three very long days, and I am tired.

The children's performance is part of the conference's closing ceremonies. As they do every year, the organizers have scheduled the three-day event again at Thanksgiving. Yes, I have to work, but this time I refused to give up the holiday weekend with my family—at least the evenings. So we're all here, together, in one hotel room. Four days ago my husband Leo, our three kids, and I made the trip from New York to Chicago in our old minivan. It took us thirteen hours. I didn't want to fly, anyway. I hate flying. Although my OB/GYN told me that it was perfectly safe to do so at this stage of my pregnancy, I felt more comfortable traveling by car. And even though Leo and the kids are not with me most of the day, having them near gives me a sense of confidence.

Each morning I rise early in our hotel room to prepare for the day. I have to do this because it takes me almost an hour to dress. Although I've been donning these Muslim robes—my disguise—as often as twice a week for quite some time now, the ensemble is still uncomfortable, cumbersome, and difficult to put together. I fight the desire to stay in bed, my body screaming, *Sleep!* as my unborn daughter consumes more and more of my energy.

Instead, I wash my face and begin dressing for this last day. Now that I'm so weary, I have to be twice as careful to put the robes on properly, to pay extra attention to the details that make this costume authentic and me inconspicuous. I know that I look like them, talk like them, and even think like them. But one slip-up, one wrong word, and I could be risking everything.

And then there's the recording equipment. The more sophisticated and miniaturized it becomes, the more complex and difficult it is to set up, and in my condition the only way I can conceal the gadgets beneath my robes is by fastening them directly under my large belly. The wires press on my abdomen, making the apparatus even more uncomfortable, but they must be like that. They secure the recorder, which mustn't fall, mustn't move. I wake Leo, put the finishing touches to my getup, and head downstairs. Leo comes a few minutes later and separately we make our way to our van, parked at the distant end of the parking lot, and he drives me to the Ramada Plaza hotel in the Chicago suburbs, scene of this year's events.

There's a lot going on in all the rooms the conference occupies. The usual stuff, jihad, martyrdom, "Death to Jews," the all-so-familiar-to-me hate speeches. But on this day, something extraordinary happens. As I'm sitting in the overcrowded hall, I hear a sudden commotion from the left, where the men are seated. We women and children are crammed in the right side of the large room, separated from the men, as is custom. Someone over on the left shrieks, "You are not a Brother! Get out!" I am too scared to even turn my head. Some more noises follow, then an argument, sounds of a fight, many angry voices, the moving around of objects, and silence. I still do not dare to raise my head and look. A Muslim woman should never be so vain as to stick her nose into men's affairs. Besides, this couldn't have been one of my people. I'm on my own at this conference. Possibly it was a journalist, because I hear a man hiss the word *recorder.* Whoever the interloper was, I hope he wasn't seriously hurt. Under my veil, I am paler than Snow White.

I hear raised voices again. Someone shouts, "The insolence! Who do they think they are? The next one we find we'll tear apart! No recording in this hall, everyone! We mean that!" My heart is beating fast, and I am sweating. I pray to God that my perspiration won't cause the $5,000 digital camcorder and backup voice recorder to malfunction and that nothing will go wrong. Putting myself in danger is one thing, but risking my baby . . . there's too much at stake. If I'm discovered, I'll never be able to do this again.

The rest of the day goes by uneventfully. The lectures in today's last sessions are general, mild, and seemingly benign; nothing comes close to the frightening statements I heard yesterday during the Friday sermon. As the day draws to an end, I'm relieved. I allow myself to relax. At one point I'd almost regretted coming to Chicago, but the material I've obtained these past three days is astounding. Even my boss, Max, usually so stingy with his praise, will be pleased. I gaze at these Muslim youth, dressed in the vibrant colors of the Palestinian flag and ready to go on with their show, and a kind of sweetness, a soothing sensation, washes over me. Behind the stage, men are setting up a large yellow backdrop. I look at the backdrop, at the bright yellow stage lights, and my eyes are filled with the color. The young kids remind me of the classmates of my early childhood . . . it's as if they're performing on the stage of my old school . . . everything turns yellow. . . .

THE YELLOW DUNES on the outskirts of al-Basrah began to wear their crimson veil only as the spring sun sank slowly and gracefully toward the horizon. Dusk belonged to the reds and browns. Sunrise, however, wrought a glorious exhibition as the rapidly advancing globe would quickly overwhelm the distant pipes of the oil refineries and paint them a shining yellow. The desert surrounding our town was yellow. The air, rippling in the heat, was yellow. The sky above, too, was a searing yellow. The houses, built of dried mud, were yellow-brown. The few bushy plants that grew here were yellow, as were the palm trees, bearing bright yellow fruit. Even the chickens running around in my grandfather's backyard, happy in their ignorance, were more yellow than white.

I wondered whether my older brother Ron liked the yellows as much as I did, but I never asked him. I liked to think of them as my private, confidential friends: if I asked him, my secret would be revealed. The yellows were an important part of my childhood, and they're among the clearest memories I have of the first part of it. My childhood, you see, can be divided into three parts. What came before the event, what came after, and what happened after I left Iraq for a place I'd never heard of during my life in al-Basrah.

Walking home from school with Ron at the end of the day, I'd welcome the lengthening shadows, the creeping browns, and the mysterious blacks of the coming evening. As much as I liked the yellow days of al-Basrah, the darker hues whispered "night" to me. Night meant cooler air, family dinner, and no more school. School days ran from eight in the morning till six in the evening, and with the approaching summer they were becoming more and more trying. Forty young kids in a small clay room baking in the desert sun with no air-conditioning meant long, torturous hours in class, and air filled with the heavy odor of sweat.

My brother and I never complained, for we knew we were the fortunate ones. In Iraq in the late 1960s, many children our age were already at work. The tasks they performed were difficult even for people three times their size and four times their age. They toiled outside under the scorching sun from dawn to dusk, for pennies a week, only to be beaten and barely fed by their parents at night. Ron and I were blessed, and we knew it. I liked my school, and I was happy to go there. In fact, I wanted to go to school even before I was old enough, and Mama and Baba had to persuade the principal that I could handle it. It was a private school, with mostly Christian children and a few of us

Jewish kids. The common denominator was that all of our parents could pay the outrageous fees the school collected for the fine education it provided. No Muslim children attended. Most of their families couldn't afford it, and those who could would never have sent their children there anyhow.

This separation from the local Muslim kids worked well for all parties involved and was a tradition kept for generations in al-Basrah. In my school, Muslims served as janitors, housekeepers, cooks, and guards, but none were found among the teachers. Teachers were mostly Christian, mostly from European countries. They were very good, and they earned European-grade salaries, ten times what Iraqi teachers could expect to earn. Our parents gladly paid for this kind of education, which included science, culture, art, and languages. By age six, most of us already spoke a little English and some French. No Qur'ân, no Islam, no jihad, no "holy" notions of an all-evil and corrupt non-Muslim world lurking beyond the borders of our homeland. Our teachers came from that outside world, and they were very worldly. School was a small intellectual haven in an ocean of illiteracy, poverty, and budding Islamic fundamentalism.

Our Jewish enclave in al-Basrah was but a remnant of the once thriving Babylonian Diaspora; the Jewish community in Iraq was one of the oldest in the world. According to tradition, Abraham, the father of the Jewish nation, was born in southern Iraq, in Ur of the Chaldees, some four millennia ago. In that fertile Mesopotamian plain between the Tigris and Euphrates Rivers, in what is now called Iraq, the Bible describes the beginning of all civilization. At that time, according to the Book of Genesis, all inhabitants of Earth had but one language and only a few words. Then the people decided to build a city with a tower so high, it would dwell in the skies. God was angered by such grandiosity, and he confused their language so that they couldn't understand one another. The city, Babylon (*babel* is Hebrew for "confusion") was abandoned and the people were scattered in all four directions.

In the sixth century B.C. the Babylonian king Nebuchadnezzar conquered the kingdom of Judea, ordered the destruction of the First

Temple in Jerusalem, and exiled most of Judea's population to Babylon. For many centuries, the situation of the Babylonian Diaspora under Muslim rule fluctuated between violent persecution and livable conditions. Although Jews were habitually subject to special taxes called *Jizya,* and to certain restrictions, many prospered and some even held high positions. Their financial situation improved under Ottoman rule and British Mandate, but when Iraq gained independence in 1932, life for Iraq's Jews went downhill at an accelerated pace.

Many began leaving the country illegally. In 1950, the Iraqi Parliament legalized immigration to Israel, and shortly thereafter the Sokhnut, or Jewish Agency, an international organization that supports the state of Israel and immigration to it, along with the Israeli government, airlifted some 130,000 Iraqi Jews to Israel. The operation was called Ezra and Nehemia, after two Jewish leaders who led a massive emigration from Persia back to Israel around 450 B.C., and it marked the end of the Babylonian Diaspora. By 1952, there were fewer than six thousand Jews left in Iraq. Today, only a handful remain there. As in most major emigration waves, those who did well were the most reluctant to go. A few of my mother's brothers and sisters did immigrate to Europe. The vast majority of her family and my father's, however, were too wealthy and couldn't bring themselves to leave, especially as the Iraqi government not only revoked the citizenship of those who left, but also took all their assets. Our families did not want to pay that price. The price we ended up paying was far more horrible.

LOUD MUSIC SNAPS ME out of my daydream. I look at the kids on the stage. Like Boy Scouts, Muslim-style, they are dancing in the traditional Arabic fashion, stamping the wooden stage with their feet, hands stretched forward, but there's no joy in their movements. Then they perform a new routine. It's called "How I Became a Martyr."

We are only weeks from the end of the second millennium, an era in which mankind eradicated major diseases, harnessed nuclear energy, made space travel practically routine, and mapped the human genome. Yet in the Ramada Plaza hotel in suburban Chicago, Arab American youth are acting out skits in which they kill Jews and become martyrs.

They're so young, yet so filled with this centuries-old hate. There's something bone-chilling in the way they portray their fury on stage. And I'd thought this was going to be entertaining! I hope that my camcorder is still working, but I'm also too exhausted to care, and once again the here and now blends with the then and there. My thoughts drift back to Iraq. How different we were from these kids on stage, how naive. And how lucky we were to have made it thus far.

I began my schooling at a very young age. My younger brother, Jonathan, was still too young to go to school. Maybe he'd have gone the next year, but at that time he was staying at home with his *nana,* a word close in sound and meaning to the word *nanny.* Ron and I had long since left our *nanas* behind—Mama said we were too old for them—but I remained fond of mine. She was a kind, old, unsophisticated Muslim woman who used to tell me spooky ghost stories at bedtime. She must have meant well by that. She told me how she'd tucked her own kids in, years before, to these same stories. *Nana* always tried to cover for me when my pranks got out of control. When we were school age we were switched from *nanas* to our own lackeys, and while they took good care of us, I didn't get along well with mine. He had no sense of humor.

Ron tried his best to keep me out of trouble, just as my *nana* did, but it was a lost cause; he couldn't keep up with me. Baba used to say that I was the devil in disguise, but I knew he didn't mean that. I think he loved me more than he loved Ron and Jonathan. In spite of my being who I was, or, perhaps, because of it. My father traveled a lot, and he always brought us presents when he returned. When Baba was on these trips, I used to have nightmares in which he went away and didn't come back. I never told anyone about these nightmares, especially my mother. I was afraid that if I did, she'd get mad at me. She loved my father very much.

I was born into al-Basrah and lived my first years there without ever leaving it. When I was there, al-Basrah was a large city with a population of nearly two million. Iraq's largest port and a terminal point for oil pipelines, the city supported a huge oil refinery industry. Like many other places blessed with petroleum, the city prospered. Its heritage was great, founded, some say, by the legendary caliph Omar in the seventh century, at the dawn of Islam. Al-Basrah even has its own honorary place in *Arabian Nights:* most of the stories in the *Thousand and One Nights* are set in Baghdad and al-Basrah. It was from al-Basrah that Sinbad embarked on his seven fabulous voyages. My memories of our neighborhood, though, are somewhat blurry. Not that there's anything wrong with my memory; on the contrary, it's one of the most powerful weapons in my arsenal.

It seems to me, though, that after the event happened, a big portion of my memory was lost. My recollections are fortified by old photos and by Mama's stories. She is a terrific storyteller. But I can no longer distinguish between which of these memories of al-Basrah are really mine, and which are someone else's.

In the 1980s, when my family and I were long gone from there, al-Basrah's good fortune seemed to run out. During the Iran-Iraq War, its oil refineries were badly damaged. Then came the Persian Gulf War, and what was left of the city was demolished by the Allied bombing campaign, bringing oil production to a standstill. From a powerful industrial and trading center, al-Basrah became a poverty-, hunger-, and disease-stricken southern Iraqi slum, compliments of Saddam Hussein. The city's population had decreased by more than half, and its children, poisoned by the contaminated water supply, are dying of cancer. Much of Iraq is in ruins now, but I cannot find compassion in my heart. The Iraqis had it coming. And they hurt me so. For me, it is poetic justice.

As lucky as my family considered ourselves to be at the time, being privileged in Iraq was nothing like being privileged in America. Life there was simple and brutal. But I had no idea about it then. That late spring evening, on the way back from school, I was as cheerful and as worry-free as my grandfather's chickens. Unaware of what was coming and how our whole world was about to crumble to pieces, I called to Ron, "Race you to the house!" We ran, laughing, and reached the gate, breathless, where a butler was waiting for us. We were happy.

At the dinner table, Mama and Baba, married then for almost a decade, sat smiling at each other. My heart rejoiced, because it was clear that they were deeply in love. Mama came from a very rich family, one of the wealthiest in Iraq for generations. Her father lived in a large mansion in the fanciest part of al-Basrah with his four wives and their children—my uncles and aunts—and a host of servants. My grandmother was the last wife, and, according to my mother, his favorite. Mama had ten full brothers and sisters and thirty half siblings, and the entire clan lived together under one very large roof. In the Iraqi fashion of those times, those who could afford it and even many who couldn't were eager to spread their seed. Grandfather, with his forty children, was accomplished at that.

Grandfather was the only *shohet*—a person trained in animal slaughter in the kosher tradition—in our community. In other words, he was a butcher. This was a sideline that yielded some additional income, but it was by no means the sole source of his riches. He used to slaughter chickens in his backyard, in front of all of us kids. We were disgusted, and he seemed to enjoy our revulsion. He used to call us weaklings and to poke fun at us. I think he liked the actual killing. I clearly recall those violent scenes, the yellow chickens scattering in the yard, petrified, my grandfather chasing them. How he smiled when he got one, how he decapitated the struggling bird, and how for a few moments afterward the chicken's torso would keep running about, headless, spraying blood all over. The scene was surrealistic, scary yet almost funny, but the touch of hot blood wasn't, and neither was its smell. It created in me a fierce sensation of death, of a point of no return, of nauseating darkness. The yellow chickens turned red.

Everyone knew his and her place in the hierarchy of my grandfather's harem, and quarrels were uncommon. Although Grandma was the most beloved wife, Mama, younger than most of her half sisters, wasn't ranked very high in the pecking order of the house. Grandfather was tight-fisted, and Mama had to participate in some of the household chores more appropriate to a servant's lot. She was also actively involved in bringing up her younger brothers and sisters. But she was content, and for her, as for most others in the household, life progressed the way it was supposed to. When Mama turned eighteen, she chose to marry her next-door neighbor, a young, handsome, wealthy, and influential businessman. They had known each other their whole lives, and they were very much in love. Mama's decision had to be kept secret while my father approached my grandfather, because according to the custom of the time, the decision was not hers to make. A marriage was to be decided between the aspiring groom and the father of the bride. The bride had no say in this matter whatsoever. And as in any other business transaction, the deal had to be negotiated wherein the groom proved his ability to provide for the bride, and the father reciprocated by coming up with an appropriate dowry. Tradition held that the groom's qualifications and character were judged by his family's reputation. Given that the standing of my father's family in the community equaled that of my mother's, the match was readily approved.

After they wed, Mama and Baba moved to a house less than a block away from where they grew up. It wasn't as big as my grandfather's, but it was newer and much fancier. It even had an air-conditioning unit—a modern convenience that was rare in those times in Iraq; even Grandfather's mansion did not have one. Mama ran our house, and the servants did everything. No more chores for her, no more being ordered about—and no chance that Baba would be taking other wives. My father was different from my grandfather. A gentle soul, kind, always relaxed, always smiling.

They'd been married only a short while when Ron was born—a short while meaning a little over a year. In those times in Iraq, childbirth occurring less than nine months after a wedding was not tolerated and would have led to grave consequences. Less than two years after Ron was born, I came, and in two years more, Jonathan joined us. Ron and Jonathan took after my father. They were quiet, well-behaved, adorable children. I, on the other hand, had a bit more of my grandfather in me. I was what people called "active" and any number of other adjectives, many of them equally euphemistic: a special handful, mischievous, daring, busy, curious, insubordinate, imaginative, bold, cheeky. None of the traits that 1960s Iraqi society would wish for in a cute little girl with black pigtails.

I soon became a regular visitor to the emergency room, and only fate saved me from serious injury. I drank a $60-an-ounce bottle of perfume. I set out to rescue burning logs from the fireplace. The logs were saved, but my hands were badly burned. Luckily, one of the servants pulled me out of the fireplace before I'd cooked more thoroughly. The burns took a long time to heal, though I escaped unscarred. Then I took to swallowing nails. Fistfuls of them. Yes, iron ones, not the kind that grows on fingers. One time I hid in a cupboard for hours, thinking it very funny when my at-that-point hysterical parents called the constables to come investigate my abduction. Another time I hid in a closet and chewed a few packs of mothballs. The latter was, in retrospect, an excellent way of determining whether I suffered from G6PD deficiency. This deficiency is a genetic disorder common in the Middle East, which can cause breakage of blood cells after ingestion of foods such as fava beans and substances such as naphthalene. Obviously, although I do carry that gene, which I passed on to two of my sons, I do not suffer from the condition myself. Or this would have been my final trick. Instead there were many, many more.

Poor Baba. He developed his own dramatic response to these incidents. Whenever he caught me in a dangerous moment, he would faint. And Mama, she certainly could have done without that. She was already busy attending to her she-devil.

What was it in my character? Was I simply curious, or was I seeking attention? Not that I lacked any. Mama and Baba loved me very much, and I knew it. I was never jealous of Jonathan, because he had a *nana* to take care of him, and Mama could spend more than enough time with me. Was it my inability to resist my "bad side"? Or was it a desire to taste the forbidden fruit? In part it was an abuse of the forgiveness my parents bestowed upon me, grateful as they were that I'd survived yet again. My skill at pulling off the most unpredictable and dangerous pranks, frequently doing so right under the noses of my parents and the servants who kept close watch over me, had been finely honed by the time I reached age four. This was also about the time I finally started to talk. Not that I was uncommunicative prior to that, but until then I must not have felt that I had anything of value to say. Or maybe I just didn't have anything to complain about. Mama took me to various doctors, none of whom could find anything wrong with me. They said that I'd talk when I was ready, and they were right. Once I started, I could not be stopped. No one, to date, can keep me from talking if I have something I want to say.

No matter where, why, or when, it takes me only a few minutes to become the center of attention, of interest, of a conversation. At first, I didn't really notice that. But one time while Leo and I were dating, he remarked on how at the party we'd just returned from, everyone was gathered around in a large circle listening to me. I began to pay attention, and, sure enough, it was true. Not long after the beginning of any kind of gathering, most of the participants would be bunched up around me. I liked the attention and the spotlight. It came naturally to me. Alas, that trait can be deadly in the line of business I'm in. It took me years to learn how to mingle, to go unnoticed, to disappear in the shadows, to keep my mouth shut.

In my early childhood, however, keeping my mouth shut was not a skill I'd yet acquired. One night late in summer, all of us, including Mama and Baba, were sleeping over at my grandfather's house, as we often did. It was because of Grandma that we loved to go there; she was one of the warmest people I've ever known. As there was no air-conditioning in my grandfather's house, when the summer nights made the air inside thicker than butter, we'd all sleep on its roof. The house was old, but it was made of real stone, not like the mud huts most people lived in. A fortress, we thought; it'll last forever. Like most things in our lives, it didn't.

That night all of us—my immediate family, my grandfather's family, a few cousins, aunts, uncles, some servants—were asleep on the roof. In my dream I heard the sound of thunder, then a sandstorm came, and then I saw the biblical scene of Ezekiel's dry bones. Just as we were taught in school, I thought in my dream, the bones were rising and pummeling me . . . and then I woke up and realized that this was not just a dream. It wasn't a sandstorm, either. The roof had collapsed!

It was difficult to breathe, and I couldn't see Mama or Baba—couldn't see a thing through the dust and debris. Everyone was screaming. A paralyzing fear cut through me: Where was Jonathan? He was then just a baby! Amid the cries of my relatives and the servants, I heard him sobbing. I stumbled as fast as I could through the rubble and I found him. He was unharmed as far as I could tell. Thank God, everyone survived the fall with only minor cuts and bruises. I smiled at Jonathan and picked him up, and he smiled back at me. I understood what had just transpired, and, with my little brother on my lap, the whole situation began to seem incredibly funny. I started to laugh. Jonathan, calmed in my young arms, laughed too. That made it even funnier, and now I was roaring with laughter.

Meanwhile, my grandfather was boiling mad. As the structure gave way and everyone came tumbling down, he was thinking of the cost of the repairs rather than our well-being. My hysterical laughter pushed him over the edge and into fury. He began chasing me as though I were one of his birds. Baba restrained him, and then he couldn't help himself and he began to laugh, too. Soon everyone was howling. My grandfather, livid, was convinced I'd had something to do with the collapse. It was so ridiculous to even think that I could have damaged the structure, causing the old roof to succumb under the weight of a few dozen people sleeping on it. Only when Baba promised to share the expenses for the repair did my grandfather regain his calm.

In spite of the incident with the roof, and my numerous visits to the emergency room, life seemed to flow in a quiet, pleasant stream for my family. Baba was what we used to call a *tajjer,* merchant. He had a trading company that did extremely well. He began to travel on business more and more frequently, and as a result of these trips, my family was better off financially than we'd ever been.

But the tranquil river of life concealed an impending disaster beneath its surface. Or perhaps we were too blind to see what was coming. We missed the writing on the wall, even though there, on the wall, it was. Christians and Jews had always survived in Arab and in other Muslim countries at the sufferance of the intolerant majority. But just as tornadoes threaten Kansas and hunger menaces Africa, riots, pogroms, and murder were always looming for non-Muslims in Iraq and most other Arab countries. Non-Muslims were blamed for whatever mishaps troubled the land. We considered ourselves Iraqi, but at the same time, we were not *Iraqi*. When times were good, when the region was quiet, it was easy to forget how easily the soil we stood on could turn treacherous to us. Of course in hindsight it is easy to say "should have," "could have," or "told you so." Yet throughout history people have misinterpreted obvious signs of the horrors to come: The fall of the Roman Empire. The Holocaust. Pearl Harbor. 9-11. When analyzed after the fact, all of these catastrophes could have been predicted and averted. Like most people, my father tried to remain optimistic, to interpret the signs he was seeing through his own moral framework—and to rely on the ostrich technique. Meaning, to stick his head in the sand until danger spontaneously disappeared. He was probably thinking, This is so unfathomable, it will never happen.

And yet it always does.

The events of June 1967 were the trigger to my family's personal tragedy. At the time, I was young and knew nothing of the region's politics; before 1967, the state of Israel was never even mentioned in my house. We felt that Iraq was our homeland. Only later, many years later, did I learn what happened then and how deep its roots went. On May 14, 1948, the state of Israel declared its independence. Seven Arab armies immediately launched a massive attack on Israel's borders and bombed its major cities. Azzam Pasha, then the secretary-general of the Arab League, publicly stated the intention of the invasion: "This will be a war of extermination and a momentous massacre which will be spoken of like the Mongolian massacres and the Crusades." The newly born state fought for its life, and managed, with few versus many, not only to win, but also to occupy some Egyptian and Jordanian territories. These two countries, along with Syria, Lebanon, and Iraq, wouldn't forgive or forget this humiliation.

Gamal Abdel-Nasser, the first Egyptian president, a hero in the eyes of his people, a nationalist who seized power after he overturned the regime of King Farouk, had spoken before the United Arab Republic National Assembly in 1964. He'd said, "The danger of Israel lies in its very existence and in what it represents." I couldn't have put it better myself. The Arab world's complaint was not about Palestine or its refugees, not about the territories occupied since 1948, not about Israel's alliance with the United States at a time when all Arab countries sided with the Soviets. The real cause, the reason for its complaint, was simply that Israel was there. It was young, modern, secular, enthusiastically democratic, and—far worse—a country strongly supportive of the West and its values of freedom and progress. For the Arab states bordering Israel, accepting its existence would have meant encouraging a disaster that could lead to men shaving their beards, women walking unveiled in public or, far worse, learning to read, and eventually—Allah the Merciful!—the selling of McDonald's hamburgers on street corners. Armageddon! Israel was for the Arabs what the United States is for al-Qaeda: a symbol of free will, of technological advancement, of a society based on justice, equality, free speech, and freedom to vote. Israel had to be destroyed before any such infidel notions could sweep the Middle East.

We in the United States have learned a horrible lesson about terrorism with the attacks of 9-11. Other countries, including Britain, Spain, and India, have suffered from terrorism, some for many years. In Israel, though, terrorism was a part of everyday life even before the state came to be. In the mid-1960s, terrorist strikes, sponsored and supported by Arab countries, grew increasingly frequent. In less than two years, more than a hundred deadly attacks were carried out against innocent civilians. At the same time, winds of war began to blow. On Israel's northern border, Israeli villages in the Galilee were shelled by Syria from the Golan Heights under its control. In Egypt, Nasser continued to incite his people, issuing such statements as "After we enter Palestine, its soil will no longer be covered with sand; it will be soaked in blood" and "The full restoration of the rights of the Palestinian people means the complete destruction of the State of Israel. . . . Our immediate aim is to perfect military might. Our national aim is to eradicate Israel." Egyptian troops moved into the Sinai desert and regrouped at the Israeli border, and Syrian troops prepared for battle along the Golan Heights. Nasser kicked the United Nations Emergency Force out of the Sinai. Hafez Assad, then the Syrian defense minister, stated that "the Syrian army, with its finger on the trigger, is united. . . . The time has come to engage in a battle of annihilation." On May 22, 1967, Egypt, violating the Convention on the Territorial Sea and Contiguous Zone adopted by the United Nations, sealed the Straits of Tiran, thus blocking all Israeli vessels from entering or leaving the Red Sea. Since 1956, Israel had had a right to transit the strait, a resolution that was supported by seventeen members of the United Nations. The Egyptian blockade was intended to cut off Israel's oil supply. On May 30, King Hussein signed a defense pact with Egypt. The Iraqi president, Abdur Rahman Aref, joined the military alliance, announcing that "Israel's existence is an error . . . our goal is clear—to wipe Israel off the map." The armies of Kuwait, Algeria, Saudi Arabia, and Iraq sent troops and arms to the front. And while the United States under President Lyndon Johnson, and France, Israel's other main arms supplier at the time, imposed arms embargoes on Israel, the Soviets were sending massive amounts of weapons to the Arab countries.

Early on the morning of June 5, 1967, a Monday, the Israeli air force launched an offensive on Egyptian airfields. Within three hours, Egypt's air force was wiped out. During the attack, a message was delivered to King Hussein saying that Israel would not be the first to initiate hostilities against Jordan. But when Jordanian radar picked up the Israeli air force returning from Egypt, the Jordanians received confirmation from the Egyptians that the planes were in fact theirs, on their way to strike Israel. Acting on this reassurance, Jordan shelled West Jerusalem and a large Jordanian force stormed the Commissioner's Palace, the United Nations headquarters in Jerusalem. Israel responded later that day, the air force bombing the Jordanian air fleet—which was still on the ground—and obliterating it altogether. During the same strike, more than two-thirds of the Syrian air force and ten Iraqi fighters were demolished. Thus in one day the Israeli air force destroyed more than four hundred enemy planes, gaining absolute domination of the skies of the Middle East. Following fierce ground battles, which also lasted but one day, Israel took all of Jerusalem.

Six days of fighting, six days only, and the war was over, eponymously going down in history as the Six-Day War, ending with an overwhelming Israeli victory and with the most humiliating defeat for

Arab armies in history. Israel now occupied the entire Sinai desert and all of the West Jordan valley, later termed the West Bank. Most important, the holy city of Jerusalem had been "liberated" or "unified" if you were an Israeli, "occupied" if you were everyone else in the region. Israel now possessed more than three times the territory it had a week earlier.

Iraq was not spared the whirlwind: it lost not only its ten downed fighter jets, but also two regiments of Iraqi soldiers, dispatched to help their Arab brothers, who were intercepted on their way to the front and destroyed. Those who survived fled for their lives, abandoning their weapons and even their shoes as they ran.

After the war, anti-Semitism, always bubbling below the surface, exploded in the Middle East. Unable to defeat the Jewish state, Arabs took revenge on their defenseless Jewish neighbors, Taliban-style. Hundreds of Jews in Arab countries were brutally attacked, raped, lynched. Iraq became a role model for the Arab world in that respect. Saddam Hussein was at that time head of security for the Ba'ath Party, which shortly thereafter took control of Iraq. Even then he had a reputation for ruthlessness and ambition: in just three years Saddam would seize power from his cousin, the secretary-general of Ba'ath, and become ruler of Iraq. But at this juncture in his career, he had a crisis to deal with—he had to save face. The destruction of the Iraqi troops was particularly humiliating for him—a devastating blow to the prestige of an egomaniac. He could care less about the lost lives; it was the embarrassment of failure that enraged him. Indeed, he went ballistic. He declared that the force had been betrayed and that he was intent on finding the traitors. Immediately many in Iraq joined the chorus, and their rhetoric meant one thing only: A large amount of Jewish blood needed to be spilled to restore national pride.

Baba was a perfect scapegoat. Even without the war, there were so many reasons for Saddam and his mob to hate someone like him. He was young, rich, respected. His business was thriving. He had a beautiful family. He had many friends in the government, in the army, everywhere. In some cases, those friendships went back as far as elementary school. Sometimes the ties were two generations deep between families. But these friends held important positions—in the municipal authorities, in the government, in the judicial system. Even the chief of police in al-Basrah was a good friend of my father's. These men knew many important secrets. My father's friendships with them therefore could be easily twisted in meaning as his attempts to spy. How convenient. Baba was raw meat to Saddam's black hunger.

On July 17, 1968, officers from the Ba'ath Party staged a coup d'état, seizing power in Iraq. Saddam Hussein and his cousin Ahmad Hassan al-Bakr became Iraq's leaders. Although the coup itself was relatively bloodless, it was followed by a reign of terror aimed at liquidating all opposition. Assassinations, executions, torture, and sham trials became an everyday routine. To divert the people's attention from the violence and the horrors of the new regime, the military junta "uncovered" an espionage network. Most of these captured "spies" were Jews.

One afternoon, the doors to our house were broken down. Officers stormed out of a dark blue Volkswagen van, charged in, and arrested my father. They tore out the transformers in the air conditioner and said that these were radio transmitters. I remember—and this I remember clearly—every detail of that ghastly scene, when the knock on the door robbed me of my innocence. That day was the conclusion of the first part of my childhood, the end of the beginning of my life.

After they took Baba, my sleep was haunted with dreams, at best, or more often, with nightmares. Even now, at night and in my waking hours, I'm dogged by these visions. Joseph's gift, I call it. Although I may have had it before then, I know for certain that I noticed it after Baba was taken. At the time, I didn't understand what it meant.

Joseph, in the Book of Genesis, was a dreamer. Literally. He had the ability to interpret his dreams and those of others. He could, through his interpretations, foresee future events. Joseph was the second youngest of twelve brothers. His father, Jacob, favored him for this gift of his, and to show it, he bought him a beautiful striped coat of many colors. Joseph's brothers' resentment of such favoritism intensified and peaked when he began to have dreams foretelling his own grandeur. His brothers, blinded by jealousy, sold Joseph into slavery, and Joseph was taken to the land of Egypt. In a strange twist of fate, Joseph's ability carried him out of the depth of a prison pit and made him the most powerful man in Egypt. His dreams turned into reality.

The day they took my father was paradoxical, like Joseph's gift. It ruined my life, but it made me into the person I am today. I now know that together with some hundred other Iraqi Jews, my father was apprehended and accused of spying for Israel. At the time, however, all I understood was that something terrible must have occurred. Because Baba was taken away, and because Mama never talked to us about it. And because Jonathan, who with his toddler's sharp intuition sensed the impending doom, tried to push the officers away. He tried to protect Baba. I remember how he was thrown on the iron railing, how he fell to the ground, and with his head split open, bleeding all over the marble floors, the not-yet-four-year-old boy tried to cling to Baba, refusing to let go or give up. And how, covered with blood, he tried to fight the officers with his tiny balled-up fists. In my memories, I can still hear the sickening crack his head made when it hit the railing. I wish to God that I could forget that scene, but I know that until my last day I won't. Jonathan carries the scars on his scalp proudly, just beneath his navy-style buzz-cut. That day scarred all of us, but my wounds are not external; I carry them in my soul. My mission, my resolve, what I do with my life now, what this book is all about, are results of those scars. My vocation is the legacy of my father.

BABA WAS GONE, and my brothers and I did not know where he'd been taken. When we asked Mama, she wouldn't give us a straight answer and would burst into tears, so we soon stopped asking. Most of the servants left the house after that day, and Mama, who never used to go anywhere before, was now going out most of the time, even though she was four months' pregnant with my little sister. She would leave early in the morning and return late at night, shattered, and then spend the rest of the night crying. Grandma moved in with us, in spite of my grandfather's protests, and did her best to help. This is when she and I became close. My most vivid memories from that cursed time in my life are of her, soothingly combing my hair, weaving it into tight braids, hugging me. She was always compassionate, always supportive. Even now, when she visits me in my dreams, she continues to smile.

Mama tried to do whatever she could to save Baba. Like a drowning man clutching a straw, she went down every possible avenue to prove Baba's innocence. His prominent friends, fearing similar fates, immediately denounced him. Maybe some of them even believed he was actually guilty of the crimes with which he was charged. Mama tried to contact those she knew well. Some refused outright, others found excuses to brush her off. One, whose brother was a cabinet member, a self-proclaimed close friend of my father's, agreed to see her. Shamelessly, he tried to exploit the situation and offered the visibly pregnant woman help in exchange for certain "favors." Mama, who would have done anything to save Baba, realized that someone so low would only use her and then do nothing. Infuriated, she left the pig's house cursing him and his seed. She must have possessed something of Joseph's gift, too, because a short time later the seemingly healthy man suffered a massive stroke and died in misery. He left his estate to his five sons, who began fighting over it, killing one brother, sending two others to prison. In a strange twist of fate, they were sent to the same prison where Baba was initially held. A fourth brother years later became an adviser to Saddam Hussein, made a wrong move, and ended up executed by Saddam personally. A great honor. Shortly thereafter, the last brother, fearing to be linked to his brother's "conspiracy," took his own life.

Baba was transferred to Baghdad, and so were we. Mama, my brothers, Grandma—who didn't have to go but wouldn't leave us—and I were all put under house arrest in a small hut in Baghdad. The Iraqi government was not content just to arrest my father. Everything we owned was taken from us, from our money to our personal belongings. The tiny house we were placed in had one bedroom and a small foyer. Behind it, instead of a backyard, grew thorny bushes. A small window in the bedroom faced these large bushes. In front of the house ran a busy road, which we viewed through a window decorated with steel bars. The house was made from stone, and its floor was of concrete tiles: an ugly, gray dungeon. The hut was in a poor Muslim neighborhood not far from the center of town and only a few blocks from the offices of Iraq's Ministry of Defense, where political prisoners were held. Three uniformed agents of the secret police guarded the house round the clock, in three shifts. No one in our neighborhood was supposed to know who or what we were, although the neighbors must have realized that our sudden appearance and all the police activity going on around the house weren't a trivial business. They were very careful; none of them ever spoke with us.

Mama still went out almost daily. She'd go, and one of the officers would follow her. We didn't know where she was going and we were fraught with acclimating to our new confinement and, more important, to the public school we were forced to attend, escorted there daily by one of the guards. The change from complete freedom, a large house with servants, and a happy family to this small cage was devastating to us children. But I soon learned that it was nothing compared to the hell of school, because in that place I got the first real thrashing of my life. Even with my grandfather's attitude and my numerous pranks, I'd never before been beaten. At home, I did get spanked now and then, but to a very minor extent, only symbolically, and in our enlightened school in al-Basrah, corporal punishment was absolutely banned. I had no idea that in the new school in Baghdad it was common practice to line up all the children in the class and hit them with a ruler on their fingers, one after the other, when one of them did something not to the teacher's liking. Teachers had full license to use force, and that they did.

A few days into the new school, I dared ask the teacher a question about something I couldn't follow. The result was brisk and vicious. As if she had just been waiting for the right moment, she jumped at me with her ruler, raining blows on my head, my face, my fingers, and screaming, "This is no place for daughters of spies, death to all traitors!" The kids in class laughed, cheered, and banged their fists on their desks. One spat on me.

I was humiliated. I realized that because I had to return to that class every day, I should keep a very low profile from then on so that no one would find excuses to attack me. When Mama got home that evening, her face, too, was swollen and blue, and her arms were battered with bruises. She looked at me, drew me close, and we both cried. It was not the pain, the humiliation, or the fear that hurt me—I was strong, and I knew deep down that I would survive this ordeal. It was what the teacher had said about Baba being a spy and a traitor. For the first time, I fully grasped that he was in mortal danger.

Too young and too overwhelmed with everything, it took me quite some time to appreciate that Mama kept coming home at night with these bruises on her hands, face, and who knew where else. When I finally asked her about it, she made excuses that even a second-grader wouldn't buy. Years later I realized what she'd been going through. While we were at school each day, she was trying to save my father. And how she tried! In prison, Baba was interrogated and subjected to the process of "convincing," the good old Iraqi way of making a prisoner confess his crimes. Knowing that a confession would mean a death sentence, Baba resisted making such a statement. He was tortured barbarically. They pulled out his nails and his teeth, applied electric shocks to his genitalia, beat and starved him, deprived him of sleep. He was told that another prisoner had just betrayed him and told the authorities "everything"—but Baba had found out that the man had in fact died weeks before, during the first days of his interrogation.

The date of Baba's trial was approaching and the inquisitors still didn't have his confession, so they tried a new method. This was one of the reasons they had ordered all of us to move to Baghdad. My pregnant mother was summoned to the prison, where on numerous occasions she was beaten, tortured, violated. They told her that if she would write a letter to her husband convincing him to confess his alleged crimes, they would stop the torture and would consider reducing his sentence. But Mama was no fool. She knew that Baba should never confess. She refused, so the torture continued. The one thing the jailers did not lie about to Mama was that my tormented father was present, behind a thin wall, every time when she was given the "special treatment." They made sure she knew he was there, and they told him that she was there. Sometimes, she heard him moan behind that screen. Sometimes, she says, she could almost feel him. Aside from satisfying the sadistic urges of the prison guards and the vile government officials, the point of this seemingly endless cycle of pain and blood was to enable the authorities to apply pressure on my father until he would finally admit his crimes.

But even witnessing her torture did not break him. He did not confess. And Mama, despite what she knew lay in store for her, despite the agony of realizing that the life was slowly being squeezed out of her husband, kept returning to the jail, hoping against all odds to save him.

The show trial was held in 1969, in the Ministry of Defense, where Baba was kept prisoner. Typical of such trials in such regimes, it lasted three days. Defense of any sort was, obviously, not permitted. There was only prosecution. The judge referred to my father as "the spy," not "the defendant." The prosecution claimed that there was strong evidence proving my father's treason, that sophisticated radio transmitters had been discovered in our house and in his office, and that his accomplices had already signed their confessions.

The trial took place behind closed doors with no public access, but excerpts of it were shown daily on Iraqi national television. On the first day of the trial, they showed how my father denied the false and transparently fabricated assertions and "evidence." That same evening, my mother received a letter, delivered by a special messenger, telling her that if she went to the jail again the next day, she might get a chance to finally see her husband. Of course Mama went there first thing the next morning. She was taken to a room where she had never been before. It was much larger and more brightly lit than any of the chambers in which she'd previously been beaten, although like the other smaller rooms, it was decorated with posters of Saddam and his cousin, the president. In the room were three large tables and ten men, all proudly mustachioed, all in the dark uniforms of the Iraqi secret service. After they punched and kicked Mama a few times, much less severely than ever before, the secret service agents sat down. The chief prosecutor—a man named Majdi Amin—entered the room, lit a cigarette, and sat quietly for a few moments, looking at Mama. Finally, he said, "There is still a possibility that you could see him before the trial is over."

He took a deep breath, cleared his throat, and continued, "We are not all monsters, you know. It does look like we may have made a mistake. I suggest you write a letter to the judge, explain everything, and ask to see your husband. I wouldn't be surprised if the judge allowed that." He smiled at her.

Mama sat down in total disbelief. This was too good to be true. It had to be some kind of trick. But what if it wasn't? The prosecutor himself was telling her this! In tears and afraid that they'd change their minds, she immediately wrote a letter in a shaking hand. She wrote that she was the defendant's wife, that they had three children and the fourth was on the way, that her husband was innocent, that he was kind and generous, that he always donated money to the poor, that he could never hurt a fly.

But then she wrote to the judge that her husband could never confess. Not to something he hadn't done. She later told me it was a premonition that made her do this: she reiterated in the letter three times, in case Baba ever saw the letter, that he was never to confess. Last, she begged the judge that she be granted a few moments with her husband, whom she missed so much. She gave the letter to Majdi Amin and waited. After less than an hour, a guard came and told her to go home. She did, with the first taste of hope she'd had in a very long time.

No sooner had Mama handed over her letter than the secret service agents gave it to my father. They told him that his wife was behind the wall. Here was the proof, they said: a letter in her own handwriting. They told him that he should seriously consider confessing this time around. Otherwise, they said, she might get the same treatment that had been delivered in that room last week. My father immediately knew what they were talking about. Everyone in the prison did. The wife of another prisoner had come a week before, and the usual roughing up had gotten out of hand. She was gang-raped by the guards, then beaten until long after she'd passed out. The woman was hospitalized in critical condition. Her husband nearly went out of his mind.

"She's right here, on the other side of that wall," one of the agents said. "You do recognize her handwriting, don't you?"

My father did.

"Refuse to confess," the agent said, "and in a few moments we'll go, cut her belly open, and bring your child to you. On a tray."

That did it.

Back in the hut, Mama waited eagerly for the report from the trial on television. Grandma told her that they had showed some of it in the morning, while she was gone, and again, Baba's plea was "not guilty." At that point, Grandma told her, they stepped out for an intermission. This was probably around the time my mother had met with the prosecutor.

And then, during the evening television report, my mother learned how her husband walked to the stand and in a clear, unwavering voice, confessed his crimes as an Israeli spy and a traitor to the Iraqi nation. That was it, Mama knew at once. It was over.

My brothers and I were not allowed to watch any of the reports during the three days of the trial, and we were kept in the dark about the entire affair. Mama herself didn't watch the final day, when my father was convicted and sentenced to death. After she saw his confession, she didn't know—she didn't want to know—what the sentence was, even though she knew in her bones what the only outcome could be.

Mama's fears about the sentence were confirmed when she turned on the television and witnessed the celebration around the execution. My father was hanged, along with eight other Jews, in Baghdad's central square. The execution was conducted in the middle of the day, in a spirit of great national jubilation, attended by half a million cheering spectators. A real holiday. Buses and trains from all over the country were free that day, so that more people could come into Baghdad and attend the hanging. And come they did. "The Israeli spies were hanged!" the frantic rabble chanted. Iraq's flag was draped everywhere, loudspeakers played lively music, and belly dancers were brought from near and far to dance under the bodies. Barbarians. The bloodthirsty mob, cheering and screaming at the top of its lungs, was nothing but a huge pack of hyenas. On television, the spectacle of nine Jewish men in red pajamas, hanged, was shown again and again. The authorities announced on loudspeakers in Baghdad that at four o'clock in the afternoon the bodies would be taken down and given to the public, so that the people of Iraq could have their way with them in the streets.

It was years before I learned the facts of this event. At seventeen, in another place, in another life, during a period in which I was searching for information on my father, I found a photograph of the execution in an old newspaper. It was only then that I accepted that the execution had taken place. With that photograph, at last, closure became possible for me.

But back then, as a small child in a concrete hut in Baghdad, I didn't know that Baba had died. It was never spoken among us that he was not coming back. I only had a vague sense that something terrible had transpired, because I saw that Mama was a shadow of what she'd been, and sadness and grief filled our days. Although I felt even then, in the way a child knows things, that he was gone forever, for me, Baba died only when I was seventeen.

WE LIVED IN the hut for over a year after my father's hanging. This was the gray part of my childhood. Gray walls, gray floor, gray existence. After the execution, we were no longer allowed to leave the hut without a special permit. We were not allowed to go to school. My brothers and I learned a little about the Six-Day War from the propaganda on television, and we learned of the defeat of the Arab armies. We used to sit at the window in the hut's tiny foyer and stare at the road and the guards, hoping that Baba would suddenly show up, smiling, and that the nightmare would be over. We began to play games of imagination. One rainy day, when even the world outside our prison turned gray, we sat in the bedroom and looked through its small window. A thought struck me and I said, "We don't need to worry. The Israeli soldiers, *our* soldiers, will come from Israel with their planes, and they will steal Baba from the bad soldiers. And then they will come and steal us and take us away from here."

"But how will they know where we are?" Jonathan asked. "Even Baba doesn't know where we are. Had he known, he would have saved us a long time ago."

Reassured by all that I'd heard and seen on television, I told him, "Don't be silly. Of course they know. The Israelis know everything."

Ron didn't say a word, as the tears rolled down his cheeks.

We kept on waiting for Baba and for the Israeli soldiers, but they never came. My brothers and I grew closer than ever before. It comforted me that we all slept in the same room. It made me feel more secure and helped me fall asleep. But sometimes at night I could hear the wolves cry. It frightened me. In Iraq they used to say that when wolves cry it means that someone is about to die; my *nana* told me about it. So I lay in bed and thought of dying. I tried to imagine how heaven looked. What if I didn't go to heaven? I remembered how I'd lied to Mama about brushing my teeth the other night. Suddenly I panicked. Why were the wolves crying? Who was going to die?

It was in this period that my little sister, Betty, was born. Mama was constantly in tears. Immediately after the baby was born, when the midwife was still washing her, my mother was already crying. Ron and I asked her why she wept; wasn't the arrival of a baby a happy occasion? This made her cry all the more. Whenever we tried talking to her, she cried. She cried all night long, every night. Worst of all, she always cried while she was nursing my baby sister.

One day a letter arrived, delivered by an old friend of my father's. It was the last letter Baba wrote. One of the prisoners who'd been kept with him, an old man broken by his torture, had been released from prison. Before he left the prison, Baba gave him the letter. The old man unstitched the rubber band in his briefs, carefully folded in the sheet of paper and the small thing wrapped in it, and smuggled them out of jail. In his letter to my mother, Baba wrote:

"I am about to die, but you have to live your own life. You have to take care of our children. Don't cry over me. Take the kids and go to Israel. You will be taken care of there. You can only be safe there." Then, in less stable handwriting, he added: "I also send you, with this letter, my ring and my eternal love." His wedding ring was in the folded paper.

After she read the letter, Mama, a young widow with four children, realized that she needed to pull herself together. The letter was the will of a condemned man; it was his last wish that she save herself and their children and get out of Iraq. It opened her eyes. It straightened out her priorities. Fight for freedom first, grieve later. Through her tears she was also beginning to see that the Iraqis were not going to suffer our presence much longer. She understood that we had to escape before some other disaster took place. And then my mother, trained only for a life of privilege and leisure, raised to be taken care of, found qualities in herself that she never knew she possessed. Secretly, she began reaching out to her many friends. Very, very carefully, because the authorities didn't need much of an excuse to finish off this business of us. Mama found a few brave souls who would help, out of friendship or indebtedness to my father, or out of opposition to the brutal regime. One friend came up with a brilliant idea. The only people who could get us out of Iraq were the *shlihim,* emissaries, who worked for the Sokhnut, the Jewish Agency. They have done this before, he told my mother. They would take any risk to save Jews from hostile regimes.

On the way to the market, Mama passed the word to a friend. His friend met her two days later, in a grocery. "I need specifics," he told her quietly. "Send your mother to the fish shop next week, it is too dangerous for us to meet again."

Mama adamantly refused to use my grandmother as a messenger. "She doesn't know about my plan," she told the man. "No one does, and no one ever will. If I'm caught, I'll be the only one to pay for it."

Ten days later, Mama met another friend of the friend. He was behind the counter in a bakery. There was no time to talk because she was being watched. She bought a loaf of bread and paid the man. Long after she left, he dared to look at the note she'd slipped in among the bills. In the note were two phone numbers and a brief message, written in Arabic letters, though the words were nonsensical to him. Still, he called both numbers, delivered the message, and hung up, shaking like a leaf. The message, which had been in transliterated Hebrew, reached its destination, the *shlihim*. The wheels of our escape were set in motion.

And then they killed Grandma. That morning they'd allowed us to go and visit the family of one of the men who'd been hanged beside my father. It was a strange privilege, but Mama didn't ask too many questions. We went, and Grandma said she'd stay home or maybe go to the market. This was the last time I ever saw her. On our way back, we saw a lot of commotion on the main road that led to our hut. Police cars, ambulances, many spectators, yelling neighbors. On her trip back from the market, Grandma had been run down by a large black limousine, right in front of where we lived. They said that she was killed instantly. As soon as we realized what happened, my brothers and I ran inside, pulled blankets over our heads, and tried to hide. We hoped this would make the terrible reality go away. Because at the time I didn't know what had become of my father, my grandmother's murder was the first time that I felt orphaned. In my hiding place, under the blanket, I sat for a few hours and began to imagine circles. The circles were rotating, turning faster and faster, and they were taking me away from there.

Mama had to leave us and go to the hospital to identify Grandma's body. The body had to be washed, according to the Jewish tradition, but the hospital staff refused to do it, so Mama had to wash her mother's dead body all by herself. She washed and cried, cried and washed . . .

Black limousines in Iraq at that time were the sole property of the government; no one else was allowed to own them. The investigation into the so-called accident was perfunctory, and the case was dismissed as a run-of-the-mill hit-and-run. Mama knew exactly what it meant. Grandma was of no interest to the Iraqis; it was my mother they were after. Forced by the authorities to wear *burqas,* the robes that cover Muslim women from head to toe, she and Grandma were indistinguishable. Mama guessed that whoever ran down Grandma had mistaken her for the widow of the traitor spy. A few days later, her suspicion was confirmed. One of the officers who guarded our hut approached her. This man had seen my father once in al-Basrah in the house of the chief of police at a time when my father was an honored guest there. The guard must have been impressed, because he showed some empathy for my mother. He was the only one of our jailers who ever said a word to us. He whispered in Mama's ear: "It is you they wanted. You are in grave danger."

Now there really was no time to lose. They had grown tired of us; our days were numbered. But there was a complication. With Grandma dead, my mother felt compelled to take responsibility for her younger brothers and sisters, five in all, still living in al-Basrah with my grandfather. Better to risk their lives for a future, she thought, than to live in this nightmare.

Her plan was almost complete. Her choice, a Friday night, when the guards would be weary from the Friday sermon and a long afternoon of prayer. But how to get rid of them? Being good Muslims, they didn't drink alcohol. Mama brewed some strong coffee into which she mixed as much Valium as she could lay her hands on, and she prayed. It was now or never. The coffee had to do its trick before the shift changed. It did; the guards fell, like flies, into a deeply drugged stupor.

Mama took the two chickens she'd cooked for the traditional Sabbath meal and a small bag with some of our clothes and urgently hustled us out of the hut. We had no idea where we were going or what was happening, but we understood that it was important and we went quietly, without asking any questions. I remember how strange it felt to see the stars and the crescent of the moon again, and how uplifting the warm breeze felt. I realized that this was the end of the gray part of my childhood. If we survive this, I vowed, I will never forget and never let the gray in my life again.

A few blocks away, a van was waiting. Inside were my mother's younger siblings, our uncles and aunts. Through her contacts, Mama had arranged for them to be spirited out of al-Basrah. Even Grandfather didn't know that we were escaping with them, a fact that ultimately saved his life. The Iraqi driver was startled by our appearance; he was paid well to wait, but he was never told that he would be transporting a group composed of nine children and one young woman. After my mother paid him some more money, he agreed to take us as far as the train station in Baghdad. Little did we children understand that we had but a few hours before the secret police would discover our flight and the manhunt for us would begin.

We boarded a train going to the northern part of Iraq, near the Iranian border. As we sat on the train, Jonathan began to cry. Mama asked him what was wrong. "You have no heart," he accused her through his tears. "How can you tell us to leave Baba behind? We never said a proper good-bye to Baba!"

Mama sat us down and quickly explained the situation. She told us that we had to be brave, that we were going away, and that if we succeeded, we would be free at the end of this long ride. She gave us instructions and told us what to say in case we were asked.

Although Mama forbade us to move about the train, my memory of that ride is of pleasure. It was movement—utterly different from our confinement of the two years since my father had been taken. Mama arranged some blankets on the floor, and for a few hours we all lay on them, holding hands. Suddenly someone was rapping on the door of our compartment. Mama threw the blankets over us, told us not to move, and opened the door. A young officer was asking her for her identification documents.

"Why, what seems to be the problem?" she asked him.

"Oh, some Jewish spy ran away with her four children," he explained.

Mama told him that she was a teacher, traveling with her baby and eight students on a field trip to the mountains. She said that all of us were fast asleep, that her bag with the documents was somewhere beneath us, and she asked whether he could come back a little later, when we woke up. With a sigh she said, "These Jews, I hope they all leave us already, and let us live our lives in peace."

As soon as the officer stepped out, she told us to split into pairs and get off the train as soon as it reached its next stop. "Go directly to the rest rooms and wait for me there," she said in an urgent tone. "Don't pee, don't move, don't talk. Just wait."

Outside, in the station, soldiers were standing in rows. Ron and I got off. A soldier approached us and asked what we were doing and who our father was. Confidently, Ron told him, "Our father lives in England. We are on our way to visit him. We just stepped out to buy a bottle of water."

Miraculously, the ten of us met up in the rest rooms and hurried out of the station, where we spotted a large Mercedes-Benz taxi with three rows of seats, a vehicle commonly used as a cab in the Middle East. The driver smiled broadly at Mama and asked, "How have you been doing lately, Mrs. Falan? Haven't seen you in quite some time!"

Falan was a famous general in the Iraqi army. His wife and my mother bore a resemblance to each other, and the driver had mistaken my mother for her. Mama played the role brilliantly and ordered him to drive us to the northern border.

"But this is a sixteen-hour drive, Mrs. Falan, it is far away!"

"Go there, and my husband will reward you nicely," Mama said.

On the way, she told the driver that we were going on vacation, and that her husband, the general, couldn't travel because of this tumult with the escaped spies. None of us spoke; Mama had instructed us to be absolutely silent. Only Ron was allowed to talk, when spoken to, since he was the only one among us mature and experienced enough to mimic the Muslim accent.

We drove for two days. Some of us were sick and vomited because of the rough and tortuous roads. The cabdriver wanted to stop, urging my mother to get some food for us. "Go on, just go on," she insisted. "If they eat, they'll throw up again."

Not far from our destination, just before the gates of the town we were headed to, we saw a roadblock. "What's that about?" Mama asked the driver.

"Oh, it's nothing. I think it's what they were saying on the radio earlier, about these Jews that escaped the other day."

"Did they find them?"

"Yeah, they did, they shot them on the spot. They should do that to all Jews."

As we approached the block, Mama asked the driver to stop so that we could all freshen up.

"Why don't you go on," she said. "We'll finish cleaning up in the rest rooms and you can meet us there."

At the inspection point, the driver told the soldiers that Falan's wife and children were traveling with him. After his cab was inspected, he continued to the rest rooms where we'd waited for him, picked us up, and went through the roadblock with no further scrutiny. As we approached the town where a *shaliah,* or emissary, was supposed to be waiting for us, Mama gave the driver the address: Abu Ahmad, a small coffee shop near the border.

"Why would you want to go there?" the taxi driver asked her. "This is a place where smugglers hang out." She made up something, paid him, and he left us there. When we all trooped into the coffee shop, the smugglers who sat there looked at us in disbelief. They'd seen some strange things, but never had they laid eyes on a bunch like us.

The *shaliah* wasn't there, but he'd sent word to a smuggler in the coffee shop to expect a woman and her children. What the smuggler hadn't been told was that there would be so many of us. He said we'd have to split into two groups.

"Under no circumstances," my mother said. "We have made it this far as a group, we're not breaking apart now."

"Then you're on your own, Madam," he said. And in a softer voice, "It is too risky for me. Please understand. Many more could suffer if they catch us. But let me get a cab large enough for your group."

He arranged for yet another taxi, and only then did he tell my mother what her next destination was. That was the way it worked. This route would be used by other escapees; if we were caught, if our itinerary was tortured out of us, it would destroy that escape plan for any others who tried after us.

At the designated place, on a remote hill some twenty miles from the nearest town, the driver let us out, leaving a big cloud of dust behind. Why he didn't ask more questions of us, I'll never know. The smuggler had said that a *shaliah* would meet us here. It was noon and very hot outside. We stood and waited. One hour passed, then two, and still there was no sign of anyone. Mama began to wonder whether this was in fact where we ought to be. It was a godforsaken place, only some shepherds with their flocks in the distant hills. The more hours passed, the more anxious she became. Had she made a mistake and somehow misunderstood the instructions? Had something happened to the emissary? Had he been betrayed? If so, it was only a matter of time before they would find us. I was clueless to the thoughts racing through my mother's mind, as were all of us children. I did know that something was wrong, because she looked very worried. Until this point, the trip had been almost fun for me. It was the most exciting thing we'd done in months. Now, though, it became a little scary. Afternoon turned into evening and then into night. The air was turning cold, and I was hungry and thirsty. We'd been on that hill nine hours, and Mama, growing desperate, feared that we'd been abandoned. Without help, she knew, we would probably die there. When she heard the heavy sound of an approaching truck, she thought, That's it. The soldiers have found us.

"Kids, come quick, we need to hide," she ordered us. We threw ourselves in the bushes. We don't deserve this, I thought. We don't deserve to die like this.

When the truck came to a halt, even I could see that it was not an Iraqi army truck. Old, dirty, noisy, outfitted for chickens, it looked to me like an angel sent from heaven. With it arrived not the *shaliah* but a group of Kurdish smugglers. These Kurds, fighting the Iraqi government, had done such things before. They had an arrangement with the Israeli government. Israel supplied them with arms, and in return they helped in such rescue operations. They were ready for us. Their big chicken truck had a small, secret chamber in its interior. "The *shaliah* could not come," they said. "Get in, there is no time to waste. Hurry."

We squeezed into the truck's secret compartment, and for two days the ten of us traveled hidden there, with no light, little air, minimal water, and no food. We were all miserable, but not one child complained. After what we'd heard our cabdriver say, we knew that if we were caught, we all would be executed on the spot.

Finally the road ended. When we emerged from the truck, filthy, sick, and cold, we were high in the mountains. A *shaliah* was waiting for us, with maps, flashlights, and some canned food. He apologized for not being able to provide us with boots or blankets. We were just too many, he said. It would have been too dangerous; the Iraqis were on our trail. The *shaliah* reassured us that once we had crossed the border into Iran, we would be safe. He bade farewell to the Kurds, two of whom would accompany us on the next leg of our flight, and wished us good luck. We embraced him, and then he disappeared.

The snow was deep as we began to walk. The two Kurdish guides knew these mountains well. They managed to get us more food from friends in the villages we passed. We walked one week, then two. To avoid the soldiers who were patrolling the border, we traveled only during the frigid nights. When we passed army camps and hostile villages, Mama would put duct tape on our mouths to ensure our silence. None of this broke our spirits. Nor did the cold or the thin air or the rocky terrain. We matured beyond our years on this journey, and we marched silently, no complaints, no tears. Whenever one of us would stumble from fatigue, Mama, my baby sister Betty in her arms, would pick up that child and carry him or her for a spell. She was magnificent. She went through so much, and she would not give up. She focused on Baba, how he'd wanted us to make it. She remembered the words in his letter, and they gave her strength.

Eighteen days after our trek began, we stumbled across the border into Iran. We were all exhausted, bruised, starved, dirty—and elated. But our Kurdish guides were restrained; for them this was not over. They still had to go back. We were now infamous—the ten Jews who escaped from under the very noses of the Iraqi guards—and if our guides were ever tied to us, they would be dead. Very little was said. We all shook hands, and then they vanished into the mountains.

Waiting for us at the border was another *shaliah*. At the time, before the reign of the ayatollahs and before the cancer of Islamic fundamentalism had eaten through Iran's bones, the Persian state was on friendly terms with Israel. The Israeli government had gotten word of our escape from the Sokhnut, and a quick arrangement was made with the government of the shah. We were taken to a gorgeous mountain resort, where a delegation headed by Israel's foreign minister himself was waiting to greet us. Even now, when I think of how we were treated in the hotel after the ordeal we'd been through, it seems like a dream. The food brought to our rooms, the warm beds, the blankets, the down-stuffed pillows . . .

Everyone, from the Israelis to the hotel staff, looked at us as if we were some species of rare bird that had just flown in. Maybe, to a certain extent, we were. Some pitied us, some found us amazing. From hunted fugitives, hungry and cold, we became celebrities, welcomed by ministers, treated like heroes. After a few days spent recuperating, we were escorted by the foreign minister to the airport and put on the plane that would take us to Israel, where we were already a big news item. On the flight, safe at last, relieved, well fed, and well dressed, Jonathan mustered his courage to ask my mother, "Are we finally allowed to say that we are Jews again?" Hearing this, everyone on the plane, including the crew, broke down and cried. Everyone except me. I didn't want to give in to emotion. I intended to remember all of this, to absorb every detail, so that when I finally woke from the nightmare, I wouldn't forget it. I would never leave this ordeal behind, and I would tell about it someday. This was a part of me, of my heritage, my pride, my father. It was his last wish that we make it out of Iraq, and we made it. We finally made it.

I looked through the porthole window, and there, in the distance, beyond the Mediterranean Sea, I saw it. I saw Israel coming into view. Immediately I knew that this was my home.

Only then did big, salty tears roll down my cheeks. Mama, who had been watching, came and sat next to me. Wrapping me tightly in her arms, she said that she understood; that she was happy, too, that we were safe now. What she didn't understand, what no one could, was that I wasn't crying from relief. I wasn't even crying for my lost father and grandmother. It was the fact that when I looked down on my future home, the tiny state of Israel, I knew even there, in the sky above, that I loved it. Because I saw its sandy beaches, its dunes and deserts, and the slanting sunbeams bathing the countryside in glorious yellows. Everything was yellow again, and I could hold back my tears no longer.

CHAPTER 2

Shattered Dreams

THE PLACE WAS CALLED Ma'on Olim, "house of immigrants," or "home for those who rise." *Olim,* the Hebrew word for "coming up" or "escalating," is also the word for immigrants and newcomers to the country. Whether they came from Russia or from Ethiopia, from the summits of the Atlas Mountains or the prairies of the Siberian Taiga, immigrants to Israel were all called "risers." The notion of going up was supposed to give the impression that once you arrived in Israel, you were on top of the world. Many a time, this view was, well, not altogether accurate. But to us, coming from where we did, going through such an ordeal, Israel sure felt like heaven on Earth.

The Ma'on Olim was clean, comfortable, and best of all, as we soon discovered, within walking distance from the beaches of the Mediterranean Sea. A five-star hotel it was not. The home was a large gray building, seven stories high, made of concrete, and with very little aesthetic appeal. A stay in the Ma'on Olim, courtesy of the Israeli government, was part of the immigration process. We were given a one-room apartment there. Not one bedroom: just one room. One mom, three kids, one baby, one small room. Not too plush, you must agree. The room was even smaller than the hut in Baghdad, but we were content, because we had our freedom and safety. The immigration process also included Hebrew lessons, given in what is called *ulpan,* or school. The *ulpan* was a friendly environment in which to study Hebrew and the basics of the local customs. Mama went there, but we young kids were sent immediately to a public elementary school not far from the Ma'on Olim. Israel's rich experience with immigrants had shown that this was the best way to get the newly arrived kids to mingle and be accepted among their peers. Also, we were expected to learn Hebrew much quicker than was Mama. As I've learned from my life experience, it's true that kids get the hang of a new language very swiftly, while adults do not. The younger we are, the less inhibited and restrained we are, and the less we are ashamed of making mistakes. Kids, therefore, are more willing to accept a change, to experiment, to explore, to mimic. Kids want to learn a new language, to speak it in its local accent, and to learn the ways of the natives, while some adults stick to old habits, never truly becoming an integral part of their new society.

So on the first day in school, I met the natives. No one knew our story, no one knew who Jonathan and I were, and I felt that we were better off that way. They quickly realized that we were newcomers, even before the teachers introduced us during the first period, for they hadn't seen us before. In class, the teacher knew that I didn't understand a word of what she was saying. She looked at me from time to time with a comforting smile. During the first break—in Israel, there usually is a ten-to-fifteen-minute recess between each class, plus additional time for lunch—Jonathan and I were each surrounded by kids talking to us, asking us questions, and trying to befriend us. We were, after all, "risers," and they didn't get an opportunity to meet such strange creatures every day.

In my new country less than a week, with a vocabulary consisting mainly of "yes" and "no," I was eager to join the jolly company in the schoolyard. I wanted to make some new friends; after all, I'd been imprisoned and had no friends, save for my brothers, for two years.

Throughout my life, it's been important for me to have friends. I am, you might say, a friendly person. So I smiled at some kids who were staring at me during my first recess in Israel. They began approaching me, and I felt exhilarated. The conversation that followed sounded, to me, something like this:

"Shdfasdu cs dcsedoc qeideuwef, dfhsauhwefuh?" said one blond, blue-eyed girl.

I looked her straight in the eye and boldly said: "Yes!"

She looked puzzled. Her friend, a dark boy dressed in shorts and sandals, asked, "Ohscsdc holacdsaijp jqped ji naslcxhnaf, hjqnlad cchie dcahac iuuiiash?"

Reassured that I had answered successfully, I replied with increasing confidence:

"Yes, yes, ahaa!"

A small crowd was gathering around me, only now they were beginning to give me these strange looks, as if my hair were green or something. I was starting to get the feeling that my strategy was not working so well. I decided to make a quick adjustment, and when another boy asked me: "Afsevn hjscds olijwef uhc?"

I responded with an emphatic, premeditated, *"No!"*

Suppressed giggles in the crowd turned into outright laughter. These kids were not mean, and they meant no harm, but I realized that I was making a fool of myself. They kept asking questions, I kept answering "yes" or "no" or sometimes a combination of the two, yet nothing seemed to work. Everyone but me was laughing hysterically. I wanted to bury myself.

At last the bell rang, sending us back to class. Only now, after what had just happened, class was a torment. The anticipation of the next break, however, was even worse.

DURING THE SECOND BREAK, I saw Jonathan wearing his backpack, looking extremely unhappy and heading straight for the school's gate. I caught up with him and learned that he'd had much the same experience during the first recess that I'd had. He'd had enough for one day, he said. Ashamed, alienated, and furious, he was headed back home, to the Ma'on Olim. It wasn't the first time that he'd lost his cool. Whether it's fair to say that Jonathan took Baba's disappearance from our lives the hardest, I don't know. But I do know that he was the one who showed his feelings the most, and Mama treated him much more gently than she treated us. Ron and I, at least on the surface, seemed to have better weathered the horrors we'd suffered. Jonathan was touchy and sensitive, and he'd sometimes have tantrums over trifling matters.

I couldn't blame Jonathan for wanting to cut school, though. It was actually starting to look like the most reasonable thing to do, all things considered.

So we went home.

That evening, when Mama returned home and learned what we'd done, was the first time I'd actually seen her lose her temper. She gave both of us a thorough thrashing.

THE TOWN IN WHICH the Ma'on Olim was located, where Mama later bought an apartment and where I lived until I got married, is called Bat-Yam. It means "mermaid," and, at least geographically, the name is appropriate. Bat-Yam, like many other cities in Israel, is on the Mediterranean. Israel is a tiny country, about half the size of Lake Michigan, but much of Israel's western border is the Mediterranean, and its coastline is remarkable. The beaches are of yellow-golden sand—a gorgeous yellow sun shining down on cobalt-blue waters.

That beautiful sea is where most Arab nations have longed for many years to see Israel and Israelis go. Their leaders have said so on many occasions. Some of these leaders still believe the waters of the Mediterranean to be the most suitable place for all Jews. The deeper, of course, the better.

While Israel is some 250 miles long as the crow flies, it is only 15 to 25 miles wide in most places. This means that Ashkelon, a southern coastal Israeli city, is only 7 miles from the Gaza Strip. Netanya, another coastal Israeli city, is 9 miles from the West Bank. Which makes it so accessible to suicide bombers, like the one who took twenty-eight innocent lives in a seder celebration—what became known as "the

Passover Massacre." Tel Aviv is only 11 miles away from what are known as "the territories."

While Tel Aviv, growing out of the sand and the nothingness that preceded it, became Israel's most prominent city, the mermaid, Bat-Yam, a southern suburb, became a working-class bedroom community for its big-city sister. Many people who work in Tel Aviv live in Bat-Yam because apartments there are so much cheaper than comparable ones in Tel Aviv. That's exactly why Mama could afford to buy an apartment there. But you get what you pay for, and our mermaid was not on the cheap side for no good reason. Many areas in Bat-Yam were plagued with poverty, violence, and drugs. True, our neighborhood, where Mama got our apartment, was not in the worst part of town. But Bat-Yam was Bat-Yam, and it carried a stigma. One thing you could never take away from our mermaid, though, was its spectacular beaches.

ALTHOUGH MAMA'S TUTORIAL about ditching school left an unpleasant pain in my behind, there was something else I found much more disturbing about her. I didn't hate Mama for what she did, and neither did Jonathan. We knew that our punishment was well deserved. She had to be tough because she didn't have anyone to help her with our upbringing. She knew that without discipline we would go wild with all the new freedoms available to us. But what did bother me was that I'd noticed, for the first time, that Mama was aging. She was in her early thirties and beautiful as ever, but something in her eyes, a spark that I'd seen even in the most difficult and dangerous hours in Iraq, was gone. She was working very hard for our survival, but it wasn't that wearing her down. In Iraq, struggling for our lives, fighting for Baba and then for our freedom, Mama had so much to divert her thoughts from herself. In Israel, far from the place she'd considered home for most of her life, Mama felt very much alone. She began to have thoughts and dreams of Baba, of Grandma, of the execution, the torture. Late at night, these thoughts crept in and haunted her. She grew sad, as I'd never seen her before, and she grew older. Sometimes I'd wake up in the middle of the night to the sound of a strange noise. I'd sneak to her room and see her sitting in her bed, talking to Baba's picture, her face covered with tears.

As if Mama hadn't been through enough already, she encountered a major setback from the Israeli government, which refused to accredit her as a war widow. This meant that she would receive none of the benefits the state of Israel accorded such survivors. Just as distressing, the state would neither confirm nor deny that my father had had any links to the Israeli government or intelligence. Though Mama believed that Baba hadn't been a spy, she'd never really know without the Israeli government's confirmation. Only after many years, under tremendous public pressure and vigorous lobbying by sympathetic parliament members, was my mother finally declared the widow of a war hero and then she began receiving a state pension.

But in the beginning she was on her own. Her brothers and sisters who'd preceded her to Israel had agreed to raise my five young aunts and uncles, and they had their hands full with that and supporting their own children. Mama had to learn to provide for her family for the first time in her life. She was not trained in any income-yielding skills, and although we were given a place at the Ma'on Olim, it was only a short-term solution. Financially, we had just about enough to keep us afloat, but no more than that. Mama, who'd known what it was to live well, aspired to something much better for us. She began taking sewing courses in the evenings, after which she'd come home and stitch clothes until late in the night. Mama would sew and sell, and gradually the jobs began accumulating. At first she was hired just for tailoring, but later, as her sewing became more accomplished, Mama's customers would order whole suits of clothes. The more she worked, the more orders she got. A far greater lesson for me than any spanking she administered was watching her work all night long. Her example taught me the value of hard work, of determination, and, above all, of courage.

We children and her work were her world. Even years after we'd been in Israel, she wouldn't consider dating anyone, although many would-be suitors were in the wings. There was a man, however, with whom she shared much in common, and the two of them struck up a deep friendship. In the sewing classes, Mama met a teacher named Zvi Wechsler. Zvi was in his sixties, and although he was always good-humored—a mensch in every sense of the word—he too bore the scars of an unspeakable tragedy. Zvi had had a beautiful wife and two pretty daughters, six and eight years old, in Warsaw, Poland. And then the Germans came. He was made to watch as his loved ones were tortured and raped before his very eyes, and when the Nazis murdered them, Zvi's soul died in him. He no longer wished to live, yet he escaped the concentration camp so that he could tell the world what he had witnessed. He made his way to Israel, where he lived with and cared for his crippled younger sister, the only other survivor of their once large family.

Although he'd seen the worst of mankind, the ultimate evil, somehow Zvi never lost faith in humanity. Twice a week he would volunteer to teach in the county jail. He couldn't accept the idea that some people are beyond redemption. During his many years working at the jail, he'd received touching letters from ex-cons whom he'd taught, saying that his classes and his compassion were the reason they'd fought so hard to reform themselves.

Like Mama, he rejected the idea of marrying again. Mama and he remained close friends for the rest of his life. Zvi wasn't a father figure for me, but he became part of our family. The only one among us, though, to whom he would completely open up was my little sister, Betty. Zvi liked to say that she was his unborn granddaughter.

When in his early eighties he took ill with colon cancer, my husband Leo's brother-in-law—coincidentally also named Zvi—was the young surgeon who took care of him. The doctors at the hospital consulted and declared, given Wechsler's age and the advanced stage of his disease, that even if he survived the procedure itself, he'd never recover from the trauma of the major surgery required. Just let him live out the remainder of his life with dignity, they said. But Dr. Zvi knew that without the surgery, his patient would most likely die a painful death within six months. Dr. Zvi, who knew this old man and his life story, persuaded his colleagues and superiors to let him perform the surgery in spite of the odds. "You have the green light," they finally said, "but if something goes wrong, you're on your own; you won't get any backup from the hospital."

So Zvi operated on Zvi. "I'm not giving up. Not on this old man," he said.

For eleven hours the patient was kept alive by noisy machines that pumped oxygen into his lungs while the surgeon operated on the tumor and the metastases that had spread throughout his body. Both Zvis fought the battle of their lifetimes. Not only was the surgeon successful, but his patient recovered—in next to no time. For almost ten years he led a perfectly normal life. When he was near the age of ninety, the cancer recurred. Again Dr. Zvi operated, and again he was successful. Zvi Wechsler lived until he was ninety-four. He never knew that Dr. Zvi was the only one who refused to give up on him.

Every year on the anniversary of his first operation, Zvi would send Dr. Zvi flowers and a bottle of wine. The surgeon said that not only was this the most touching token of appreciation he'd ever received, but also that it came from a truly great man.

AFTER LESS THAN A YEAR in the Ma'on Olim we were seniors in the home's hierarchy, which qualified us for a bigger apartment. This one had two rooms, what in the United States is considered a one-bedroom apartment. We had no living room, just two rooms we used for sleeping, but this was a giant improvement over the first place. This was considered the "business class" of the Ma'on Olim, and everyone called these apartments "the suites." They had blue doors. All the other apartments, on floors two through seven, had orange doors. Moving to the new apartment, located on the first floor, meant that we were the elite of the home; but being closer to the ground also symbolized, maybe, that our time in the home was almost up.

I was still in the Israeli equivalent of grade school, but I wanted to help Mama, who was working ever harder. As Hebrew bears some similarities to the Arabic we'd spoken in Iraq, we kids caught up with the local language in a flash. I soon felt confident enough in my new language to offer my services as a tutor to the daughter of newcomers who'd just arrived. They came from what was then Soviet Georgia, and they brought a lot of money with them. I taught the girl for weeks, and when I finally received my payment, it was something like a buck and a half. Even in those days in Israel it wasn't much, but I was proud of my earnings. When Mama came home from work late that night, I tried to give her the money. She wouldn't accept it, but I saw that spark in her eyes again. She hugged me as she used to in the hut in Baghdad and told me to spend it on myself. So the next day, after school, Ron, Jonathan, Betty, and I went to an ice-cream parlor and had a party. I will never forget that vanilla scoop. It had the sweet taste of victory.

Without anyone's help, taking large, high-risk loans, Mama soon opened her own clothing business, through which she began to design, manufacture, and sell small quantities of clothes, earning just about enough to support us. After a couple of years, Mama took on the risk of a big mortgage and even more loans and bought us a relatively large three-bedroom apartment. She was determined that we not suffer for lack of a father and that we live in relative comfort. Occasionally, on Saturday evenings, she would put down her work and the five of us would go to the beautiful promenade that ran along Bat-Yam's beach, where we'd walk and then reward ourselves with ice cream.

One Saturday we went to Jerusalem, our first trip to this enchanting place. We traveled the city by foot for a while, and then Mama decided to splurge on a cab to take us to another part of town, to visit the windmill that Sir Moses Montefiore, a Jewish philanthropist who lived in England, had built in the nineteenth century. The cab we hailed was a particularly large one, with three benches rather than two, and there was a passenger in it already; many cabs in Israel are communal. I got in and so did Ron, but Jonathan would not. He started to scream, and scratch, and kick, and it took all of us to restrain and calm him. Mama quickly figured out what had happened. In Jerusalem, a city with a great mix of orthodox and secular, of Jews, Christians, and Muslims, and of Israelis and Arabs, a good number of taxi drivers are Arabs. Many Arabs wear bushy mustaches. In Iraq, practically all the officials, policemen, and secret service agents, like the ones who took Baba away, wear mustaches. Jonathan looked at the cabdriver and at the Arab passenger who sat inside, both of them with thick black mustaches, and he lost it. He'd had a phobia that dated back to that night when the Iraqis busted his head on the marble floors, only we'd never known it.

So there we were, with all our emotional scars and baggage, a family of immigrants reconstructing their lives in Israel. Mama worked fifteen-hour days, making sure we were always dressed in the best of fashion, had the best snacks and expensive fruits packed in our lunch bags, and had everything we could dream of. Our family was even the first in the neighborhood to own a VCR—back when those contraptions were the size of small cars. She somehow did this and managed to keep up with our lessons, too. Ron, who is very smart, was flourishing academically and socially. Jonathan, however, struggled. Mama sat for long hours with him, and he still barely passed. I did okay, but not great—the necessary minimum to get a reasonable grade. My social life was much more important to me, and this made Mama furious.

What can I say? I sought the spotlight as a butterfly does the sweet nectar in a flower. There was no school production in which I didn't play the leading role. I loved to dress in costumes, and I loved being on-stage, riveting the audience with my performances. Never had a hint of stage fright. I became popular, perhaps too popular, because I spent more time with friends than with my homework. I also began to notice that I preferred going to the homes of girls whose fathers were home. I had a burning desire to use the word *Abba,* the Hebrew word for Baba. I was never able to use that beautiful Hebrew word, and I envied those girls who had an *abba* and could call him that whenever they wanted. Sometimes, hoping that no one would notice, I'd whisper *"Abba"* to these men, just to see what it felt like.

Further adding to Mama's tsuris, my new popularity and confidence caused an old trait to resurface. Hot and sunny Bat-Yam was the perfect ground for my mischievous tendencies, which had been utterly suppressed while under Iraqi house arrest. I returned to my old tricks with a vengeance. Because I wanted to avoid a repeat of the pain Mama had administered to my gluteal region, I adopted a more chary approach. Mischief itself would not cause trouble, I'd figured out. It was *getting caught* that was the problem. So I refined my techniques. I skipped school and went to the beach, often persuading my many friends to join me. Then we'd come up with some excuse that the teacher couldn't dismiss because of the vast number of students supporting it.

Realizing the power of money and the virtues of a free market, I used my time away from class to sell a variety of items on street corners. At one time I sold cactus pears, which are sought after as a snack in Israel. But being less than expert in handling such prickly creatures as cactus fruit, I picked them up with my bare hands. The pain and swelling in my palms didn't go away for weeks.

Sometimes I'd buy products in the supermarket and resell them at school for a slightly higher price. My school had had no specific prohibitions against such enterprise; it was not smiled upon at home, however, and whenever Mama caught me at it, yet another spanking was in the offing. These prank-punishment cycles became routine enough that I learned to dodge Mama's whacks. She too adapted to our little dance. Her favorite educational aid became her shoe, and her aim at a fast-moving target (your humble servant) became eerily effective.

Many times Jonathan and I would gang up on Ron. He was so serious and responsible, he was just asking for it. The night before he went on his first date, Jonathan and I casually told Mama, bent at her sewing machine, that we'd go with him.

"Ahaa," she said, preoccupied, not really hearing what we were saying. Our gambit had worked; that distracted "ahaa" constituted permission. The next day we followed Ron, and when he met his date, we jumped them and made them take us to the matinee. This was the last Ron saw of that girl. We played many other practical jokes on him, but he was always tolerant and understanding, always with a sense of humor. The night Mama told us he was going away, the news hit us like a ton of bricks.

It was customary back in Iraq among the wealthy families to send the older boys overseas, in order to get them the best education money could buy. When the time came, Ron was sent to school in England. Mama had a brother there, and Ron could stay with him. I know Mama thought this was the best thing for Ron, and she may have been right. But my poor older brother! He'd just started to feel that he was part of a happy family again, and now, once more, it was to be denied him. And as for Jonathan and me—we were heartbroken and for many nights buried our heads in our pillows and cried ourselves to sleep.

Ron left, and he left a void in me. His departure acutely sharpened another facet in my life that I'd been noticing for quite some time. Before he left, he was the one in charge, the one we could always turn to, the father figure we lacked. Now he was gone, Mama was working insane hours, and, in a sense, I was alone. Jonathan, in the nature of boys will be boys, declined to do any household chores. Mama had to spend so much time with him on his homework and was so preoccupied with assuaging his moodiness that she didn't have the will to fight with him over the chores. Betty, by now in school and a brilliant student, was so engrossed in her studies—Mama sometimes caught her reading late at night under a blanket using a flashlight—that she was always too busy studying to contribute to the upkeep of the house. Anyway, she had absolutely no touch for it. So there I was, taking care not only of all house chores, but also of my younger siblings.

Out of the house I was always queen of the clique, of the school production, of the prom; at home I was a poor student, a budding delinquent, and the informal housemaid. I felt that I was constantly being spanked or yelled at, and I began to think that Mama hated me and that she was ashamed of me. I felt like the black sheep of the family. So when Mama spent her savings on a gorgeous and overgenerous bat mitzvah party for me, my whole view of the world was shaken. Maybe she was proud of me after all.

It was during this time that I became increasingly preoccupied with the question of my father's involvement in the Arab-Israeli conflict. Ron was away, in England, doing very well in school, and not in the least interested in reopening the wounds of the past. Jonathan too had no wish to delve deeply into the subject. Betty was a baby when it happened and had never known her father. But as time passed, I thought more and more about it. Between school and friends, boys and housekeeping, I had very little time left. Still, I began searching for information. I went through all our family albums, compiling photos and notes, and asked Mama for any information she could give me about the people in the photographs. I gradually put together my first dossier, never imagining that dossiers would become an indisputable proficiency of mine. Next I scoured libraries and public archives, reading every document I was able to find about the Six-Day War and its aftermath, looking for clues regarding Baba. Old newspapers, periodicals, articles, reviews, files, history books, photos, I went through them all. I read in Hebrew, Arabic, and English, and experienced for the first time the power of being able to read a document in its original language. How valuable I'd find this skill later in my life! To broaden my knowledge, I wrote to politicians, historians, and experts, requesting copies of documents, asking their opinions.

Unfortunately, the files were all stamped confidential, not to be released to the public for fifty years, and my search ended without any significant leads or useful information. But all things, I believe, happen for a reason. Not even in my wildest dreams had I envisioned then that this search would have such a fundamental impact on me. Literally, it determined the course of my life. I feel that nothing could be more important than what I do today, and I love every second of it, but I would give anything for Baba not to have died and left me with this legacy. It is a very heavy load.

Although my search, until that point, was futile, I wasn't willing to give up without a fight. I volunteered to work for a member of Israel's Knesset, or Parliament, and as that politician's aide I gained access, for the first time, to the Knesset's library and archives. Some documents there could not be found elsewhere.

As I sat in the library one evening looking through some records, I suddenly saw it. The photograph struck me with tremendous viciousness. I looked at it, and I couldn't breathe. I tried to inhale, but no air was coming in.

That was it. That was the proof. There was the picture, in black and white. So long had I been hunting for an answer, and now that I'd found it, I wished I'd never sought it in the first place. It was a photograph of the hanging, in the central square in Baghdad. Underneath the image I read my father's name and a caption describing the event.

I tore out of there, my eyes filling with blinding, painful tears. I sobbed, for the first time, over Baba. Even now, when I remember how I first laid eyes on that horrendous picture, I cannot help but cry.

I THOUGHT I heard him. Yep, there he was, honking again. I'd just come out of the shower, water dripping from my hair on the bathroom tiles. Hadn't it occurred to him to come upstairs and get me, instead of laying on the horn? He shouldn't have been so lazy. After all, he wasn't even eighteen—three flights of stairs wouldn't kill him. He was rushing me, and I didn't like to be rushed. I looked at the clock. Oops. It was quarter to nine; I'd told him to come around eight. I had no idea it was so late. It was summer, and there was still so much daylight. I stuck my head through the bathroom window and yelled, "C'mon up, it'll take me a few more minutes."

"Take your time, I'll wait here," he yelled back. What a gentleman.

Now I was even more stressed out. I grabbed the first shirt and pair of jeans I found in the closet and hurriedly put them on. On the way out, I stopped and checked myself in the mirror. What did they all see in me? I had no idea. My eyes? My breasts? Legs, skin, what was it? In my teens, I was somewhat full figured. I wasn't fat, only rounded here and there, mostly in the right places. Boys were hitting on me all the time. Not that I was provocative or easy; I was neither. I'd been dating Yossi, the boy who was honking outside now, for almost two years. He was of Iranian ancestry, tall, with green eyes and dark, curly hair, and at the time I thought I loved him. Mama was strongly opposed to that relationship. She just didn't like Yossi, for reasons beyond me. I looked in the mirror again. What did they all see that I was missing? I honestly couldn't understand why so many boys were swarming around me. I rushed downstairs.

Yossi had a small car, even by Israeli standards. In Israel, a Volvo is practically considered a limousine; most cabinet members are driven in Volvos. In such a universe, Yossi's two-door Ford Fiesta was considered a respectable car. The most frequently used device in his car, as you might have suspected, was its horn. Most Israelis use their car horns liberally, either to signal danger, to register discontent with the driving of others, to express admiration for a beautiful girl on the sidewalk, or just to call a friend to come downstairs—even if that person lives on the third floor.

Yossi and I used to take his car and go to the beach, the movies, the park, and parties. I could hardly be bothered with my studies, and my grades showed it. I was preoccupied with Yossi and with partying, which is probably why Mama resented him. She knew that the only way to success was through education.

After Yossi and I broke up, suitors literally lined up at our door. I did try dating some of them. I dated tall and short, thin and chubby, rich and poor, sophisticated and simple. Some of them were nice, but I hadn't fallen for any of them. After a date or two, I'd end it. I began to feel that I was wasting my time. But the more I said no, the more they seemed to want to date me. It became a nuisance. I decided to stop with the dating and, at long last, pay attention to my schoolwork.

I was still hunting for information about the circumstances surrounding Baba. Mama was absolutely certain that he wasn't a spy, but I'd started to develop my own suspicions. The more I thought about it, the more I realized that the way to get to the bottom of the mystery was through academia. So I studied Middle East affairs at Tel Aviv University. I grew fascinated with the subject, and although my high school grades were far from outstanding, in Middle East affairs I did exceptionally well. I gained extensive knowledge and the cerebral tools to become an expert on the issue. Had my professors known what I'd end up doing, they'd have put me on their CVs.

A familiar joke at Tel Aviv University was that students, particularly of the feminine persuasion, who were attending certain schools were doing so only to obtain an educated spouse. Some of the schools, particularly those related to social studies—among them Middle East affairs—didn't promise their graduates a lucrative future. These disciplines were sarcastically nicknamed "the schools of marriology." And as they say, there's truth in every joke. . . .

Leo lived in our neighborhood in Bat-Yam, and I'd seen him around, here and there. The only time I really met him, if you can call it that, was during my freshman year in high school, when he came to give us a lesson in biology. We were both at the same school, and my biology teacher, who thought very highly of him, asked him to give us a lesson in something she felt he knew better than she did. I remember thinking it was pretty cool that this guy knew so much, but I didn't give him much more thought. The next time we met was years later, on the bus to the university. We struck up a conversation. He told me that he had a car, that it was in the shop that day, and that when it came out of there, he'd be happy to offer me a ride, perhaps, maybe, if I wanted to, that is. After some time, I took him up on his offer, and Leo started driving me, once or twice a week, from home to the campus.

He really was a strange bird. He grew his blond hair longer than I wore mine, and I have no memory of his ever running a comb through it. He was the only one in his graduate school who showed up for class in a tie. Dress codes in Israel are much more lax than those in the United States, so at first his fellow students thought he was a weirdo; but by his second year, nearly half the students in his class were dressing up, too. He hated small cars and was completely in love with huge American dinosaurs, gigantic by any standard, but even more conspicuous in the Israeli milieu. He never, ever, honked his horn. He despised it. He'd come as a boy from Russia, and he had some Russian friends with whom he liked to drink. As he could hold his liquor very well, he used to drink quite a bit. At first, he used to tell me jokes I couldn't really follow, and I was under the impression that he was trying to poke fun at me, although I wasn't quite certain what made me think that.

After he'd driven me home a few times, I asked him up one night. Mama had suggested that I do that so that she could meet my dedicated driver. I wasn't even sure I liked the guy. He came up, sat for a while, talked to Mama and Jonathan, and went home. He came again, and I still had no idea what, exactly, we were doing. And then Mama urged me to ask him out on a date.

Joseph's gift? I still don't know why she asked me to do that. She later told me that the night before Leo first came to our house, she saw Baba in a dream. He smiled at her, waved good-bye, and then he turned his back and slowly went away. Mama told me that such a dream meant that it was time for her to let go of someone, or, in other words, that I was destined to leave the family in order to start my own.

I didn't believe a word of it. Every time she wanted to persuade me to do something she would come up with a dream that would provide an excellent reason to do whatever that thing was. I think she was making these dreams up as she went along. But why did she like Leo, of all people? I'd had nicer, richer, older boyfriends, but none were to her liking. Leo was younger than I was, in the beginning of his graduate school studies, and not someone you'd expect to be mature enough for a serious, long-term relationship.

I ended up asking Leo out. That was a new one for me. Usually I'd been in the position of turning them down, and here I was, asking someone out I wasn't even sure I liked. His sense of humor annoyed me, I thought he was dispassionate and arrogant, and he hated Middle Eastern and Arabic music, my favorites. We went to a nice place in Tel Aviv called Rothschild's Pub. We drank a few beers, he told me a few stories, and before I knew what was happening, I was all over him. I don't know whether it was the alcohol or the place or his blabber or the gorgeous Eric Clapton music in the background, but my doubts—and inhibitions—all but vanished. When we met a few days later, I saw that Leo was a bit embarrassed and that the question of whether I actually remembered what happened on our date was on the tip of his tongue. But like a true gentleman, he never asked, and I never told him. Of course I remembered.

On Israel's Independence Day, usually in late April or early May, depending on the Jewish calendar, people usually take a few days off and go on trips. The weather is nice around that time of year. Leo and I had been dating for a few weeks, and I was expecting him to call me to discuss mutual plans for the holiday. Instead he disappeared. Never called, never gave a sign of life. I hadn't made any other plans for the holiday, so I ended up staying at home. The nerve of that guy. No one had treated me that way before. I decided that whatever his reason or excuse might be, I no longer wanted anything to do with him.

A few days later, he showed up in our apartment. I came out of the shower, and there he was, standing in my room. I was very frosty to him. He was mystified; what was the problem? Two people who are involved in a steady relationship, I tried to explain, don't just abandon each other, certainly not on a holiday. He was taken aback. He apologized, said his friends called and they had spontaneously decided to go on a trip to Eilat.

Eilat! The rogue! Eilat was my favorite city! This city, on the astounding beaches and coral reefs of the Red Sea, is probably the most amazing place in the Northern Hemisphere. That was it. I was through with him, and I didn't want to talk to him again. But he kept apologizing, kept saying he thought I wanted to spend the holiday with my family, and on and on.

In war and love, said Miguel de Cervantes, a fortress that embarks on negotiation is bound to be taken. It's true. We met later that day, we spent some time talking, and then I went to his place. We talked some more, we started to kiss, and we ended up in bed. There awaited me yet another surprise. He was gentle, caring, and considerate, but that wasn't the surprise. He wasn't my first, and he didn't mind. It was obvious to me that he, too, had some experience. But then we did something new to me, and for the first time in my life, I understood what was the big fuss about sex. I was completely shaken. Literally. And it made me feel more like a woman than I'd ever felt before. Later, when Leo went to his desk, pulled out two cigarettes, and lit one for each of us, I suddenly saw the light. Not that of the Zippo, but of finally knowing what it was that I saw in him. This arrogant, selfish, inconsiderate brat would be the father of my children. I looked at him and I saw them—running around, playing with a ball, spraying water on one another, laughing out loud. I couldn't explain what it was that I saw, but it was there, crystal clear. He *was* the one. How had Mama been able to foresee that?

While Leo and I were still dating, I had to go and serve my time in the army, as all Israelis must. The first part of the service is a breaking-in period of training; this can be harsh for many girls, even ones who are not spoiled, because the general idea is, well, to break you in. You shoot, you run, you climb ropes and walls, you wash toilets and huge pots and pans, you eat very little, and you sleep even less. You get, as part of the training, plenty of abuse and attitude from your superiors, girls whose only advantage over you is having been inducted into the army a few months before you. Many girls cry half the time during these training periods.

I lucked out and was assigned to a base located only some five miles from where we lived. Every night, when the other girls were complaining about the training, feeling sorry for themselves, and counting blisters, I would receive a visitor. Leo, an officer in the army, had free access to that base, a perk that most relatives of the other girls didn't have. He'd bring me flowers, goodies, candies, nice stuff, even wine, but mostly, he'd bring himself. We would find a quiet corner somewhere and make out. How could I take the army training seriously when I had so much fun almost every evening? The other girls were so jealous, seeing me return with leaves and blades of grass in my hair, that even the candy bars and snacks I used as appeasement bribes barely spared me their ire.

After I got out, Leo and I got married. We were both still young, both still students. We moved into our own little place. Two years later, I gave birth to my eldest, a boy named Jordan. I continued with my studies, and it was in these years that I had my first encounter with intelligence agents. It wasn't a very pleasant one. Leo was and still is a great believer in the need to give the Palestinians a state of their own, but during that time, similar to the McCarthyism of the 1950s, perhaps, there was hysteria in Israel regarding left-wingers such as Leo. Those who in the early seventies, not long after the Six-Day War, supported an independent Palestinian state were likely to be considered traitors and potential security hazards. I was approached by two intelligence agents who asked me to "keep an eye" on leftist activists, including Leo. I was disgusted and told them to go look for their mole elsewhere.

Becoming a wife and a mother was wonderful, but it brought new responsibilities. We needed to make a living. Academia was what I wanted to do, but that doesn't put a loaf of bread on the table. Leo, too, was still a student, and we barely scraped by. I was forced to switch gears toward a more money-generating occupation. I decided to shoot two birds with one arrow and go into Mama's business. Hit hard by wild inflation and a shaky Israeli economy, her clothing company was just hanging on. I was hoping to provide some income for my family and to improve Mama's situation at the same time.

Clothes, on the one hand, and business, on the other, were entirely new to me. Sure, I wore clothes, but that was about all I knew about them. In my mind, the making of clothes meant sitting through the night in near darkness, designing, cutting, and sewing—as Mama used to do. Not a very desirable life, I thought to myself. So I decided to concentrate more on marketing than on the actual manufacturing process. Cluelessly, I started my career as saleswoman. I trudged from one neighborhood of fashion shops to another, lugging a heavy suitcase filled with dress samples I knew almost nothing about. I used to show the samples, and then, when questions were asked, I'd stop my presentation and call Mama for the answer. I knew nothing about prices, sizes, material, quality, warranty, credit, availability, quantity, nothing. Some store owners looked at me with pity and then made all kinds of excuses to get rid of me. Others thought I was a complete moron, and the less than polite ones were happy to share that opinion with me. I knew I was ignorant and cheeky, but I also knew that I wasn't stupid. I kept going, and gradually I learned about interest rates and consignment, fabrics and dyes, ornaments and accessories, and most of all, I learned how to engage and entice even the most stubborn, disinterested shop owners. I started to get some orders. Small amounts at first, from hesitant salesmen and for ridiculously low prices. But then the volume of orders increased. Mama's merchandise was of high quality. Those who placed orders always called within a few days, saying that they'd sold the entire stock, asking to reorder.

Before long, our clothes were selling like crazy, more orders came in, and we got busier and busier. I began knocking on the doors of the largest department store chains in the country. These giants were always leery of working with small manufacturers, which were frequently unreliable. Mama had tried several times in the past to sell them some of her stuff, but they'd never ordered a thing from her. I walked into those fancy offices and told them that I didn't need them, that it was they who needed me. That I was going to make this pitch only once, and that if they missed this opportunity, there would be no second chance. I told them that our line was selling like hot cakes—the first sentence in my presentation that vaguely resembled the truth—and that the sales of our clothes by their competitors would cause tremendous damage to their business. I don't know how and why, but they bought it—the story and the clothes. With combination of the quality of the goods and my chutzpah, I managed to bring home some very large orders. Almost too large for us to handle. I began to work twice as hard; I went to the fabric and accessory manufacturers and wholesalers myself, and I had to learn that part of the business fast. There was no time for a learning curve, and I couldn't afford to get conned. With such a volume of orders and our margins stretched thin, if we produced defective goods or lost money on this, it would mean going out of business. At this point, I was no longer just helping Mama to design the fashions. Now I had the last word, and I'd decide what was to be done and what would sell.

We made it. The success was phenomenal. The clothes were flying out of the stores even before we could supply new stocks. We were getting calls from many branches of these chains, begging for more, saying that people were coming in and asking for our line. The family's standard of living increased so that we were all able to afford nice houses in the suburbs—very nice houses, in fact, in a very nice neighborhood. So long, Bat-Yam. Leo and I moved into a house next door to Mama.

At this point I did something that would have a bearing on my future, but for reasons I could never have imagined at the time. I decided to penetrate the largest and most difficult clothing market in Israel: that of the ultra-Orthodox community. Those folks, as you might guess, believe in procreation. Unlike secular families averaging a child or two, the ultra-Orthodox routinely have twelve, fourteen kids, even more. Moreover, they dress for the holidays, usually a new outfit for every child, boy or girl, for every holiday. Holidays in Israel, thank heavens, are numerous. This market was therefore a potential gold mine, but it had one great disadvantage. The ultra-Orthodox will buy goods only from their own people. They wouldn't deal with secular merchants, mostly because they wouldn't find styles to suit them—long dresses, long sleeves, lace, head cover, the whole nine yards—among such manufacturers. Second, they'd have to deal with people who don't look like them, dress like them, speak their language, or think like them. I realized that, and I took the time to study their ways. When I felt I was ready, I put on a long dress with long sleeves, I covered my head and neck in the spirit of tradition, and I marched into their neighborhoods. To make a long story short, we became a hit with the ultra-Orthodox as well. Here is where I learned to camouflage, to mingle, to blend, to accommodate, to assume a personality.

Early in the morning, I'd put on my usual tight jeans and a short-sleeved T-shirt, I'd go to our little factory, check the seamstresses, make a few remarks. Later, I'd throw on a jacket and go meet the CEOs of the large department store chains to discuss sales and distribution and fashions. Then I'd change in the car, assume my disguise of an ultra-Orthodox woman, go to our stores in the neighborhoods of B'nai-Braq and Jerusalem, make sure everything was running well, and help with the sales. Later still, I'd put on my jeans and T-shirt again and return to the industrial district of Tel Aviv to meet with fabric manufacturers. During this period in my life, I got accustomed to changing into someone else within minutes.

Business was booming. I ran the show. Our family grew, and we had three kids, Jordan, Gil, and Charlie, all boys. Jordan was already in school. We had many friends, and we went out very often. We had fun, lots of fun. Life was good.

Alas, the idyllic life was not assured. The apple was big, beautiful, and juicy, but it was being eaten from within by a vicious worm.

AFTER HE RETURNED from the war in Lebanon, Leo grew restless in Israel. He began to talk to me about trying to live, at least for some time, elsewhere. It wasn't just the war. He was fed up with the Israeli rudeness, wild driving and honking, and Middle Eastern manners and behavior in general. I was absolutely opposed to the idea. I was a patriot, Baba had died because he was a Jew in the Diaspora, and financially, things were going well for us in Israel. No way was I going to leave. But Leo kept on bugging me about moving, even though for years he wasn't even sure where he wanted us to go.

It didn't happen overnight, but seams started to appear in my wall of resistance. Not that I was foolish enough to think that Israel was the Promised Land. If you were to summarize life in Israel in one sentence, the words *hardship* and *war* would definitely be in it. I was still a child when the Yom Kippur War erupted. I'd lived through that time, and it had marked me. I saw young men join the Israeli Defense Forces, IDF, and never come back. And the sound of sirens . . . Then there was the war in Lebanon. Leo fought in it, and I went a few times to the north to pick him up and drive him home for short leaves after he'd flown in from the war zone. Twice he nearly died there. Then the Gulf War, and the sirens, again. This time we civilians were on the front lines, Scud missiles flying everywhere. We were all made into soldiers, involuntarily.

Because Leo was an officer, and the IDF knew the 1991 war was coming, he was summoned early in January, before the first bombardment of Baghdad by the Allied Forces. Two days after it started, in the middle of January, the first Iraqi missiles arrived. Scud missiles from a scum leader. We knew Saddam Hussein was trying to use weapons of mass destruction, so when the sirens went off, everyone hid in what we used to call "the sealed room." Not bomb shelters anymore. The thought now was to be ready for poisonous gas or some nasty bug. So everyone sealed all the windows in one room in their apartments with plastic sheets and duct tape. When the sirens went off, we'd go into the room, put on our gas masks, shut the door, and put a wet towel on the floor near the door to prevent gas from seeping into the room. We were to keep the masks on until the signal was given that the missiles had been checked for gas and biological content and cleared. We needed to do all this in less time, practically, than it took you to read those two sentences; we had only thirty seconds. Any longer, the authorities told us, and it would be too late for us. But there was more. In some places, the sirens were too remote and not easily heard, so the radio was to be set on "the silent wave," a channel that would transmit absolute silence around the clock. When the warning was given by the IDF radar, the silent wave would immediately broadcast the wailing of the sirens. We all slept with the radio on and at our bedsides, tuned in to the silent wave, waiting. Most attacks happened at night, so we couldn't even get a decent night's sleep during that time.

There's more yet. We grown-ups could somehow manage with the gas masks. But what about kids? Charlie wasn't born yet, but I had Jordan and Gil. For older kids like Jordan, they came up with smaller-size masks. For the very young ones, they invented a contraption that looked like an oxygen tent in a hospital or a plastic incubator. It had a smart lock-in device that would allow you to quickly open the device, put the infant or toddler in, and safely seal him or her inside within seconds. Or so it said on the brochure that came with the thing. I did my best to manage with it. Mama moved in with me so that we could help each other and worry about sealing only one room. The first time the sirens sounded, it was a fiasco, total chaos. When the sirens sang their chilling tune, we tried to go by the book. I started with myself, as we'd been instructed. Then I tried to put the infant, Gil, in his tent. Mama was in a lot of trouble trying to put her mask on. Jordan somehow managed to put his on by himself. I lost concentration for a fraction of a second, and the lock-in mechanism of the tent snapped and clamped down on Gil's neck. Frantically I tried to pull his head out, but the harder I struggled, the more tightly it pressed on his neck. He was screaming. Jordan sat quietly in the other corner with his mask on. I thought he was okay, but when I looked more carefully, I saw that his face was dark blue. The mask was on, all right, but its valve was still shut. I'd forgotten to turn it on. He didn't know what wearing the mask was supposed to feel like, so he was tolerating it obediently, and suffocating. About 120 seconds into the emergency mode—90 seconds too late—Mama was still struggling to fix her mask, Jordan was being asphyxiated, and Gil's head was pinched between two plastic collapsible poles. If those Scuds *had* been armed with gas, you wouldn't be reading this book.

Then Leo called. He was very worried. He himself was safe in his bunker—they had sophisticated filtering mechanisms and didn't even need to wear masks. But, he asked, how were things back home? *Great,* I lied.

We had the opportunity to get better with our apparatus because there were attacks almost every night, sometimes even three or four a night. But with small children and temporarily husbandless, under the constant threat of a chemical attack, I was living in a nightmare. The entire country was at a standstill because of the fear of attacks. For long weeks, schools were closed, businesses were closed, everything was shut down, people went out only for necessities and rushed back home immediately. Israel became a giant ghost town. Everyone just sat at home and waited, for the next attack, for the next report. Was there poisonous gas yet, or wasn't there?

Leo and I spoke daily on the phone, and he was telling me that everything was cool, nothing to worry about, that this thing would soon be over and he would come back home. Now it was his turn to lie, and I could easily tell he was lying, but I had no idea about what. I only learned the truth long after the fact. During the war, Leo was assigned to head a research team that would design facilities to treat massive casualties. He was called one night to meet with some generals, all with very grim expressions, and they asked his professional opinion about one threat: anthrax, they said. Their prediction for casualties was between five thousand and fifty thousand per set of missiles. He was asked to assess the threat and come up with a quick solution for effective treatment facilities for such numbers. When he came back after the war, Leo had gray hairs that hadn't been there before. For him, that war was the last straw.

A year after that war, we decided to take a trip to the United States. We packed a few things, took our boys, and went. The five of us traveled coast to coast, a wonderful experience. We felt that if there was heaven on Earth, it must be somewhere in Yellowstone National Park. Or along the Pacific Coast Highway in California. Or the Grand Canyon, perhaps. And then Manhattan, coming into view from the Verrazano-Narrows Bridge, on the Brooklyn-Queens Expressway—a breathtaking sight. Its skyline filled with majestic giants, from the Twin Towers to the Empire State to the Chrysler Building . . . unbelievable.

Symbols of the greatest nation on Earth. Leo was captivated, and he decided that *this* was where we were heading. The United States of America.

Still, I resisted. But then things started to happen, one after the other. I lost a newborn baby, the result of medical malpractice. I never sued; the money wouldn't have brought him back. I never got to see him, for they took him away immediately after the operation, and I was too sick. But Leo sat with him for the long hours during which the intensive care pediatricians fought for him.

Then came another blow, a great tragedy had happened in Israel. A right-wing fanatic murdered Prime Minister Yitzhak Rabin. Most Israelis will never forget what they were doing and where they were at the time of the assassination. We were with friends, having fun, and we heard shouts on the street, and Mama called, and we turned on the TV, and they were announcing that he was critically injured. Then a spokesman, his voice breaking, announced Rabin's death. Something very big cracked in all of us that night. Gone was the age of innocence, of pure and conscientious Zionism, of an idealized picture of our small country and our countrymen. Gone were the dreams. That day we came of age, and in a most horrible way.

The writing on the wall is always there, but we all tend to miss it. A few years before that murder, a right-wing psychopath had thrown a hand grenade into a peace rally, killing one activist. In right-wing rallies, months before Rabin's killing, they were showing posters of him and of his partners for the peace process dressed in Nazi uniforms and with targets on their faces. When Rabin died, the country woke up, but then it was too late. Israel wept. The day he was buried, a million and a half Israelis, a third of the entire state's population, passed in a procession by his grave to pay their last respects, on the blackest day in Israeli history.

The next blow? The Israeli tax authorities, as is their wont, decided to investigate Mama's business, searching for illegalities. I later learned that this was a common practice of theirs with regard to businesses that show a sudden large increase in revenue. I was interrogated for months, as if I were a criminal. I was forced to return time and again to the tax offices, bearing heavy binders with details of our accounts and transactions. We were finally given a clean bill, but I was deeply hurt. To conduct their investigation in such a way, and to us, of all people . . . I felt betrayed by my adoptive country. I began to feel for the first time that something was wrong, a kind of unlucky streak. I wanted to change it, to stop this negative series of events. Why not try someplace else for a while? Two or three years in America could boost Leo's career tremendously and put him in an excellent position when we came back to Israel. Leo sensed an opening in me and pushed harder and harder. On the other hand, I'd miss my family, I reasoned with myself. Mama's business would be badly harmed. And it'd be difficult for me to get a job in New York. . . . Oh, the dilemma.

And then Rothschild's Pub was shut down. That place, our favorite, where our love story began, meant so much to Leo and me. Bad, bad sign, I decided. It was time for us to go.

CHAPTER 3

A Tendentious Translation

Where observation is concerned,
chance favors only the prepared mind.
—Louis Pasteur

MOVING TO AMERICA, in a way, meant exchanging a life I knew for something different and unfamiliar elsewhere. The last time I'd moved from one country to another, the choice was simple: Leave or die. This time around I was making the move for reasons not nearly as dramatic. Still, transplanting myself from Tel Aviv to the suburbs of New York City was a fraught endeavor, no matter how voluntarily we were going.

It's hard to imagine how much stuff can accumulate in a house over the years, especially a house like ours—a fancy, seven-bedroom modern structure with two Jacuzzis. The things we wanted to take with us, such as our memories embodied in photos and videos, we sent by sea. The rest we sold or simply gave away. Everyone we knew came to this giveaway carnival. Our friends, neighbors, and acquaintances, their friends and neighbors, the people we employed in our stores—you get the picture. They came with vans and pickup trucks and hauled away just about anything they could put their hands on. Surveying our house afterward, I could easily imagine how Rome looked after it was stormed and looted by the Vandals and Visigoths.

Our U.S. visa had been delayed for bureaucratic reasons. When it finally arrived, we bade farewell to family and friends—again—and set out for the airport. The procession that took us there included Leo, me, our three boys, ten medium-size boxes and four large suitcases, Mama and Leo's mother, Jonathan and Betty, our closest friends, and our not-so-closest friends. At the airport it was easy to make out who was with us and who was not, because when it was really time to go, almost everyone in our bloated delegation started to sob. By the time we left the passport checkpoint, there was a little lake where we'd all stood, and they later named that lake after us. . . . I do get a bit carried away. But all of us did cry bitterly.

We happened to be flying on July 4, and as we approached New York's JFK Airport, we could see fireworks going off in several spots below. It was a spectacular sight that made us feel as if America were welcoming us heartily. This thought was silly, I knew, but nonetheless our arrival couldn't have been any nicer.

THEN AMERICA REALLY welcomed us, in the way it has greeted so many immigrants before: Find a house for rent that's smaller, older, and far less nice than the one you left behind. Obtain all the necessary documentation to rent it. Then find out that it will cost you nearly two-thirds of your salary. Quickly spend most of your savings, which you thought were going to last a long time, on furniture, a car, and, because your boys are accomplished at piano, throw in a piano. Enroll in a mandatory and most embarrassing course on drinking and driv- ing, surrounded by eager teens who have yet to drink or drive, and then take a road test after having had a license for nearly two decades. Register for a Social Security number. It seemed like there was no end to it. But finally we had all our IDs and permits, our long-distance provider, our gas, electricity, cable, and bank accounts. We even bought a used minivan.

The boys, who knew not one word of English, adapted to the foreign culture about as readily as my brothers and I had when we came to Israel. Jordan, our eldest, came home one day and told us he wanted to cut off his long hair. In Israel his long black curls falling at his shoulders were nothing out of the ordinary. Here, Jordan realized as his English improved, his hair made him look like a geek. His next makeover focused on his attire, and while we could barely afford Kmart and Payless, he demanded Abercrombie, Nautica, and Nike. He knew what he wanted, and he was 100 percent right. When he changed his physical appearance, he became popular almost overnight. Gil intuited the cultural stuff quickly, thanks to the paths cut by his older brother, though it took him two years to become fluent in English. My youngest son, Charlie, found his own way. The boy he was seated next to in class was Chinese, also a new immigrant and also with no English. They spoke—all day, every day. They developed their own patois, consisting of neither Hebrew nor Chinese.

So there I was, at last, settled into my suburban home. More or less the American dream, right? I sat back and made a conscious decision to rest. For the first time in my adult life, I wanted to relax, do nothing, and take it easy for a while.

That resolution held for almost two weeks.

LEO WAS at work, the kids were in school, and I was . . . bored.

Loneliness began creeping up on me. I am a person who craves company. I need friends. I need to go out. In my new home in the United States, sitting idly, I had too much time to think. I began regretting the move. I began feeling that Leo had tricked me into it. I became depressed, and I spent much of my time crying. I wanted my life back. My work, my business, my friends, my house, my family in Israel. When I complained to Leo in the evenings, he'd become annoyed and make fun of me. I'd thought I wanted to slow down, but the quiet wasn't doing me any good. It was doing the opposite: driving me crazy. Apart from my homesickness for Israel, and besides the fact that doing nothing was antithetical to my temperament, there was also the issue of money. Our finances were very tight, and Leo and I had started to worry that we'd be unable to afford the things our kids needed.

Thus, I decided to look for a job. Leo was fine with it either way; he'd supported my staying home, he'd support my going to work. Even during the early stages of my first pregnancy many years ago in Israel, I'd asked him what he thought about my working after we had a baby. "Whatever makes you happy," he'd said, and he meant it wholeheartedly.

I began looking through the ads in the morning papers. Lots of positions for a part-time teacher, tutor, teacher's aide. I didn't know much about teaching, I had no references or documented qualifications, and anyway, I had no work permit. I'd applied for one—Leo's visa allowed that—but I hadn't received it yet. Obtaining a work permit is a very slow, tedious process that takes three or four months. INS inefficiency at its best, trying to make the lives of newcomers as miserable as possible. Give me your tired, your poor, your huddled masses, indeed. I kept on looking through the ads. One Sunday I saw something. An institute was looking for someone interested in doing research on the Middle East. That's me, I thought. I graduated from the faculty for Middle East affairs at Tel Aviv University. I'm fluent in the two languages of the Middle East, Arabic and Hebrew. But who would hire me with no papers? I was also concerned that my English wasn't polished enough to do that kind of thing. And computer skills—they did ask for computer skills. I typed okay, in Hebrew, that is, but I had no experience with typing in English, or with programs such as Excel, PowerPoint, and the like. No, I was not yet ready for that job.

Monday morning, strolling around the center of the town we lived in, I stumbled upon a gift shop. It was small, but its location was superb. I walked into the shop and met Catwoman.

Linda was the owner of a small shop and a large body. She was at least ten inches taller than I was and she weighed some two hundred pounds more. Very big woman, she was. Even if you think about tigers—the largest cats—there was nothing feline about Linda. So why Catwoman, you ask? The answer is simple. She had four cats. All her cats lived in the shop, never going out of it. Yes, I've heard the fairy tale about how self-reliant cats are, how clean they are, how faithfully they use the litter box. Well, Linda's cats never read that particular instruction manual.

Linda, I would soon discover, cared more about her cats than she did about her customers. Or her salespeople, for that matter. But these cats were the least of my worries when I entered the shop and met Linda for the first time. I decided to take a direct approach. Simple, honest, blunt, Israeli. Did she need any help? I asked. Because I was looking for work.

Linda looked me over from head to toe and said that, yes, she might be interested. How long was I planning to stay? Was it only for the summer? I told her that we'd be here for two, maybe three years. Could I sell? she asked. I smiled from ear to ear. Could I sell? Now that was a good one.

One of the biggest differences between Israel and the United States is in the quality of service. Even in Europe businesses are not as service oriented as they are in this country—hence the American tourist's reputation for being fussy and spoiled. Linda, however, was an isle of rudeness in an ocean of quality service. Take the elderly man who came into the store, asked for silver candlesticks, and within five minutes had bought a set for $1,700. Before leaving the store, he asked Linda to gift-wrap his purchase. Slowly she rose from her armchair, gave him a bone-chilling look, and roared, "We don't gift-wrap! Does it look to you like we have time for that?" The man grabbed his candlesticks and shot out of the store, afraid even to look back. Linda was like that to everyone. What bewildered me was that she was able to keep her customers. She didn't even have a register in the store. All the money we made was put into a large drawer.

The first thing I did when I went to work for her was to be nice to the customers. I gave them a smile even if they bought nothing. For some reason, Linda was careful when she interacted with me. She somehow deduced that I wouldn't let her treat me as she treated everyone else. She also noticed, immediately, that sales were way up. I was not only pleasant to customers, I could also sense what they wanted.

Like this guy who came in once, a macho dude in his thirties with a big gold chain dangling on a chest fuzzier than an angora sweater and with more hair on his knuckles than on his scalp. He was looking for some CD we didn't carry. I persuaded him to instead buy a whole bunch of women's magazines. I told him that the knowledge he'd acquire within them would have an immense impact on his popularity with the ladies.

Things were going relatively well in Linda's store, but a feeling of dissatisfaction was building in me. I was on my feet all day long, six days a week. Although my work reinforced my belief that I could sell ice to Eskimos, I didn't meet too many Eskimos in New York, and Eskimos traveling to New York didn't need to buy ice anyway. I didn't really want to spend my life in some small retail business, especially when the business wasn't mine. My unhappiness came to a head one Sunday, after I'd been with Linda a few months. That morning my middle child, Gil, woke up sick. Leo was at work, and Sunday was the store's busiest day. I decided not to let Linda down, so I brought Gil in with me. I thought that he could stay in the back room. When I arrived, Linda angrily asked why I'd brought him to work. I explained, but she looked at me and barked: "Whadya bring him in for? D'ya wanna give us whatever disease he's got?" That was it, the last straw. I was going the extra mile for this woman, and she was treating my son as if he had the plague. It was back to relaxing and resting for me.

Only . . . it wasn't. Our financial situation was precarious even when I worked for Linda; now it was in serious jeopardy. I began to choose at the supermarket only what we really couldn't do without. I would compare prices among brands and buy the cheapest one or the product for which I had a coupon. At the register, I'd scrutinize the checkout girl as she'd scan items. It's amazing how many mistakes they make at the register, even though they use the bar codes and everything is computerized. I could always find a dollar here, fifty cents there, and in those days, every penny counted. I became obsessed with not spending money. Our house in Israel with the two Jacuzzis and all those bedrooms seemed another lifetime away.

We stopped making all discretionary purchases, ran the dishwasher and the dryer only at night, when electricity rates were lower, and planned carefully when we used the car so that we could combine trips. Going out for dinner or a movie was completely out of the question. I became more and more depressed. Was this what we'd come to the United States for?

One evening the kids and I went to the supermarket. At the register, my credit card was declined. I didn't know we'd reached our limit. "Never mind," I said, "let's use the debit card." It too was declined. Nervously, I apologized, "Something must be wrong." Something was. At the in-store ATM I checked our bank balance. We had ten days to go until Leo's next payday, and there was $13 in our account. I've never felt so ashamed. I returned the items I'd intended to purchase, and the kids and I left the store. When we got home, I locked myself in the bedroom and burst into tears. I couldn't take it any longer. I wanted my old friends, my relatives, my mother. I wanted my old life back.

Leo returned late that night to a silent, somber house. The boys were in their beds already. We'd kept them in the dark about our financial difficulties because we didn't want to worry them. So what they'd witnessed in the supermarket had come as a shock to them, and my reaction had scared them, too; they'd never seen me like that. They were quiet all evening, and they put themselves to bed early. When Leo, who had no idea that our bank account was so low, came in and found me absolutely distraught, he was perplexed. I hugged him hard, and with large tears rolling down my cheeks, I pleaded, "Leo, I can't take this any longer. I want to go home." He held me for a while, then he asked what had happened, and I told him about the declined cards, about the thirteen bucks, about the humiliation.

Patiently and in a soft voice, he started to tell me how all great businesspeople had endured rough times in the beginning, how they'd tried and failed, on average, seven times before they finally made it to the top. That was what we needed, he said: perseverance and patience. The thirteen bucks were a sign, a good one, because in the Jewish tradition, thirteen equals good fortune. These magical numbers include five, like the number of fingers on one hand; seven, like the number of days in a week; and thirteen, like the number of years in a bar mitzvah.

Leo knew I believed in such things, but he himself was always cynical about them. So his attempt to mollify me with numerology was obviously a sop. But it did its job; it even made me laugh. Maybe he was right. This was only the beginning, and beginnings are always difficult.

If I got a job, I thought, things would work out better. I went back to reading the want ads in the newspaper. There it was. Again. The ad for the Middle East research institute, the one I'd noticed upon our arrival in New York. I wondered. . . . How come it had been sitting there, waiting, for so long? *You, yes, you,* it whispered to me. *Are you ready now?* It had been six months already. How was it that they'd not filled the position? Was it really meant for me? What was going on? I talked about it with Leo. Maybe the salary was too low, he said. After all, the ad did indicate "a nonprofit organization." Or perhaps, Leo said, they'd hired someone who'd come and gone already. I decided to send them my résumé and find out what the deal was.

Two weeks passed, and I'd heard nothing. I thought they weren't interested. I was just about to try my luck at a Muslim school not far from our house, where I could teach Arabic to kids, when Berta called. She sounded very pleasant on the phone, with her unmistakable accent of a native Nu Yawkuh. She asked me whether I was still interested in the job, went over some of the things I'd written in my résumé and cover letter—my knowledge of Hebrew and Arabic, my education— and then she asked whether I would like to come in for an interview.

"How about tomorrow morning?" I asked.

LEO CAN MAKE FUN of my premonitions and superstitions all he wants, but there it was. Joseph's gift. I had a very strong feeling about this. There was something mysterious going on. That ad—my name was practically written all over it. I knew in my bones that there was something different about this job opportunity, and I didn't want to mess up the interview. I sent the kids off to school, I dressed in my best formal suit, and I took the train into New York.

The directions from Grand Central were clear. I took some extra time, allowing for traffic, and when I arrived, I saw a tall building, uglier even than the Ma'on Olim, the public housing my mother, brothers, sister, and I had been placed in when we'd first arrived in Israel. I counted the floors: one, two . . . six, eight . . . eleven . . . thirteen floors. Thirteen, of all numbers! Another sign? I entered, told the doorman where I was going, registered, and made note of all the security cameras. Very fancy, marble floors and dark carpets, heavy chandeliers. Much more impressive than the building's facade had indicated. I took the elevator to the third floor, found the suite, and knocked on the door.

"Coming," a man shouted. "Who is it?"

"It's me, from the ad," I replied as the door swung open. Neither the huge, dark, unshaven young man in shorts and sandals before me nor the office itself—the little of it I could make out beyond the man's frame—looked anything like I'd imagined. In my mind, a research institute would be filled with nerdish-looking guys in suits and ties sitting at tidy desks stacked neatly with a few open books, writing or dictating some report to an assistant to be typed later. The place looked nothing like that. In fact, there was not a soul to be seen.

"So what was it that you wanted?" the young man asked.

I tried again: "I am here for an inter—"

"Oh, I see, come in, come on in."

I looked around. The place was a war zone. A terrible mess of books and newspapers and files and boxes and electronic equipment tossed and piled all over the office. No desks were identifiable under the rubble of papers and machines. I knew that they had to exist, however, because here and there I saw computer monitors bravely peeking out, which implied that some sort of desk must have been supporting them from underneath. Looking more closely, I noticed many periodicals, some of them in Arabic. Tapes of various sizes crowned a few of the mounds of paper. On the walls hung posters of bearded men I'd never laid eyes on before. Some posters displayed Qur'ânic verses, in Arabic, and one of them had a picture of the famous al-Aqsa mosque in Jerusalem. I started worrying about whether I'd made the right decision to come here.

Meanwhile, the hulk, who himself looked Middle Eastern, was still eyeballing me. Although he was smiling, I began to wonder. What was this place, Hamas headquarters? Berta had told me virtually nothing about the organization. "Just come in and we'll go over the details when you're here," she'd said. Maybe I was better off teaching Arabic to Muslim kids. But what I saw made me curious. What did people do here? And where *was* everyone? This place was a puzzle that I wanted to solve. So far, it was just me in my suit and the hulk in his shorts. He looked at me. I looked at him. He still smiled. I wasn't sure what, exactly, it was that he wanted of me.

Because he really did look Middle Eastern, I asked, *"Tahqi arabi?"* (Do you speak Arabic?) He stared at me as if I had just grown horns. Maybe Hebrew, I thought—some Sephardic Jews are very dark skinned—and asked, *"Ata medaber ivrit?"* I was met by yet another silence. Clearly he didn't speak either language. Now it was his turn to wonder whether I was in the right place; maybe I was meant to be in the psychiatrist's office on the fourth floor?

Suddenly a woman popped out from behind the no-longer-smiling giant. Thank God; it was Berta. The impression I'd gotten over the phone was accurate. She was a warm woman. She asked whether I'd met Judah. Sort of, we both muttered, finally looking at each other with a "Nice to meet you" and a handshake. Berta apologized that everyone was busy in a staff meeting and invited me in. She told me that in this organization, they were doing mostly research, and asked what my interests were, my expectations, and for a little background about myself. She had absolutely no interest in my visa status or, for that matter, in my computer skills. Such a waste, because in the days before the interview I'd gotten Leo to teach me the basics of Excel and PowerPoint. After we'd spoken for a half hour, she said, "I think they're done. You can go and talk to Max now."

Max, the man behind this peculiar place, was a short, chubby man in his late sixties who still had an impressive mane of gray hair. Our interview was short. He asked me a bit about my personal history; he knew most of it from my résumé, which he was holding when I walked into his office. Then he inquired about my political views regarding the Middle East conflict. I told him that my inclination was toward the left wing, in the sense that I believed in the need for a Palestinian state. He then asked how good my Arabic was, and I said that I was equally fluent in that language and in Hebrew. I had the impression that he liked what he heard, but I wasn't sure. Next, to my amazement, he asked me when I could start and told me to go and work out the details with Berta. Max, I would soon come to learn, didn't want to be bothered with the details.

The salary Berta offered me was higher than what I'd been making with Linda. I was pleasantly taken aback by the figure, and my surprise must have registered on my face, because Berta immediately told me not to worry. They needed to see what I could do, and if things worked out to everyone's satisfaction, the issue of my salary could be revisited in the future.

What was it that they expected me to do? I asked. I hadn't had the slightest idea of what they were working on there, and my interview with Max hadn't made it any clearer.

"Mostly, I think, it will involve administrative work," Berta said. "I understand from your résumé that you have a bit of experience with such. Filing, photocopying, arranging folders, that kind of thing. Hang around here for a while and you'll see for yourself. Don't worry, you'll be fine."

Down on the street, I called Leo from the first phone booth I found. "Oh my God, I got it! I got it!" I yelled into the receiver. "And do you know how much they are going to pay me? Nonprofit or for profit, we, for sure, are going to make a profit!"

I still couldn't believe that they'd actually hired me. Recent immigrant, no degree from an American college, limited computer skills . . . None of it apparently mattered. Leo was happy for me, and I was happy for us. Neither of us had the faintest idea what I was getting into.

I WAS WORKING for a nonprofit organization studying the Middle East. But what were we doing, exactly? I expected, or hoped, that on my first day at the office someone would take me under his or her wing, show me around, give me some background. No one did. Not just on the first day, but for months I remained in the dark. The way the office functioned was that everyone worked on his or her own projects. Each had a small niche and expertise in a limited number of subjects, knowledge that he or she would never think to share with others.

The office is entirely different now. Based on my nonwelcoming welcome, I introduced a system where each new researcher is assigned to a veteran researcher who shows him or her around and teaches what we do and how we do it.

Complete silence was what greeted me. The little I could grasp was that the organization operated in a state of permanent crisis, responding to an endless flood of requests for research, mainly from the media. Everyone at the office was tense and edgy. Including Max. The workload, even years before 9-11, was phenomenal, and Max's behavior as a leader didn't help, either. He was not . . . well, a direct and organized person. Even had they wished to show me the ropes, my new colleagues would have found it difficult to find the time to teach, guide, or involve me in what they were doing.

That first day at work, I asked Judah for some answers. He was smiling at me again, but I learned that he was the computer guy and really knew very little about what kinds of research were going on at the office. Next, I approached Amy. Blond, blue eyed, an attractive young woman, Max mentioned her to me as one of the most experienced researchers there. He'd suggested that I stay close to her so that I could learn the basics of the job. I asked her to show me around, to tell me what she was doing. She looked at me as if this were the most outrageous request she'd ever heard. She uttered some excuses and went back to the mountain of papers on her desk. Defeated, I retreated to the seventh floor, my place in exile.

The organization occupied a suite on the third floor and one on the seventh. I quickly discovered that as in the Ma'on Olim, the closer you were to the ground, the higher you were in the hierarchy. I was on seven, in Siberia. Most of the others at the office, including Max, were on three. I'd been plopped at someone else's pigsty of a desk—it would be months before I'd have my own—and sitting there, I felt like an idiot. Was this job a huge mistake? Should I quit right now? What is it with these people? Why are they so unfriendly? Why isn't this desk neat, professional, and, most of all, mine? And what is all this junk, anyway?

Absentmindedly, I picked up a booklet lying in the papers piled before me. Its title: "The Holy Land Foundation for Relief and Development: Programs & Objectives." Holy Land Foundation, HLF. Relief and development. Relief to whom? I wondered. Development of what?

On the cover of the report was a sweet picture of a group of Arab boys kneeling, wearing backpacks, one of them holding a pencil case. HLF's logo was of two hands cupping a structure that looked vaguely familiar. The kids in the picture were busy, they weren't looking in my direction, but it was almost as if the booklet itself were. It was smiling at me, teasing me. It was printed in two parts: one half in English, the other in Arabic. I turned it over to look at the Arabic-language cover. Same picture of the boys, same logo, Arabic font. Nothing unusual.

My first instinct was to hurl the thing back onto the heap of the garbage on the desk, go talk to Max, and tell him what was bothering me. I wondered how long the brochure had lain there gathering dust, and who, if anyone, had looked through it already . . . and then the office, my aloof colleagues, Max, all of it ceased to annoy me, because that damn booklet *was* looking at me. It was now struggling to free itself from my attention, practically begging me to throw it back on the desk where it had gone undisturbed, literally for years, until I showed up.

What was happening? I looked at the booklet again. It was still smiling, but this time there was no purity in that smile. I peered at the logo again. And the picture. Oh my God.

In the time I spent in the Knesset's library and archives searching for information about my father, combing through documents and reports like the one before me, I'd come to know poison like this. The surface is always cheap propaganda and innocence-splashed outer layers, but read between the lines and the true intent is vicious, venomous, tendentious. How could I have missed it? Even the photograph seemed to have two meanings. Same picture on front and back of the booklet, yet the image had been flipped left to right. Sloppy publishing mistake— or maybe a hint?

I now realized what the two hands in the HLF logo were holding. It was a likeness of the al-Aqsa mosque. This mosque, in Jerusalem, is one of the cornerstones of the Arab-Israeli conflict. It is the place where the second *intifada* began, thus giving it the name "the al-Aqsa Intifada."

Okay, you say, so they want the mosque on their logo. What's the big deal? Couldn't it just be an expression of patriotism? But if you were to look carefully, you would see that the shape formed between the two hands supporting the mosque was of the map of Palestine. From the River to the Sea. As in the Jordan River and the Mediterranean Sea. Anyone who is well versed in the Arab-Israeli conflict would know that such a map allows for no existence of Israel: "From the river to the sea," as the Palestinians cry at their rallies. As I held the brochure tightly in my hands, I wondered, why would a foundation devoted to relief and what-have-you use such a provocative logo?

Two languages. That intrigued me. Arabic with an English translation. Or was it just that? Two languages. In the Middle East I've encountered it so many times before. There's what is said, and there's what is said between, behind, and beneath the lines. Vice President Dick Cheney visited the Arab world a few months after 9-11 in an attempt to set the stage for an assault on Iraq. He quickly learned that what is said doesn't necessarily mean what in fact is agreed. Upon returning from these talks, Cheney said that he was happy not with what was actually said to him, but with what he assumed was thought by these leaders behind their closed curtains and screens. Say one thing, mean another within your own cohort, let the other party give your words yet a third interpretation, and eventually take a fourth action that diverges from any of the three courses discussed or implied.

Let's be blunt for a moment. In Western culture we simply call that behavior lying. Take, for example, the document I was holding in my hand. You publish such a booklet, in which you spell out your organization's message and goals in English. You say similar things in Arabic, only with a few alterations, and suddenly the publication has two messages, one for the Americans you hope to fund-raise from, another for those people who literally speak your language. I looked at the booklet and knew it was lying to my face. What was it that it was trying to hide?

I worked on it for a few hours. I read it very closely, first in Arabic, because that language is easier for me than English, and also, as I correctly assumed, because Arabic would reveal the truth behind the goals of the Holy Land Foundation. Afterward I read the English translation. I pored over the two versions again and again. Almost hesitantly, I began to write a report. It took me a few days to craft it. I read other documents, searched through books and files, and substantiated what I had to say. If no one in the office was going to help me, fine, I'd just help myself—to anything that would facilitate my research. I had no clue whether what I was doing would lead to a promotion or to a sacking, but I had a hunch and I wanted to follow it. Here are some of the things I expounded in the report that I put together less than a week after I began to work in the office. I called it: "HLF—Where Does the Money Really Go?"

> In its publication, the "HLF News," from 1992, the Holy Land Foundation claims to have used the funds they collected "for the overt poor and the devastated needy" in Palestine. Has it indeed?
>
> This manifest, published in Arabic and English, lists Palestinian organizations, located in the West Bank and in the Gaza Strip, which received funds from the HLF. The list in English consists of thirty organizations. The corresponding list in Arabic reveals *thirty-nine* organizations.

I showed that some of these nine organizations that were omitted from the English version had been transferring funds to families of Hamas terrorists who were involved in deadly attacks against Israeli citizens. One of the organizations even provided safe houses for terrorists and hiding places for their weapons. Another was outlawed by the Israeli authorities and was headed by one of the spiritual leaders of Hamas.

Other organizations mentioned in the publication were also connected to Hamas. One of those was the Islamic University of Gaza, a known Hamas stronghold: some 60 percent of the nearly four hundred Hamas deportees of 1992 were its staff or students. Even Yasser Arafat, in an attempt to restrict Hamas, ordered an invasion of the university and the destruction of some of its equipment in 1995.

I then listed some of the organizations that were mentioned in the English version, where they were portrayed as innocent charitable foundations. In truth, I asserted, they supported Hamas and were headed by Hamas leaders. I presented evidence of these charities' involvement in terrorism. I included five appendices of the documents from which I obtained the information. Finally, I added a note:

> This is the summary of my findings of the illegal fund transfers by the HLF to Palestinian organizations involved in terrorism. I think that we should initiate a larger investigation based on this preliminary report. Please let me know your thoughts.

And I left the report on Max's desk.

MY INITIAL IMPULSE was to not go to San Francisco. I'd had a bad feeling about the trip. I'd been with the office for quite a few months by then, but I had very little experience in the thing I was about to do. With time and practice I'd learned to prepare for these gatherings, but not yet at that time. Everything was done in great haste because I'd found out about that event only the day before. I'd made every mistake in the book. And I'd had a terrible fight with Leo. He wouldn't listen and he wouldn't believe that I was going, on a day's notice, to cover a Muslim fund-raiser in San Francisco. The trip wasn't the only reason for our fight; tension had been building between us for a few weeks. My demanding new job, the long hours I spent in the office, the difficulties the kids had in school, our financial situation, all added up and made both of us overwrought. The trip, however, sent Leo over the edge.

The first few weeks in the office had indeed been very difficult. People still were not helpful, I got involved in repeated conflicts with some of them, and there were so many things I needed to learn. And when, a full month after I'd left my HLF report on Max's desk I was finally summoned to his office, I was sure I was in big trouble.

Max closed his door. He sat behind his desk, from which he'd cleared off just about enough stuff to enable him to actually see me. He was wearing a somber expression.

That's it, I thought. I've really done it this time. I shouldn't have filed such a blunt report on a Muslim charity without knowing the goals and principles of the organization that hired me. This was a research institute, I reminded myself, not the CIA. What was I thinking?

Max didn't start by berating me. Instead, he insisted on knowing why I'd made this report. I told him the story, how I'd found the booklet and noticed the discrepancies between the charity's stated mission and its intent. Max asked who had given me the idea to study the HLF—who at the office had helped me with my research. Again, I explained that this was purely my initiative, my research, and that no one else was to blame for it.

Max looked confused. Blame? "This report," he said, "is very interesting. It is an eye-opener, really." I learned later that for him to utter such positive remarks was exceedingly rare. Max is a no-news-is-good-news kind of boss.

But now I finally began to understand what we were supposed to do in that office.

IT TOOK ME some time to figure out what was so eye-opening about my report. To me, an Israeli, the idea that Muslim charities were operating as fronts for terrorism wasn't a surprise. This was an accepted fact back in Israel. What was amazing to me was how these groups operated with such ease, with such nerve, on U.S. soil. I didn't realize then, years before 9-11, that in the United States—which lacked experience with Islamic terrorism and where people had a tendency to believe in the integrity of religious and relief organizations—no one imagined that a group called the Holy Land Foundation could be used so cynically as an instrument of destruction. Years before the attacks on the World Trade Center and the Pentagon, I'd tried to get the FBI and the State Department interested in my research on the use of charities as front groups. Neither did anything with my material.

Within days after 9-11, George W. Bush signed an executive order designating a number of charities as front groups for terrorism. To most Americans, even some in law enforcement and in Congress, this came as a shock. Charities using funds to pay for murder? Not long after the president's executive order came amendments to it that caused even greater shock. These amendments designated several other so-called charities. HLF was among those charities, yet its inclusion on the list opened a new frontier in the war on terror. The charities designated in the original order, you see, were based in Afghanistan and in Pakistan. Out of sight, out of mind. HLF, however, was based here in the United States, operating under the noses of the authorities and sometimes with their full cooperation. An American-based charity, tax-exempt, that was raising U.S. dollars for terror.

When I first talked to Max about that HLF report I'd compiled—years before 9-11—he promised to forward my findings, together with the HLF booklet, to "the right people." I am still not sure who these "right people" were, but when I got my hands on the Justice Department's HLF report, submitted in support of the president's executive order, parts of it looked awfully familiar. . . .

The day HLF was designated as a terrorist organization was a big day for me. Yet it also broke my heart. Why, I thought, did it take 9-11 to make that happen? Why would it continue to take the government so long to understand what I'd seen almost instantly in the booklets and solicitations openly distributed by these charities? Why couldn't they see that the terrorists were hiding in plain sight?

FATE, I THOUGHT, was mocking me yet again. Leaving Iraq for Israel, I'd believed that I was through with persecution, fear, and terrorism. Then came the 1973 Yom Kippur War, which reopened my old wounds, and then the Gulf War. Finally, the move to the United States.

Far from terror, I thought, in the land of opportunity, the land of tranquility and peace . . . and a land of minefields for me, I discovered. In America, of all places, I came closer than ever before to terrorism. History kept repeating itself.

On the Friday I went to San Francisco, I got up at dawn and made a nice Sabbath dinner for Leo and the boys: *kebba,* a traditional Iraqi dish with meat wrapped in farina, soup, salads. Leo brushed me off when I left for the airport. He shouldn't have done that to me; he shouldn't have let me go like that. We'd have to discuss that when I got back. I wouldn't have missed that event, that HLF fund-raiser, for the world. At that point I knew already that HLF was a front for Hamas. I'd learned a lot about it in the time since I'd spied its booklet, and I felt that my knowledge wouldn't be complete without going to San Francisco, meeting the people I'd read so much about, and listening to what they'd say.

But the bad feeling I'd had about the trip kept intensifying as time went by. It seemed as though nothing was going right. Berta had gotten these plane tickets the day before, so not only were they outrageously expensive, they weren't even for a direct flight. God, how I hate to fly. Although the security in the checkpoints I went through was pathetic compared to what I was used to on El Al, we still managed to get into Denver a half hour late. I missed my connecting flight, and the next flight out would get me to San Francisco more than an hour late. The meeting would already have started by the time I got there.

I landed, hailed a cab, and in a great hurry, put on my Muslim disguise and my recording equipment as I was riding in the backseat. How dangerous and amateurish to do such a thing. I should have waited until I checked into my hotel, and I should have dressed in my room, carefully, discreetly. Walk in as Ms. West, emerge as the Queen of Sheba.

Meanwhile, the cabbie was driving around in circles. Tensely, I asked what was wrong, and he was apologetic. He swore he wasn't trying to cheat me. He was at the address I'd given him, but there was no such hotel there. He radioed his dispatcher, who told him his customer had the wrong address. The street name and number were correct, but the address was in *Berkeley,* not San Francisco. That meant another forty minutes in the cab, and I was becoming hysterical. I'd fought with Leo, flown to the other side of America, spent so much of the office's money, was about to be away from my kids for the entire weekend— and thanks to this screwup, I was going to return empty-handed. Bad, very bad.

I looked at my watch—nine P.M. in New York; Leo and the kids had probably finished dinner. From the back of the taxi I called him—yet another dangerous mistake, I knew, but I needed to hear his voice. A good word from him would have made me feel much better. No answer. Where could they have gone? I looked out the driver's front window at a sea of red taillights. Great. A traffic jam. What else could go wrong?

I was such a neophyte then. I didn't know that these meetings rarely begin on time. Now I know that even when the information I get about these gatherings is accurate, a rarity in itself, very little goes according to the original plan. I'm no longer surprised when the featured speakers don't even show up. Ah, the magnificent value of experience. As Oscar Wilde so nicely put it, experience is simply the name we give our mistakes. And I was on the verge of making a very big one.

The fund-raiser was supposed to be a large, open meeting. When I finally arrived, almost two hours late, I was hoping to hear at least the closing remarks. Expecting to find a few hundred people there, I opened the door of the meeting room, dressed in my Muslim robes, hoping to walk in unnoticed. What I saw froze me in my tracks. My heart stopped beating. Icy needles of fear pricked my spine.

I stood there, looking. It was a large, beautiful hall. Brilliant chandeliers, heavy carpets, at least a hundred dining tables made of dark wood. Very luxurious. The tables were formally set for dinner, but all of them, except one, were empty. At that one table sat about fifteen men, all staring at me. For a split second I thought I was in the wrong place, but then I knew, looking at these Arab men, that I was not. This was the right place. I recognized some of the men. In the previous months, I'd been going over files and reports, learning, absorbing, soaking up knowledge. Some of these people sitting around the large table had been the cover boys of those files. One character was a short and chubby middle-aged man with gray hair and a trimmed beard. I recognized him as a Jordanian politician. Others were some of the leaders of HLF. All of these people were obviously here for the meeting, so where was it? Was it over? The room was warm, my robes were heavy, but underneath them I was freezing.

Some of the men looked at me with curiosity and interest. Others, with overt suspicion. We were all well aware that I didn't belong there. What could I do?

Two options. Stay or go. Walk in and try to sound credible—or get out. Say I was there by mistake, perhaps, in which case my undercover career would be over; I wouldn't be able to show my face again in any of these meetings. Or run like hell in the other direction, in case they tried to unveil me. This could cost me my life, because they'd certainly outrun me, encumbered as I was by my robes and recording gear. Before I even realized it, I found myself striding intrepidly into the room.

"A'-Salamu Aley'kum." (May peace be with you.) I spoke to them directly, as if I'd known them for years.

"Wa-Aley'kum as-Salam." (And peace to you too.) My confidence puzzled them.

I continued in Arabic. "I'm not from here, Brothers. I was staying with friends, and they'd told me about a fund-raiser. Is this the HLF fund-raiser?"

"Yes, Sister, this is it." So far they were buying my act. "Thank you for coming."

"So is it over already? I wish I'd come earlier."

"No, as a matter of fact it didn't even start yet. People haven't arrived yet. Please, feel comfortable, be seated, you can wait with us."

I sat at the adjacent table. No sitting with the men, obviously. They were clearly suspicious of me, and for close to an hour they spoke only among themselves. In Arabic, of course, and in a near whisper. I could barely hear a thing. Recording was out of the question. Under my robes, I clutched my thigh so tightly that the bruises from my fingernails lingered for a week. Were they talking about me? What if they suddenly decided to ask me more questions? I kept thinking about my cover story. Would it hold? And what if they'd already figured out who I was?

They kept whispering. I kept listening. What I could make out was that they were terribly disappointed with the event. They said that the previous event at this location had raised $100,000. Money that went to Hamas, I thought.

I sat at the table and waited for other people to show up. I waited for a long time, yet no one came. The men continued to converse, and after an hour, they suddenly raised their voices to an audible level.

"It seems that no one else is coming, so we might as well have dinner now," one addressed me. "You're welcome to join us."

"No, thank you, but I really think I should go." It was my opportunity to get away.

"No, we insist." They weren't letting me go. "You've come all this way, you've got to stay and eat dinner with us."

I excused myself to go to the rest room to wash my hands before the meal, stepped out, and called Leo. He picked up the phone. The kids were asleep.

What was it that I wanted? he asked. Very cold, very distant. I had no time for that now.

"Listen to me," I said in a low voice. "I'm in the meeting. If I don't call back within two hours, call Berta. She has the address and all the details. Only make sure she knows it's in Berkeley, not San Francisco. She'll know what to do and who to call. Her emergency number is in the top right drawer in the desk downstairs."

I could feel Leo, three thousand miles distant, listening very carefully. He wasn't sure what to make of what I was saying—was I making this up to tease him? I didn't have any time to persuade him that I was telling the truth. Let him figure it out by himself. I quickly hung up and returned to the conference room before anyone became suspicious.

Then the dinner arrived and I had the odd sensation of being scared yet grateful for the superb food—Middle Eastern cuisine with shish kebab and falafel—almost like the food at home, in Israel.

Having a good meal in their bellies seemed to cause the men to let down their guard, and we began to speak. I talked only a little, very humbly, extremely cautious to make my cover story credible. There I was, sitting with members of Hamas, the terrorist organization that had claimed more innocent Israeli lives than any other. I, a Jew and an Israeli, a woman alone with fifteen men. Very dangerous game I was playing in this unbelievable scenario.

We finished the meal, spoke a bit more, exchanged addresses and telephone numbers, and I donated a nice sum in an envelope to "the cause," to jihad. We stayed there awhile longer, and then the meeting was "adjourned." In the cab back to the hotel, I called Leo. By now it was very late in New York, but he picked up the phone before it even rang once. He must have been sitting by it, watching the clock, waiting.

"I'm fine," I told him, "you can go to sleep. . . . Yeah, don't worry, everything went smoothly. I'll tell you about it when I come back."

I kept looking through the taxi's rear window to make sure that I wasn't being followed. I still couldn't believe that I'd come out of this encounter unharmed. As I put more distance between Berkeley and me, I began to feel victorious. True, I hadn't taped anything I could later use, but I did pass the most important test; they'd taken me for one of their own. Now that I'd sat with Hamas members, right there in the lion's den, I could go anywhere, penetrate any gathering, tape everything. The evening was my baptism of fire and my graduation from spy university, cum laude. From the center of attention, queen of the prom, I'd become the mistress of the shadows. My transformation was complete.

I LATER FOUND OUT what had happened at the fund-raiser and why no one came to it. It was planned to be a large event and many people in that community were supposed to come, but it seemed that the daughter of a rich and influential Muslim living in the area had scheduled her wedding for the same evening. The father had invited everyone in the area, and they chose the wedding over the fund-raiser. Which reduced attendance to the fifteen Arab dudes and me.

Leo picked me up at the airport, but he would barely speak to me.

The hastiness, the strange way in which the trip had been arranged on one day's notice, my mysterious call, it all seemed too fishy to him. What was he thinking? On the way back from the airport, our words sharpened into insults, our voices soon turned into hollers, and the fight resumed at the exact point where we'd left it before I went to San Francisco.

Leo finally spat it out: He suspected that I was having an affair. Listening to this nonsense, I lost my temper completely. We screamed at each other, and I demanded to get out of the car. He pulled over, I got out, he drove away, immediately made a U-turn, and returned to pick me up. We hadn't had such a bad fight since we'd left Israel. Why do people who love each other stoop so low sometimes?

Our snarling lasted only a few more minutes, though, and then we made up. When we reached home, I hugged Leo and cried on his shoulder for a long time. I'd taken this job as an additional source of income, and look where it had gotten me. What if something had happened to me? No money in the world was worth that. I was afraid at the fund-raiser, but my fear wasn't for me. It was for my kids. I'd gone through the hell of losing a father, and I knew how terrible it was. I'd do anything to make sure my kids didn't become orphans. The trip, the stress of being late, the encounter with the Arab men, the pointless fight with my husband . . . it all overwhelmed me and I cried like a little girl.

There was more to it than just the relief of tension. I cried, too, because I finally understood that nothing was coincidental. My Arabic, my knowledge of the Middle East, the decision to leave Israel, the ad for the research institute . . . it all had a purpose. Call it fate, karma, Joseph's gift, divine intervention, whatever you want. The bottom line was that I was here for a reason. This was my destiny.

History just wouldn't let go.

But this time history wasn't going to play one of its dirty tricks on me. This time I would make history, and I would shape it to my liking.

Baba, you'd have been so proud of me had you only known.

CHAPTER 4

Dar al-Hijra

PALESTINIAN ISLAMIC JIHAD. Sami al-Arian. Islamic Committee for Palestine. Islamic Concern Project. Ramadan Abdallah Shallah. World and Islam Studies Enterprise. Fat'hi Ibrahim Shikaki. Sound like Greek to you? It sure did to me only two weeks into my work for the office. In these two weeks I'd acquired some familiarity with HLF and Hamas, but as far as the above names were concerned, I was completely ignorant. And then came a request to translate some documents. Documents that concerned these names and entities. I promise you that by the end of this chapter you will have become familiar with these names.

No, I will not try to make you an expert on that subject. If I did, you might end up competing with me. I won't tell everything about those names I've listed, but I promise to tell you more than enough to make you know what they mean to my story—and to the safety of Americans.

A little over a week after I'd started, Berta called and asked me to come to my first staff meeting. I was thrilled. I was finally about to learn a bit about what was going on down there on three. The guys there didn't share anything with me. Fine. But now, when they discussed it, I'd learn and absorb.

We waited until everyone had joined us to begin the meeting. Excited, I looked forward to hearing the first item on the agenda. It was choosing a single font for the office's documents. I thought this was some kind of a joke. Times New Roman versus Arial. Being unfamiliar with the technical terms and the various intricacies of Microsoft Word, I failed to understand quite a bit of this discussion. Next, my colleagues moved on to discuss the need to maintain cleanliness in the kitchen, and then continued on to equally weighty matters. Have all these people lost their marbles, I thought, or was it I who failed to see the import of the issues at hand?

The eve of Purim was a few days later. Purim, the Jewish holiday when people dress in costumes, go to synagogue to read the Megila, or the Book of Esther, and celebrate the deliverance of the Jews of Persia some 2,500 years ago. Purim is a happy celebration accompanied by yummy pastries. I was looking forward to taking my kids to temple. As I was getting ready to leave, late in the afternoon, Amy came up to my office in Siberia and handed me two documents.

"Max asked me to give these to you," she said. "They were just faxed over to him and he needs to know what's in them. He said you know Arabic. You do know Arabic, don't you?"

I thanked her and took the documents. I looked at them. This was my first assignment in the office. A test, in a way. The HLF report I had done without anyone asking me. Now I'd been asked.

"What are these?" I asked.

"I'm not sure. All I know is that they'd been seized two years ago in some raid in Florida."

"Why is the translation urgent, then?"

Amy had no idea; she was just the messenger. I looked at the documents again. The type on the faxes was tiny, and the quality of the copies very poor. I asked Amy whether there was a better copy, but she said that this was the only one.

I began to translate the documents, and the more I worked on them, the more complicated the process seemed to become. The documents had large passages that were illegible. Even in the better parts I couldn't read half the sentences. And though I was fluent in Arabic, I couldn't translate many of the terms and words because the material was so unfamiliar to me. I'd never done anything like this, and I didn't have a dictionary at hand for whenever I got stuck. My annoying insecurities began tormenting me: Was this job too big for me? I became frustrated, angry with myself, angry with everyone else. What was so urgent in those documents, I thought, that they had to be dug into, all of a sudden, on my night of Purim? And why do I have to take everything so seriously? I couldn't come up with a good answer. But I wanted to do a good job, so I went in search of relevant documents in the office. I needed some background in the subject in order to understand what I was doing.

At two A.M. I finally finished the translation and left it on Max's desk. I wasn't happy with it. To date, I don't know what, if anything, Max did with it. Of course, I missed the Megila reading, the synagogue, the feast, everything. My children were terribly disappointed. Miss a kid's baseball game because of work, there's always another. But Purim happens only once a year. They did go with Leo, but they said the celebration wasn't complete without me. I still remember that day as one of my worst on the job.

Like so many things we hate while we do them, only to realize later that we benefited greatly, the ordeal turned out to be a crucial stepping-stone. Everything happens for a reason. It didn't matter what Max had done with my translation; for me the process opened a door onto the world of Palestinian Islamic Jihad, or PIJ, and its ties in the United States. I fell in love with PIJ. I fell in love with PIJ's Tampa cell. From that night on I read, listened to, and watched absolutely everything we had in our office that concerned PIJ. And we had quite a lot, you see, because PIJ was designated by the U.S. government as a terrorist organization way back in 1995. I began ordering documents from all over the world: magazines, academic and political journals, books, and articles, in English, in Hebrew, and most often in Arabic. I read them all. I read every single document the government ever released on PIJ and the groups affiliated with it. I learned, and learned, and I wanted to learn even more. Within only a few months of that rotten night at work, I'd become the authority on PIJ in the United States. Not even government agents who are assigned to investigate the group, I daresay, know as much as I do about it.

And now for the documents themselves. What I'd translated were PIJ communiqués claiming responsibility for terrorist attacks in Israel. These were fax transmissions, seized by a U.S. government task force from the Tampa, Florida, offices of the Islamic Committee for Palestine (ICP) and the World and Islam Studies Enterprise (WISE). The documents concerned "the martyrdom of the commander and hero, Issam Mussa Barahima . . . of heroism, sacrifice, and self-sacrifice . . . in the Jenin district . . . the Israel Defense Forces believed that the commander Issam Barahima had already been martyred . . . but the Zionists were shocked when the martyr and hero started to throw hand grenades at them and when he launched a hail of bullets from several machine guns . . . the commander of the Israeli special units for fighting 'terror' . . . was killed . . . and 4 soldiers were seriously injured."

The documents then conclude that "the Saif al-Islam [Sword of Islam] Brigades, the Brigades of Islamic Jihad in Palestine, follow the Zionist enemy and fight it in order to prove that the only way for liberation of Palestine is through armed Jihad . . . all our hero Mujahideen who promised with their souls in the blood of the Shuhada [martyrs] . . . long live Palestine from the Sea to the River . . . long live the Intifadah."

In the days following the translation, I began looking in our archives for anything we had regarding PIJ, ICP, and WISE. I read documents, I listened to tapes, I watched videos. On one of the tapes, dated December 1992, I heard a speech in Arabic, made by one Ramadan Abdallah Shallah, at the opening session of the fifth annual conference of the ICP. The conference took place at the McCormick Center Hotel in Chicago. Here are some excerpts of Ramadan Abdallah Shallah's speech, translated from Arabic:

> Perhaps some of us heard this name . . . the martyr Issam Barahima
> from Palestine . . . Barahima was martyred during a battle with the

occupation forces . . . Barahima was a Palestinian Muslim youth who lived in the last two years in caves in the high hills of the West Bank. His weapon was a machine gun and his Qur'ân, which he carried in his chest pocket . . . the Zionist enemy admitted that in the last few months Issam Barahima was responsible for all the military Jihad operations against enemy targets . . . the occupation soldiers were surprised to discover that Issam . . . was throwing hand grenades and firing at them [from the audience come shouts of "*Takbir,*" or "Praise to Allah"]. Issam killed one Zionist and injured four others. And his God purified him as a martyr.

Sounds awfully familiar, doesn't it? A rhetorical twin of the PIJ communiqué. It made me wonder whether ICP played for PIJ the same role that HLF did for Hamas: a front group designed to deceive the authorities.

I soon learned what ICP was. In a videotape of a fund-raiser that ICP held in Cleveland, the local imam, an associate of the 1993 World Trade Center bombing conspirators, said, "The Islamic Committee for Palestine [ICP] . . . is the active arm of the Islamic Jihad Movement in Palestine [PIJ], and we like to call it the Islamic Committee for Palestine here [the United States] for security reasons. . . . Donate to the Islamic Jihad. If you write a check, write it for the Islamic Committee for Palestine, ICP."

So ICP was the "active arm" of PIJ in the United States. The active arm of an illegal terrorist organization, proudly residing and practicing in America. Nice use of our democratic freedoms.

Next I turned my attention to this Ramadan Abdallah Shallah. Who was he, I wondered, and who was Sami al-Arian, another distinguished panel speaker in the opening session of this conference? What did these men have in common?

What I learned took me months to digest—there's a wealth of information on this subject—but I will do my best to give you the essentials. This book is not a textbook on terrorism, nor is it *The Encyclopedia of Vile Creatures.* But this is my story as I see it, and these people have come to be a part of it.

Sami al-Arian is a professor of computer science at the University of South Florida, in the beautiful city of Tampa. In the early 1990s, Sami arranged U.S. visas for several people, including Shallah and Bashir Nafi, who lived at that time in Britain. They knew one another from way back, in the late seventies. Nafi and Shallah lived in Cairo and attended Egyptian universities; Sami was a student in North Carolina, but he traveled to Egypt frequently, staying there for several months at a stretch. It was at this time that this jolly group of Palestinians came up with the idea of founding Palestinian Islamic Jihad. Years later, Sami also started WISE and ICP. We already know what ICP is: a front for the terrorist organization PIJ. So that, by itself, is more than enough to justify labeling Sami a terrorist. But what is this other organization he created, WISE? He always describes WISE as a research institute specializing in the Middle East. Nice and benign sounding, right? Why, you could describe the place I work the same way. Through Sami, WISE made a contractual agreement with the University of South Florida's Middle East Committee, in which WISE employees were entitled to the perks of university faculty and to the use of the campus facilities.

Shallah and Nafi were sponsored for U.S. visas and invited by Sami, their old friend, to join him at WISE and become members of its board. Shallah is an economist; Nafi, a theologian and Islamic scholar; Sami, a computer scientist. They needed someone with a formal education in Middle East politics to join them in order to make the thing look credible. That was Khalil Shikaki, a Middle East scholar with a Ph.D. in political science from Columbia University who is considered by many to be a moderate Muslim. A perfect choice.

Shallah lived next door to Sami in Tampa, until a man named Fat'hi Ibrahim Shikaki, the head of PIJ, was assassinated in Malta in October 1995. Fat'hi was Khalil's brother. So what does Shallah, the distinguished speaker at the ICP conferences, a close friend and associate of Sami al-Arian, a board member of WISE, and a teacher at the University of South Florida—what does he do the next day? He goes to Syria and becomes Fat'hi Shikaki's successor, taking over as secretary-general of Palestinian Islamic Jihad, in Damascus. Do you understand how big this is?

Imagine that you have a pleasant and mild-mannered neighbor, a scholar, an intellectual. And you never hear any complaints about the guy. Actually, you happen to like this Joe Shmo. Maybe your kid even took his college course. And then one day, the leader of a terrorist organization—say, for sake of argument, Usama Bin Laden—is shot dead in whatever cave he happens to be hiding. What does Joe Shmo do? Without a second thought, he takes the first plane to Afghanistan, or Pakistan, or any other of the hell-holes where the vipers of al-Qaeda nest, and moves seamlessly into place as their leader.

So WISE, it turned out, was a sister organization to ICP in the shape of a think tank, and thus one more front for PIJ. Confusing? How about the fact that Sami incorporated ICP as the Islamic Concern Project, Inc. yet never in practice used the name? Sami always referred to ICP as the Islamic Committee for Palestine, although there is no public record for that organization.

Shortly after Shallah's appointment as head of PIJ, federal agents raided the offices of ICP and WISE in Tampa; Sami's house was raided, too, because ICP's U.S. headquarters were located there. Among the documents the agents removed were the communiqués I was later asked to translate.

This raid was the end of ICP and WISE. Neither was ever formally or legally shut down, but in effect they ceased to operate.

When Shallah went to Syria to become the leader of PIJ, Sami said he'd known nothing about it. He publicly denied, on several occasions, any knowledge of Shallah's activities and ideology. In TV interviews he said that all this came "as a great shock" to him. A great shock to the man who created PIJ in Egypt with his old mate Shallah? A great shock to the man who invited Shallah to America and helped him get a U.S. visa? A great shock to the man who lived next door to Shallah, who hired him and participated with him in WISE, the think tank they started together?

A FEW MONTHS in the office, and I still didn't know that the only effective way to communicate with Max was through e-mail. I was on the seventh floor, in Siberia, and although I finally had my own desk, I was out of the loop. So I had very little contact with Max. He didn't know what exactly I was doing upstairs, either. He will never admit it now, but I know that his impression of me back then was that I was sitting in my office all day long doing very little productive work. One day I bumped into Berta, who asked me what I was working on. I told her: reading magazines, watching videotapes, fishing—for information. She told me that Max had mentioned that he felt I could do more to help with the research, that I wasn't putting in enough effort.

It didn't come as a big surprise to me when on my way out of the office late one evening, I discovered Max having a meeting with three government agents about PIJ and Sami al-Arian—*my* topics—yet I hadn't been invited. I knew of these agents because I was quite familiar with their investigation, but I had never met any of them before. The last thing on Max's mind was to tell me about that meeting.

So I barged in. The agents looked at me. Max introduced them: Barry Carmody and an agent I'll call Kirk, both FBI; and John Canfield, from Customs. Max said that these were the guys working on Sami and PIJ, and he obviously expected me to smile politely and leave.

On this day I happened to be wearing a tight white shirt, tight jeans, a wide, western-style belt, and high-heeled boots. The agents couldn't take their eyes off me. And then Canfield asked, a little patronizingly, "So, can *you* tell us something new about Sami?"

Max moved uncomfortably in his chair and said, "No, I don't think she would know much about Sami, she's not currently working on that."

In the months leading up to that evening, I'd been eating PIJ, drinking WISE, breathing ICP. Every night I read through my files on them after Leo and the kids were asleep. I was going to bed more often with Sami and Shallah than I was with poor Leo. That night, for instance, I was carrying home a four-inch-thick binder on PIJ. Canfield's timing was exquisite; I erupted like a roaring volcano. I was sick of my seventh-floor exile, of meetings about font style, and of being unappreciated and invisible. I knew my hour had finally come.

"Yes, I guess I can tell you a few things about Sami," I said, staring at these four men. "You asked for Sami? You'll get just that."

John, Barry, and Kirk never knew what hit them. I started to show them the documents I had on their man. In the very folder I was carrying, I showed them the complete file on Barahima, the so-called martyr in the documents I'd translated. They'd known about Barahima, but they didn't know that at an ICP conference his story had been repeated, almost verbatim, along the lines of the PIJ communiqué. I then showed them the University of South Florida–related documents about Sami. The agents had copies of these documents and should have known what I was about to tell them. They didn't.

When Shallah, Sami, and their connections to PIJ came under scrutiny of the government, the University of South Florida hired a lawyer to investigate Sami, ICP, and WISE—and, university officials hoped, to clear the school's name. The lawyer wrote a two-hundred-page report on the matter. His finding: There was no way the University of South Florida could have known that Shallah was who he was. As part of his exploration, the lawyer interviewed Khalil Shikaki, one of the pillars of WISE, whose brother had headed PIJ until his assassination. He asked Shikaki when he'd first met Shallah. Shikaki had lived in the United States since 1985; Shallah arrived in 1991. Shikaki told the lawyer that he'd met Shallah for the first time when they both started to work for WISE.

However, I had a transcript from a 1990 ICP conference in which Shikaki sits down after a speech, and Shallah, on a panel of speakers with Shikaki, rises and says, "I agree with what my brother Khalil just said." I showed Max and the three agents the section in the lawyer's report where Khalil says that he is not ashamed of his participation at ICP conferences and that these were academic gatherings of the purest intellectual nature. Another lie. I gave the agents books they didn't have. Among them, the punchy-titled *Islam and Palestine Series—The ICP Speeches of the Third Annual Conference: Islam—the Way to Victory*. In it were the conclusions of this conference, which took place in Chicago in December 1990. Here are some excerpts, translated from Arabic, from the conclusions of this highly academic gathering:

The conference was convened in one of the most critical times that the Islamic and the Arabic worlds are witnessing. It comes at a time of daily and continuous massacres to our nation of Jihad . . . and to where sea fleets and Western military forces were deployed in the heart of the Arabian desert, to be stationed in the Islamic holy area. . . .

The participants hailed the blessed people of the Intifada and their determination to continue their Jihad and sacrifice in spite of the terror inflicted upon them by the enemy, and the embargo imposed on them by their friends. They also invited all sectors of the *"Ummah"* [Islamic nation] to unite in solidarity and to organize themselves in one line to confront the new crusade invasion to the lands of Muslims and Islam [U.S. forces in Saudi Arabia]. . . .

The participants assert that Jihad is the only way to get back the whole Palestinian holy land, which is a property of the whole *Ummah* and no one has the right to surrender or yield a span of a hand, or recognize the existence of Zionism or any part of it, because this is considered as treason for Allah, his prophet, our Muslim nation, their Jihad, their martyrs and their sacrifices which didn't stop at any time. . . .

The participants call upon all honest people of the *Ummah,* their organizations, Islamic and national institutions, especially in the American continent, to pool their resources and energies for the support of our people's Jihad inside Palestine, and make financial support available for them to enable them to overcome the acute and dangerous economic crisis facing them, and which exacerbated during the Gulf crisis, and they call upon all Muslims to support the Jihad of our brothers in Kashmir, Afghanistan, Eritrea, Lebanon, and Sudan.

The conferees affirm that the invading foreign forces [U.S. in Saudi Arabia] are aiming in the first place at destroying the Iraqi military power which threatens the security of Israel, and to occupy the Arab and Islamic oil sources, extend the American hegemony, leadership, and influence over the world, and not to liberate Kuwait. . . .

Whoa! Jihad, *intifada,* crusade, jihad, martyrs, more jihad. Highly academic, indeed. Second only to the teachings of Socrates and Plato. And holy. As in holy war. Jihad.

I was only warming up. I showed Max, John, Barry, and Kirk the agreement Sami made with the University of South Florida, where he presented the CVs of Bashir Nafi and Ramadan Abdallah Shallah. Nafi notes that he is an editor of the *al-Mukhtar al-Islami* (the *Islamic Digest*) and the *a-Taliya al-Islamiya* (the *Islamic Vendor*). Ramadan, in his, says that he was one of the editors of *al-Mukhtar* and of another publication, *al-Nur* (the *Light*). My point was to prove that save, perhaps, for Khalil Shikaki, all the players, all the so-called scholars of ICP and WISE, were strongly connected to PIJ long before they'd been given visas to come to the United States. Anyone who'd studied this stuff, from the government to the university's Middle East Committee, should have known that.

"Had any of you," I asked the agents, "ever seen these publications?" No, they hadn't.

I excused myself for a minute, ran up to my office, grabbed a few copies of these journals and newspapers, and returned to my still-seated audience, who were either under a spell—or simply afraid to move. Max included.

I pulled out an interview with Fat'hi Shikaki where he declares that *al-Mukhtar al-Islami* was used by PIJ to disseminue its ideology. ICP and WISE personnel were editors and contributors (sometimes using pseudonyms) to *al-Mukhtar* prior to their involvement with WISE and ICP.

Al-Mukhtar was based in Egypt. When PIJ's leaders left Egypt, Bashir Nafi began publishing and editing *a-Taliya al-Islamiya* in London, England. At the same time, parts of *a-Taliya* were published in Israel under the name *al-Nur*. Nafi was in England, Shallah in Jerusalem, and they kept up a lively fax correspondence, ensuring that their publications were on the same page. Several history books, in English, Hebrew, and Arabic, that talk about PIJ, refer to these publications, *a-Taliya* and *al-Nur*, as official PIJ publications. I showed some of these to the four men. I showed them a few issues of *a-Taliya* and told them that I'd obtained every single issue of that journal. I then showed them that the address in the United States for back issues of *a-Taliya* was in

Raleigh, North Carolina. In the same zip code where Sami happened to be living before he moved to Tampa.

The long-standing involvement in PIJ of Sami, Nafi, and Shallah was perfectly obvious.

Sami managed to surround himself with an impressive roster of terrorists, it seemed. One of the dignified gentlemen whom he invited to WISE to conduct roundtable discussions at the university was Hassan Turabi, the head of the fundamentalist party in power in Sudan. You don't have to look too far to learn who Turabi is. According to a State Department fact sheet on Bin Laden, released in 1996, Turabi hosted Usama Bin Laden in Sudan for five years starting in 1991. Sami invited Turabi to Florida in 1992.

And there was even more. WISE was working in collaboration with the University of South Florida's Middle East Committee (MEC), and in 1991, one of the theses approved by a committee composed almost entirely of MEC members stated that Bashir Nafi was closely associated with Fat'hi Shikaki and that he published a-Taliya "specifically for the group." Yet the members of MEC on the committee that approved this thesis didn't make the connection between Nafi and PIJ.

Now for the punch line. As part of its agreement with the university, WISE members were given access to the school's resources. This is how Shallah, a terrorist leader, was given a VIP tour of MacDill.

"Mission First, People Always." The slogan of MacDill Air Force Base, in Tampa, Florida. Home of the Sixth Air Mobility Wing. People always. Including Shallah, the man soon to become the secretary-general of the Palestinian Islamic Jihad. Smiling, shaking hands, taking photos, and committing to memory who-knows-what. What does such a man look for in an American air base? A man who serves, even now, as the leader of a major terrorist organization—an organization that works in close collaboration with al-Qaeda!

At this point in my impromptu presentation, Max and the agents were practically agog. They'd been assigned to investigate PIJ, they'd been working on it for years, they were the government's ultimate experts on the organization and its lieutenants. Yet in a few months, using only public-domain documents, I'd learned more on the subject than they'd thought possible. I just spilled what I knew off the top of my head, and I flooded them like a tsunami.

But there was another reason those agents felt uncomfortable. When I'd first entered Max's office some forty-five minutes earlier, they'd been . . . well, they'd been ogling me. Mother Nature had endowed me with certain ample physical attributes that some men deem appealing. You'd never guess in a million years that I had three children then. I have four now, and my figure still hasn't changed much. Maybe that was why John tried to crack a joke about me teaching them about Sami. Anyway, as the agents were trying to disconnect their gazes from my cleavage, I bombarded them with knowledge. I now looked at them with combined sympathy, glee, and pride. Yes, the old me was back. I could definitely manage a little spotlight. The long months of being invisible hadn't eroded my ability to command attention when I wanted it. I'd mastered the two techniques. Almost like having a split personality that I could control. That night was fun, I must admit. John Canfield kept looking at me with apparent disbelief, and after a long pause, he said:

"I surely hope there's only one of you. There is no way anyone else like you can fit on this planet."

MAX CALLED ME to his office the next day. I saw that he was struggling to talk about the previous night, but he was unable to find the right words. Instead, he told me that the office had been asked to provide some additional information on PIJ. Some agents were coming again early next week; could I join the meeting this time and provide my insight? Oh, and maybe I would like to move to the office on the third floor? That way, whenever we met I wouldn't have to schlep between three and seven.

I smiled at him. It felt as if I were experiencing a déjà vu. It was exactly as it went at the Ma'on Olim. Rising up in hierarchy by going down. In addition, Max said, did I need someone to work with me? Anyone in the office? He'd free up a researcher if I wanted. He then struggled a bit more.

"About yesterday," he began.

"Yes?"

"You saw what the rest of us here missed, and you knew what to do with it."

I laughed.

"One last thing," he said. "Since you are the only Israeli in our organization, I thought that maybe you'd be able to figure out a way to get some documents from Israel. We've been trying to get them for a few years now. They're very important. Even the federal agency assigned to that investigation was unable to get them."

"I'll do my best," I said.

Max gave me the specifics of the court documents that were needed for the investigation—the summary of the Israeli Supreme Court decision in the case of Odah. Abdel Aziz Odah was the spiritual leader of PIJ. (See, you are not an expert about PIJ yet.) Odah was sentenced to be deported from Israel in the mid-1980s. He appealed to that country's Supreme Court, was again convicted as a terrorist and a leader of PIJ, and was deported, along with our now dearly departed acquaintance Fat'hi Shikaki, in 1987.

The INS maintains a database that is used to filter out all kinds of nasty characters who try to enter the United States. Anyone who has been arrested in his country of origin and convicted of terrorism is supposed to be automatically banned from coming to America. So how did Odah repeatedly enter the country between 1988 and 1992—at the invitation of Sami al-Arian—to participate in ICP conferences after he'd been convicted as a terrorist? The INS, we have learned since 9-11, isn't always the most effective filter. There's no record of an Abdel Aziz Odah entering this country. Yet there are videotapes of him attending these "highly academic gatherings," proving he was here. It is believed that he used a false identity to come. This lack of documentation on Odah was why the Israeli Supreme Court documents had become so important to Max. Now, how could I get those?

Remember my little sister, Betty, the one Mama used to cry over while she was nursing her? Well, Betty was a brilliant student, and she wanted to be a doctor. In Israel, it's very difficult to get into medical school. There are only four of them in the country, and competition is fierce. Betty, however, breezed her way in. She began her studies while she was in active military service. Army in the morning and in the afternoon, medical school in between. While she was at it, she discovered an interest in the law. She decided to get into law school—while she was in active service and in med school. Again, she was quickly accepted. Maybe she had too much time on her hands doing only the military service and the medical school, I don't know. Anyway, she graduated with the highest honors. So when I needed those documents, I gave her a call. After all, she was a lawyer; she might know how to get them.

Piece of cake, she said. There's a public database in Israel, just as there is one here in the United States, that posts Supreme Court rulings. Betty accessed the database, copied the parts I needed, e-mailed the files to me, and sent me the disk through FedEx for my future reference. Three hours after Max asked me to help locate these documents, I went downstairs and paid him a visit.

"I thought about it," I said. "Thanks, but no thanks. I don't want to move to the office downstairs. Too much chaos. I won't be able to work there as well as I do where I am now. I'm happy upstairs. Upstairs, I have my own little kingdom, I organize things my way, I can run tapes on the VCRs all day long, I can listen to them undisturbed, and as I do that I can go over the documents that are arranged to my liking. So I think that I'll stay there awhile longer. As for someone to work with, yes, I definitely could use some help. I want George."

George was one of the top researchers in the office and one of the first people with whom I'd bonded there. Although he was a Christian, he knew a lot about Judaism and Israel because he'd spent nearly a year in Jerusalem as a political science student. He'd had the dubious privilege of witnessing a terrorist attack—a bomb exploded on a bus near him—which I think led to his decision to work in our field, although he denies that this was the impetus. George told me that one of the things he found most amazing about Israelis was that they were far less religious, in the churchgoing sense, than Americans. This is true. A much smaller percentage of Israel's population goes to synagogue compared to the number of Americans who regularly attend religious services. It was in my talks with George that I realized how magnificently religious the United States is. While maintaining secularism in schools and government, Americans still hold dear Judeo-Christian values. The separation of church from state is, oxymoronically, religiously observed here. This makes America all the more admirable.

I knew George and I would be able to combine our talents. He'd worry about the English documents, I'd tackle the Arabic. Together, we'd make a lot of progress. "I like George. He's very bright," I told Max. "And I know that he knows PIJ well. I'd appreciate working with him on this investigation.

"Oh, and one more thing," I said. "Here are the documents you were looking for. I hope they're helpful." I gave him the files Betty had e-mailed me.

"How the hell did you get these?" Max was stunned.

I could swear that his right arm, stretched to take the files from me, was trembling.

FOR MONTHS I'd been going through piles of material that was languishing on shelves and in overflowing bins. I'd found the HLF booklet accidentally, and through it I'd discovered the Hamas front and cover-up. I was asked to translate the Barahima file, and I'd learned about PIJ operatives in the United States. As I progressed in my work, my searches were becoming more expert, more targeted. Learning the systems and convoluted methods of this shadow world, I began to realize that there was a code to break, a message to decipher.

In my mind the pieces of the puzzle were gradually coming together, and a broader picture emerged. I knew now that there were many U.S.-based organizations and groups and cells dedicated to the destruction of America, the West, and everything that we hold dear. This did not surprise me. I came from the holy terror-land. I lived terror, I was burned by it. I realized, on the day I picked up the HLF booklet, that these charities in America were used as front groups for terror and as a means to collect funds for terrorism. But this wasn't all;

these groups were also busy lobbying and building an infrastructure for something I didn't fully grasp at the time. What became clear to me, though, at this early stage of my career, was that many leaders of terrorist groups resided in America and used it as a safe haven for their operations. The ease with which they operated in America was astonishing to me.

There was still much I didn't know. I sensed that something in my education was incomplete. My advantages in this game of cat and mouse? A familiarity with Arabs and Muslims. My intellectual background in the history and politics of the region from which Islamic terrorism hails. My language skills. My resolve. My determination. Increasingly, I felt that I was made for this kind of work. I felt that I was ready to take a risk, even to make a sacrifice. So there I was, sitting in the office with George, going through folders and transcripts, accumulating knowledge, when I realized what needed to be done. I knew that I was ready. Enough with the desk work. I had to hit the streets.

In the time before 9-11, religious and charitable institutions were completely off-limits to government agents. Raiding a mosque or a conference sponsored by a religious or "charitable" organization would have spawned outrage from religious groups across the board as well as from civil libertarians. Moreover, agencies such as the FBI had a long-standing reluctance to investigate before an actual crime was committed. Thus, a conspiracy to bomb the World Trade Center or U.S. embassies in East Africa was not worthy of investigation—not until the embassies in Kenya and Tanzania were blown up. Not until the Twin Towers came down. This attitude has done a 180 since September 11, but before that, radicals could operate freely in this country, with no fear of detection or apprehension. And so they did. I knew what was happening and I knew they had to be stopped. If the authorities couldn't or wouldn't do it, I thought, let me try.

I had to prepare very carefully—I had to be a lot smarter than I'd been on my undercover trip to the HLF fund-raiser in Berkeley. I had to create a false identity: fake address, fake personal and family histories. I fabricated an elaborate story and I practiced it until I had it down cold. I could talk forever about the neighborhood I claimed to be from, the town in which my mosque was located, and my Arab family's history back in the Middle East. I even frequented "my" mosque, just to cement my cover. I talked to the other worshippers, finessing my conversational Arabic. As for my costume, I was confident. I'd had enough practice assuming another form when I was selling to the ultra-Orthodox Jews back in Israel. To look like a Muslim woman was easy. After weeks of preparation, I felt that I was ready.

I was not the first to try to infiltrate these groups. Some who had attempted had been caught. The lucky ones had simply been expelled; others had been badly beaten. As a woman going undercover in a culture that did not tolerate its own women well, I was in great danger. Even in the years before the televised lynching of two Israeli soldiers in Ramallah, these people were deadly serious. They say that a coward dies a thousand times. But to go undercover and pretend that there's no risk is plain foolish. History has a nasty tendency to repeat itself, and I didn't want to end up like my father. If something were to happen to me, what would become of my kids? In all the years since my first undercover job, the fear has not diminished. The robes I wear not only help hide my identity; they also help hide my fear. In my kind of game, danger is lingering, and even when I'm not undercover, it's still there.

So I made myself two rules. One, never undertake any operation in my own neck of the woods. Too risky. I could later be seen, in the supermarket, at the mall, without my disguise. The second rule was to disconnect. When I'm out there, I am who I claim I am. I'm the Muslim woman I pretend to be, and as such, I have nothing to fear.

THE NARROW DRIVE was packed with cars. Far more crowded than one would expect on a Friday afternoon. Agitated-looking policemen were busy directing numerous vehicles to the mosque and its adjacent parking lots. As for the drivers themselves, they were sticking their heads and hands out of their cars and using their voices and fingers in various imaginative ways. I knew immediately that something unusual was happening.

In the morning, before I'd left for the airport, I'd hugged the kids. I'd held them in my arms for a long time, as Mama used to do with me long ago. They'd asked me what was wrong. Leo knew where I was going, but they didn't, and they felt that I was acting strangely. Leo and I had decided it was better to spare them the anxiety. If all went well, I'd be back before dinner.

Rising above the maddening bumper-to-bumper traffic, everyone honking, exhausts belching, there it was: Dar al-Hijra. It wasn't so impressive from a distance—big, white, rectangular. Mundane looking, even, not unlike a public school. But as I drew nearer, I saw that my first impression was wrong. The closer I got, the more I could see that it was a large, luxurious-looking, beautiful contemporary structure. I saw that there were two gates, one for vehicles, the other for pedestrians. I parked my rental car and walked toward the entrance. The door nearest to the parking lot, at the front of the building, was for men. The women's entrance was on the other side of the mosque. To get there, I had to go around the whole building. Thus I could appreciate how large the mosque really was. I spied a nice playground for kids, which I later learned cost some $70,000, a gift of the Nike Corporation. I found my entrance and went in. To the right, said the sign in the corridor, was where women with children needed to go. That corridor didn't lead to the actual prayer hall, but rather to a room equipped with speakers through which the Friday sermon, or *Khutbat al-Jum'aa,* would be broadcast. To the left was a path, for women only, that led into the main prayer hall. Like the men, we had to take our shoes off before we entered the holy ground of the mosque. On the way in was the *hamam,* where we all were supposed to wash our hands and faces before entering the mosque. Stairs led to a gallery some twenty feet above the main hall. It was difficult to see the preacher from there, but the gallery afforded a good view of the men downstairs, and that was where I settled myself.

Three days earlier, Max had told me that he'd received a call from some people at a Middle East institute based in Washington, D.C. I knew about that institute—in some ways it resembled ours—but I'd yet to be in touch with the people there. Max was asked whether we would like to meet with them and exchange information about HLF and other related organizations. Max couldn't go, but he told them who I was.

He asked me whether I was willing to go and meet them. I could fly, take the shuttle from La Guardia to Reagan National, hop there and hop back in time for Sabbath dinner. He already knew I had that thing about Friday nights—that I wanted, if possible, to have Friday night dinner with my family.

Before I went, I spoke with one of the Washington people on the phone. Harry sounded like a nice young man. He was a lawyer. We discussed what files I should bring with me, and then he said, "If you have enough time after the meeting, you may want to visit Dar al-Hijra. You may find it an interesting experience."

Our meeting wasn't very fruitful, even though Harry was knowledgeable and in spite of our mutual interest in HLF and its mother organization, the Islamic Association for Palestine, IAP. There was a world of difference between how the Washington people and I perceived the job we were doing. For them it was more academic. They didn't believe in acting on their information. I told them that I would very much want to interest the appropriate authorities in what we had. They told me that they didn't think it would be taken seriously. They were right. It wasn't. At least not then.

And so I decided to go to Dar al-Hijra. A game of words, in a sense. Hijra, A.D. 622, 1 A.H, the year from which the Islamic calendar is dated. One A.H.—After Hijra, after the journey—marks the date when the Prophet Muhammad made his historic move from Mecca to Yathrib, during which time he abandoned pagan ways in favor of Islam. *Hijra* also means "immigrants." Dar al-Hijra therefore means "house of immigrants." As does "Ma'on Olim" in Hebrew, I thought. A sign, maybe?

This Dar al-Hijra was also the house of Muhammad al-Hanooti. I didn't know who he was when I went to the mosque that first Friday. I'd asked Max, before I left, what he could tell me about Dar al-Hijra. Not much. I looked in our database. Not much there, either.

As soon as I entered the mosque I could see that, yes, this mosque was rich—extravagant, but in a tasteful way. Must be sponsored by some very affluent people, I thought. What I also noticed was that this Friday service appeared to be unusual. The mosque was packed. People were squeezing their way in and collecting donations even before the sermon started. Not the norm at a mosque. I donated $5. Many women were sobbing. Some sounded like professional wailers, and they were pounding on their chests and faces. And all this commotion was taking place before the imam, al-Hanooti, had even showed up.

It was in December 1998, the first Friday after the renewed American bombing on Iraq. Saddam Hussein was looking for ways to build and improve his arsenal of doomsday toys, and he'd expelled the United Nations inspectors who had tried to figure out what he was hiding up his sleeve and down his palaces. The retaliatory strike soon followed. It created a major turmoil not only in Baghdad, it seemed, but also here in northern Virginia. At Dar al-Hijra.

I later learned that al-Hanooti had been born in Haifa in 1937. Following Israel's war of independence in 1948, his family fled to Iraq. In 1965 he moved to Kuwait and from there, in 1978, to the United States. In 1992 he founded the Greater Washington Islamic Center, otherwise known as Dar al-Hijra. His affinity with Iraq was great, so when he finally came that Friday afternoon to preach, he began, in English, with a story about Iraq, from which he had recently returned. He was devastated to see the suffering of the Iraqi people, he told us. The war and the embargo had created a shortage of food and medicine, and because of that, the Iraqi children were dying. The audience, emotional even before he started his talk, became increasingly aroused. Everybody around me was weeping. I had to join them, in order to be inconspicuous. So when al-Hanooti talked about Iraq, I thought of my childhood in Iraq. What I went through, what the Iraqis did to me. What they did to my father. Soon enough, I too was weeping. And then the women around me began hugging one another. I hugged them, too.

At this point al-Hanooti switched to Arabic. Through my tears, I looked around. At least half of the people in the mosque were African American. I wondered how many of them spoke Arabic and would be able to follow the next part of the speech. The more I heard, the more upsetting the sermon became. Here are some of the things he said, translated from Arabic:

> The Iraqi people have been suffering for many years, from one war to the other, and why? Just because Israel and the United States are planning to destroy every Muslim center in the world. . . . History teaches us that they are all against Islam and Muslims. But Allah has the power, and He will get even with them. . . . We have to do everything in our power to save the Iraqi people from the tyrannies [United States and allied forces] . . . all of us have to be ready for jihad with our money and our souls. . . . Dar al-Hijra will be the greatest example of loyalty, of liberation, and of bringing forth the jihad which Allah calls for.

Dar al-Hijra, an example for jihad? At that point, al-Hanooti's speech turned into a prayer. Everyone in the mosque—the men down below, the women in the balcony—stood. I realized that I had made a terrible mistake.

My disguise? Perfect. My cover story? Airtight; I'd even just cried with them. Yet I'd never thought to prepare for the actual practice of prayer. How to stand, where to move, when to bow to the ground. My feet became heavy, my breath shallow, my fingers numb, and my vision blurred. I was hyperventilating, and I knew it. In this charged atmosphere, these women would not let me go unharmed if they found out I was an impostor. I had to think fast. I completely cleared my head of any other thoughts. I'd seen Muslims pray in the past, I just had to remember. Yes, the drivers who'd delivered clothes to my mother's little factory. The construction workers who'd built my house in Israel. I began to recall their movements. Quickly! It's going to begin! It was as if I were looking at myself from outside my own body, saying, "Come on, girl, you can do it."

Al-Hanooti began leading the prayer. I remembered that it is custom for Muslims to move close to one another during prayer so that they touch shoulder to shoulder. But Dar al-Hijra was so crowded that this step was unnecessary, which gave me a few extra seconds to think. After each sentence al-Hanooti uttered, the audience answered, "Amen."

"The Iraqi people are suffering . . . but Allah will take revenge."

"Amen."

"Allah will rain his curse on the Americans and the British."

"Amen."

"Allah will give us the victory over our tyrannical enemies in our country [Iraq]."

"Amen."

"Allah, the infidel Americans and British are fighting against you."

"Amen."

"Allah, just like Allah promises us, He will fulfill his promise, and His curse, the curse of Allah, will become true on the infidel Jews."

"Amen."

"Allah, the curse of Allah will become true on the tyrannical Americans."

"Amen."

"Allah will help the Iraqi people to win their victory."

"Amen."

"Allah will help Iraq to be liberated from the tyrannies."

"Amen."

This was followed by a traditional, run-of-the-mill Friday prayer. By now, I was remembering everything. I bowed, I moved, I looked exactly like them. But the sermon had shaken me. How many people here really understood what was said? I guessed that most of the African Americans didn't follow a word of it. But what about the Egyptians, Palestinians, Iraqis? How many did actually come to pray, just pray and practice Islam, and how many supported these state-ments? No question as to where al-Hanooti's loyalties lie, I thought as we all worshipped. Isn't supporting an enemy, publicly, during war-time, an act of treason? How far can the freedom of speech be stretched? Al-Hanooti urged his followers to collect money for the Iraqis. He called for jihad, holy war. He promised Allah's curse on the "tyrannical Americans." He urged his followers to make Dar al-Hijra the model for jihad. To me, that was nothing but a declaration of war against America, against the West, against civilization. If this is what he preaches, if this is his *Khutbat al-Jum'aa,* I thought, how would his fatwas look? A fatwa—religious edict—by a respectable imam could have tremendous power.

Does it really matter whether most of the worshippers in Dar al-Hijra didn't fully understand, or agree to, everything that al-Hanooti said there? It requires only a few followers who agree and abide by such a *khutba,* or a fatwa in the same spirit, for havoc to ensue. The followers who are intent on seeing fatwas through will not be discouraged and will stop at nothing. Anyone inflamed enough to carry out a fatwa would be more than willing to give his life for the cause. The only way to stop them, therefore, is to prevent such fatwas from being issued in the first place.

Preachers like al-Hanooti and mosques like Dar al-Hijra promote fundamentalism that may prove extremely dangerous. A new generation grows on these sermons; in Dar al-Hijra there's also a school. I wonder what is being taught in a school in a mosque where the imam is al-Hanooti. And we wonder now where the Americans who went to train in Bin Laden's camps in Afghanistan ever got these crazy ideas of theirs.

On the way out of the mosque, I was preoccupied with what I'd seen and heard. I know that I looked upset because people were staring at me, although they assumed that I'd become distraught over the sermon and the sufferings of the Iraqis. It was the sermon all right, but I had my own reasons. I recognized some of the people leaving the mosque. The pillars of the Muslim community in the United States, some of its most prominent leaders. One particularly gaunt man looked familiar, but I couldn't remember immediately who he was—in my mind's eye the face was fuller—and then it came to me. Abdalhalim al-Ashqar. Recently released from prison after he'd gone on a hunger strike and the prison physicians hadn't wanted to take unnecessary risks. No wonder he lost weight. Al-Ashqar had been jailed in New York when he refused to testify before a federal grand jury looking into the connections of Musa Abu Marzook, the political leader of Hamas and one of the leaders of IAP, HLF's mother organization. More pieces of the puzzle. The more I gathered, the more enmeshed I saw they were. The players may have had different names, addresses, and affiliations, but they were all playing the same game. I just needed to find the source.

I caught the shuttle back to New York and from there I hailed a cab. I told the driver, "Get me home in time for dinner and I'll make it worth your while." The guy drove as though the devil himself were chasing us, and when I got home, dinner was waiting. The real world, where love and happiness prevailed, was still there. It filled my heart with joy.

The next morning, a Saturday, I went to the office. I made a report of what I'd heard and taped. I translated the Arabic parts. Then I started looking deeper at my material. I cast a thin fishing line, hoping to catch some sardines. The thing I began pulling out of the water eventually emerged like some mythological sea creature, beyond my wildest dreams, greater than anything my colleagues or I had ever seen. That thin line led me eventually to discoveries that drove one of the greatest antiterrorism operations in U.S. history. I made the link, I deciphered the code, I found the key. Sami al-Arian, PIJ, Muhammad al-Hanooti, Abdalhalim al-Ashqar, HLF, al-Qaeda. Many players, one plot. And one address, in Virginia. Open Sesame. The password that brought me to the source. I revealed the Saudi connection.

The following story perhaps doesn't belong here chronologically, but I would like to close this chapter with al-Hanooti. A few days after my visit to the mosque, I tried to interest the FBI in my transcript of the imam's speech. As Harry had predicted, they pooh-poohed it. Freedom of speech, not enough to initiate an investigation, no crime committed yet . . . blah, blah, blah.

After 9-11, they called me. Begged me to give them these tapes. "Happy to help," I said, "but it's a bit late, don't you think?"

When I met with Attorney General John Ashcroft after 9-11, one of the issues I raised was al-Hanooti. I gave him the tapes the FBI didn't want. Two weeks after that, I was called by some INS people. They told me that the information I'd given Ashcroft had been forwarded to them. They said they were trying to block al-Hanooti's application for citizenship. Maybe he'll even be deported someday. But we're not done with him yet; although he was expelled from Dar al-Hijra and lived in upstate New York for some time, I've learned recently that he was appointed "the Grand Mufti of Greater Washington" and that he's going to return to . . . Dar al-Hijra.

Perhaps you may be thinking that all this business with al-Hanooti and Dar al-Hijra is just a minor thing that I've blown out of proportion. So here is a piece of information about the mosque that may help you make up your mind. A Jordanian guy named Eyud Alrababah approached the FBI a few days after 9-11. He told them that he'd recognized on TV the faces of two of the hijackers who crashed the jet into the Pentagon. He told the FBI that he'd met Hani Hanjour, the Pentagon attack ringleader, and Nawaf Alhazmi, also on that flight, in his local mosque. There he befriended them. He invited them for tea, helped them rent a flat, traveled with them to Connecticut. The mosque where they'd met was none other than the Dar al-Hijra Islamic Center.

And in Dar al-Hijra, a year after 9-11, it's business as usual, where the new imam preaches jihad and hatred toward Israel and its allies.

CHAPTER 5

A Diplomatic Incident

IN THE FEW MONTHS since I'd started this job, I'd spent count-less weekends in the office. I don't like working on weekends. Week-ends are for rest, for family, for fun . . . and for chores.

Leo tries to help me with the housekeeping—he's good with a vac-uum, I'll give him that—but some things he never managed to learn to do up to my standards. Like mopping the wood floors. Like folding the laundry. So he drives the kids to their piano lessons and other various activities and takes care of handyman stuff around the house, does the lawn and is in charge of the bills, and sometimes even prepares a sim-ple dinner when I'm working late. But that still leaves me with a house full of chores and four kids to feed, dress, and help with homework. For the first year we were in America, Leo and I would sit with the kids and help them with their homework for hours every evening—even in subjects such as math: a child who doesn't speak the language can't solve the problems. Gradually, things improved. Not only are my children doing well in school, they've made tremendous progress in their extracurricular activities. One of them actually played piano in a recital at the Carnegie Hall.

Sometimes I don't get home until ten P.M. Then I start to clean the bathrooms, and mop the floors, and cook, and scour the kitchen after I've finished cooking. I can't stand a dirty kitchen. As a matter of fact, I can't stand a dirty anything. I have a thing with tidiness. When I first started working in the office, I saw a place devastated by a volcanic eruption. As I advanced and got my own space and team of researchers, my department began to look more and more distinct from the rest of the office; it was clean and tidy as a museum. At home, no matter how tired I am or how late I get back from work, I still have to bring the house to order before I feel I can go to my bedroom.

There I slip into something more comfortable and do my other duty: I get to work on my PC. Do all the things I had no time to do during the day, such as browse radical and terrorist-affiliated Web sites, read e-mails, check the news. Deepen my knowledge. I'm a control freak as far as keeping up-to-date about Islamic terrorism. I have to know absolutely everything about it. As I rose in my position at the office, I found myself working more and more hours. Not just late nights and weekends, but holidays, too. Even High Holidays. I even went to the office on Yom Kippur. This day, the Day of Atonement, is the holiest of all Jewish holidays, when people are supposed to fast so that bodily issues are set aside. It's when they contemplate their relationships with God, with others, and with themselves, and ask forgiveness for the past year's transgressions with a resolve to improve in the future. Not improvements such as "Let's lose five pounds," but rather focusing on how to become a better person. Three years in a row I ended up in the office on Yom Kippur: hungry from fasting, angry with myself, and remorseful that I was at work instead of home, where I should have been. Every year I promised myself not to do it again, and every year an emergency occurred that needed my immediate and personal attention.

There is, however one unbeatable advantage to being in the office when everyone else is not, and that's zero interruptions. No phone calls or pages or meetings or bureaucratic matters. Just me, the documents, and the quiet.

And thus, on that Saturday after my visit to Dar al-Hijra, I shut the windows so that even the sounds of the busy street below couldn't intrude, and I read, thought, and concentrated. I finished translating the Arabic parts of al-Hanooti's sermon, I summarized the transcript of the events and statements made in the mosque, and then I started to look. I thought of al-Ashqar, the man who was released from prison following a hunger strike. Why him? Maybe because I needed to take a break from al-Hanooti, maybe because I was impressed by the tenacity of al-Ashqar's refusal to eat. Or maybe it was just a hunch.

Don't get me wrong; I wasn't letting go of al-Hanooti, not in a million years. I was just looking for a starting point, and al-Ashqar seemed as good as any. I studied his background. I discovered that he ran a charitable organization called al-Aqsa Educational Fund. According to Justice Department documents, this fund was a cover operation for Hamas in the United States. Like HLF, I thought.

I looked for al-Aqsa Educational Fund's tax forms—its 1023, which is an application for tax-exempt status, and its 990s, which are returns that must be submitted for every fiscal year in which an organization's income exceeded $25,000. All charitable organizations in the United States must submit tax forms; 1023s and 990s are in the public domain and easily retrievable in most cases. Yet in my experience, government agents investigating terrorism rarely look at these forms.

On al-Aqsa's 1023 a certain address popped up. In Herndon, Virginia, Grove Street. One of al-Aqsa's board members listed his address there, at 555 Grove Street. I knew I'd seen that address somewhere before. I knew I had. How could I ignore a number like 555? Five is a magic number, not only in the Jewish tradition, but also in Arab cultures. *Hamsa,* as the Arabs call it, is a symbol of good luck used to drive demons away. I racked my memory . . . yes, it had to be that. I went to get the folder. Second file cabinet from the left, upper drawer, two-thirds of the way back. Bingo! Sami al-Arian and WISE. Remember them?

In 1991, our old pal Ramadan Abdallah Shallah, then WISE's executive director, wrote a letter to Mark Orr, director of the International Affairs Center of the University of South Florida. Shallah, as you will recall, is currently secretary-general of the terrorist organization Palestinian Islamic Jihad, the same person who proudly announced, in June 2002, from his hidey-hole in Damascus, Syria, that it was he who gave the order to blow up a bus in Israel, killing eighteen civilians and gravely injuring more than thirty. In that letter to the university, Shallah noted that the largest contributor to WISE "is the Washington-based International Institute of Islamic Thought (IIIT)." He enclosed with his letter a brochure describing IIIT and its activities.

Copied on that letter was Bashir Nafi, one of the four founders of WISE and of PIJ, who was deported from the United States in 1997. I ran a quick search and found that Nafi had been employed by IIIT—which listed 555 Grove Street in Herndon, Virginia, as its address. I then cross-referenced the address with al-Hanooti just for kicks, to see if there was any connection. Surprise, surprise: The return address on al-Hanooti's mortgage payments was 555 Grove Street, Herndon, Virginia. Seemed like that address peeked at me from everywhere I looked. Was this a coincidence? Something peculiar was going on there, at 555. I made a mental note to remember that address.

DAN CADMAN WAS an INS agent in Washington, D.C., when I met him, but he'd begun to investigate terrorism on U.S. soil during his years in south Florida, where he'd crossed paths with Sami al-Arian. In fact, Dan devoted himself to counterterrorism work years before anyone else at the INS thought that it was a serious domestic threat. He is a dedicated, extremely capable investigator. America needs more people like him.

Part of Dan's job in Florida was to review applications for citizenship, and one day Sami's landed on his desk. Sami claims frequently in the press that he's a U.S. citizen. Well, he's not. He's voted in presidential elections, which is illegal; this right is reserved for U.S. citizens only. He and his family even had a heart-warming picture taken with George W. Bush Jr. and his wife, Laura, before they became president and First Lady.

Sami is not a U.S. citizen thanks largely to Dan Cadman. In a section of the application for citizenship in which the applicant is to list any organizations with which he or she is affiliated, Dan noticed that the only group Sami wrote down was the University of South Florida's Computer Engineering Society. Following a hunch, Dan looked into Sami's application file and learned that the professor had been the sponsor of many visas issued to men from the Middle East who came to America to serve as members of WISE. Dan looked a bit further and discovered that not only was Sami affiliated with WISE and ICP, he was their founder. Because Sami lied about his affiliation to these organizations, Dan blocked his application for citizenship. Sami, in turn, sued Dan and the INS. Sami lost. The judge agreed that withholding such information, particularly in light of WISE's and ICP's ties to PIJ, constituted a lie. Sami never got his citizenship.

Sitting in his Washington office, Dan hatched an idea to create a counterterrorism unit within the INS that would track down terrorists in the United States and expel them from the country. To this his new superiors, who didn't share his enthusiasm for counterterrorism work, said, Sure, why not? Let this guy worry about counterterrorism to his heart's content. To aid him in this venture, they even gave Dan an entire desk all to himself.

Dan sat at his new desk and devised a plan. He well understood that Sami was just one example and that there were many more like him out there. He wasn't going to get any help from his superiors, he knew, so he began contacting various INS field offices, looking for collaborators. He went from one office to another, briefed agents about what he was doing, and organized a large conference in New Mexico to which he invited hundreds of INS agents as well as nongovernment counterterrorism experts. He worked hard to make himself known. As he gathered information and began to get field offices interested in his work, his superiors started to notice. After a year, two agents and an analyst were assigned to him.

At that conference in New Mexico, Dan met Max, my boss. Dan told him that he was trying to learn as much as he could about Sami and PIJ's Tampa cell, to figure out how these guys operated in the

United States. Dan wanted to learn their way of thinking, on the one hand, and, on the other, to review the mistakes INS made in allowing Sami to sponsor U.S. visas for so many of his PIJ colleagues, so that similar errors could be avoided in the future.

The little tutorial I'd given John Canfield, Barry Carmody, and Kirk in the office was still fresh in Max's mind. "I have just the right person to brief you on Sami," he told Dan.

Veronica Cates, the INS analyst assigned to work with Dan, showed up in my office relatively early in the morning. She was tall, blond, elegant, and very smart, and left me with the impression that there was something noble about her. Soon after she'd joined Dan's team she was hooked on the work they were doing. She stayed with George and me the whole day, taking a crash course on Sami, until it was time for her to catch the last train back to Washington. We taught, she absorbed. She took notes and asked for copies of documents. There was so much she needed to learn, but she loved every bit of it.

ONE DAY Max asked me to prepare a report on Hamas and its front organizations in the United States. I was the Holy Land Foundation expert, HLF was a Hamas cover, so Max decided that I was the right person for the job. Although I knew HLF, I also knew that there were other organizations operating in the United States with the same mandate: Raise money for Hamas. I dug into our files on HLF, including my own earlier reports, and one thing became immediately clear. HLF was connected to another charity, IAP, or the Islamic Association for Palestine.

As soon as I discovered that, I took a break and went to read the newspapers. I love reading newspapers. Not the daily American papers; those I read at night. What I began reading was old Arabic newspapers going back years. These publications can lead you, if you know where and what to look for, to the source. So I began with a periodical published by the IAP Information Office called *al-Zaytuna*. The *Olive*. Very symbolic. Not for the olive branch, symbolizing peace, but for the olive trees so prevalent in the West Bank, in Palestine. The *Olive*, fascinating reading material to me, was the successor of another paper, named *Ila-Falastine, To Palestine.* In this *Ila-Falastine* I found tons of Hamas propaganda, including interviews with Sheikh Ahmad Yassin, the spiritual leader of Hamas; updates about Yassin's detention in Israel; several Hamas communiqués; and instructions for donors.

In one edition of this periodical, dated October 1988, I read the "Hamas Charter of Beliefs." It said, "The first principle is that Hamas is part of the Muslim Brotherhood organization . . . Jihad is their way . . . the only way to solve the Palestinian issue is through Jihad."

In the November–December 1989 edition of *Ila-Falastine,* I found an advertisement for IAP. "Our Palestinian people," the ad read, "are presently entering the third year of the Blessed Intifada under the leadership of Hamas. . . . We assure all Arabs and Muslims that our Jihad proceeds. . . . The Palestinian land is part of an ancient struggle between justice—the Muslims, and the loafers—the Jews and their allies. . . . The only way to liberate Palestine, all Palestine, is by way of Jihad. . . . Every Muslim and every Arab is committed to the Palestinian issue and Jihad for the sake of Allah. The Islamic Resistance Movement [Harakat al-Muqawama al-Islamiya in Arabic; "Hamas" is the acronym] is the conscience of the Palestinian people, and it is the hope against all those who betrayed . . . [o]h our Arab masses wherever you are. . . . The enemy has destroyed thousands of houses and thousands of olive trees. . . . Carry on with sacrifices until Allah announces victory over the Jews and their allies. . . ."

After this long-winded pitch came practical instructions for donations. "The IAP in North America will keep you informed of the activities in the Intifada until victory. . . . We call you to Jihad for the sake of Allah by donating any amount you can in support of the Intifada. . . . Send your contributions to The Occupied Land Fund," which was an early name of the Holy Land Foundation, until the organization got savvy in 1990 and gave itself a more benign-sounding moniker. The ad listed a P.O. box in Los Angeles. It was signed "Islamic Association for Palestine in North America." IAP.

It's amazing how much information a properly trained researcher can retrieve simply from looking at public records. Even before the Internet made my job easier and faster, I could discover real gems just by reading archival documents. At that point in my investigation I'd learned that HLF and IAP were connected to Hamas. I was familiar with HLF and Hamas, but not IAP. So I decided to dissect IAP using the scalpel of public records. I began gathering everything possible about IAP. I obtained its articles of incorporation. As was often the case in my investigations of such charities, the deeper I looked, the more complicated the situation turned out to be. These front groups and charities hide their actions in a maze of such complexity and deviousness that I can almost understand why U.S. government investigators can't combat them effectively. I know of government agents who did succeed in shutting down an organization or a Web site, only to see the thing reemerge a few days later under a different name. It's like the mythological Hydra story; you chop off one head and two others grow in its place.

Although I didn't have Hercules' powers, I was no less persistent—and much more curious. I read and studied, and traced and analyzed, and as the days outside grew shorter with the approaching winter, my days in the office got longer as the job of deciphering IAP became more intricate. One by one I tracked down the names and addresses and officials of this complex organization. Finally I produced a forty-nine-page report on IAP and its connection to Hamas. I called the file "IAP, the Never-Ending Story."

The way the IAP perpetually switched names and locations and directors is very, very knotty and convoluted. I'll keep it as simple as I can. IAP was first incorporated in 1981 as the Islamic Association for Palestine in North America, in Illinois. A year later, the registered agent's name was changed, as was the IAP's mailing address—to that of the residence of the then president of the Illinois organization. An IAP annual report shows that in 1991 the office was dissolved. In 1993 it was reincorporated, this time as the American Muslim Society, AMS. However, the February 1992 issue of *al-Zaytuna* noted that "the Chicago branch had been operating formally since the 9th [of February 1992.]" Obviously, the IAP branch in Chicago had remained active between its pseudodissolution in 1991 and its formal reincorporation in 1993. In 1994, the organization reincorporated yet again, this time as the IAP in Chicago, stating that it now intended to also do business as the American Muslim Society. Thus, the IAP in Chicago and the AMS were one and the same.

Outside Illinois, the IAP had incorporated in California as a non-profit corporation in 1986. Meanwhile, the IAP headquarters, in Texas, established five distinct corporations, all of which were plainly other IAP branches. The first of those corporations was the American Middle Eastern League for Palestine, AMELP, established in 1990. Ghassan A. Dahduli, who lived in Richardson, Texas, was the registering agent. Little did I know, as I was taking all this in, that Dahduli was going to star in my future counterterrorism activities. He'd be one of my home runs.

In the same year that Dahduli was setting up AMELP, the IAP Information Office in Dallas was incorporated, as was the Islamic Association for Palestine in North America. The latter was also owned by Ghassan A. Dahduli and listed a P.O. box in Dallas—the same address used by the AMELP. In 1993, the IAP, as such, incorporated in Texas. On top of everything, IAP operated without incorporating out of bases in Indiana and Arizona.

All these corporations' names were swimming around in my head. Many facades, one entity. The result was that it was almost impossible to follow their activities—it was like watching five shell games on a street corner at once, trying to keep track of both the hustle and the prizes beneath the shells.

While studying IAP, I was astounded to find out that Muhammad al-Hanooti—the imam from Dar al-Hijra who'd invoked Allah's curse on the tyrannical Americans and who'd called for jihad and for the mosque's worshippers to support Iraq in its fight against the United States—had been the head of the IAP in the early nineties. This case was becoming more and more intriguing. And then I'd found Sami's name, too. Yes, Sami al-Arian again. He too had been with the IAP in its early years, before breaking off to start his own organization, PIJ.

That was interesting: What was causing such major changes in the IAP leadership and its affiliations in the late 1980s? I pored over editions of *Ila-Falastine,* I listened to tapes, watched videos, searched public records. I read articles of incorporation and hundreds of documents in English and Arabic, and finally, it all became clear. The key to this story was the formation of Hamas.

The IAP served as a nucleus of Palestinian fundamentalists in the United States who provided ideological and financial support to Palestinian radicals in the Gaza Strip. Before the establishment of Hamas, Sami—a Palestinian—and his PIJ were part of it. In the late 1980s, with the eruption of the first Palestinian *intifada,* Hamas emerged out of the Muslim Brotherhood movement, which is the ideological progenitor of today's most violent Islamic extremist movements. Sheikh Ahmad Yassin, then the leader of the Muslim Brotherhood in the Gaza Strip, saw that the *intifada* could easily sustain a new political and military organization, and thus he founded Hamas. The name, in addition to being an acronym for Islamic Resistance Movement, also means "zeal."

Almost immediately after Hamas's establishment, the IAP began serving as the de facto financial arm for Hamas in the United States. IAP's offshoot, HLF, was also raising funds for Hamas.

In the heat of the *intifada,* a split occurred between Hamas, rapidly gaining popularity and influence, and PIJ, Palestinian Islamic Jihad. In the occupied territories, PIJ and Hamas were competing over funds from abroad and over local support in terms of recruiting mujahideen. Each of these organizations even celebrated a different day as the beginning of the *intifada,* according to what they perceived as their contribution to it. A similar struggle took place on U.S. soil, within the IAP.

When Hamas's interests took over IAP, Sami, who sided with PIJ, split and created ICP, the Islamic Concern Project, later called Islamic Committee for Palestine. Long wise to America's reverence for religious institutions, Sami chose a name that made his organization sound like a religious venture so that he could avoid paying taxes or provide documentation to the government that would reveal the organization's financial transactions. Very smart, very convenient.

So Sami, Dahduli, and al-Hanooti all had roots in IAP. Tentacles, tentacles everywhere. I couldn't find a stone under which creepy crawlers weren't scurrying away. IAP's "never-ending story" was finally ready to tell.

I CALLED Veronica. I'd come up with an idea I wanted to run by her. Years ago, in the pre–9-11 era, INS tried to block the entry into this country of known, convicted terrorists only. Supporters of terrorism, issuers of fatwas calling for jihad against Americans, and people who made verbal threats against the United States could obtain U.S. visas with no difficulty. In part, this was because the INS had no efficient way to screen these people; the intelligence agencies didn't believe that Islamic fundamentalism was a significant threat to America and didn't follow such people as carefully as they should have. The INS didn't even have a unit that collected information on these people. Dan Cadman had established such a unit, but a problem remained: INS does not gather intelligence information. That's the job of the CIA and the FBI, but these agencies do not share intelligence information with the INS. Or with anyone else, for that matter. INS had long been the subject of severe criticism for its failure to block certain people from coming to America, yet in many cases, INS just didn't get the information from the intelligence agencies it needed in order to do so.

I told Veronica that I had a proposal for her.

"Go on," she said. "I hear the sound of the wheels turning in your head." I could almost see her grinning on the other end of the line.

"We need to figure out a way to block terrorist supporters from coming here," I said. "Some are as dangerous as the actual terrorists. If these people hate us so much, what business do they have traveling here to disseminate their hate ideology, to call for jihad, not to mention raising money here to fund it?"

My idea was simple and straightforward, really. The State Department had a watch list of terrorists it banned from entering the country. What if the list were expanded to ban supporters of terrorists, potential terrorists, and those who issue fatwas promoting terrorism? People who could pose a real danger to the United States?

Veronica loved the idea and immediately took it to Dan. Soon they called back. They were eager to begin getting information on such people from me. Did I have anyone specific in mind?

As a matter of fact I did. Dr. Ishaq al-Farhan and Sheikh Yousef al-Qaradawi. They could be a good start. Two well-known Muslim scholars, Farhan and Qaradawi. Two distinguished gentlemen. Farhan, a political leader in Jordan. Qaradawi, a resident of Qatar and a revered cleric with a worldwide following. Both frequently traveled to the United States and participated in important Muslim meetings and conferences.

You may be wondering why I would want to undermine the sincere wishes of two honorable Muslim leaders to speak their minds in the land of free speech. Well, while Qaradawi may be one of the most respected clerics in the Muslim world, he is also one of the religious leaders of the Muslim Brotherhood. Same old Brotherhood. Long before this Brotherhood gave birth to Hamas, it was an international Sunni Islamic extremist movement, founded in Egypt in 1928. In the aftermath of World War I, as the European imperialist powers were carving up the Middle East, the Muslim Brotherhood rose in opposition to the West's nation making—borders that still exist today. For the Muslim Brothers, only one Arab nation, *Ummah,* governed by the laws of the *Shari'a*—the rule of Islam—was acceptable. The Brotherhood still opposes all Arab governments today, and for that, in most Arab countries, its members are hunted down and on occasion executed. In addition to begetting Hamas, PIJ, and the Egyptian Islamic Jihad (the group that assassinated Egyptian president Anwar Sadat in 1981), the Muslim Brotherhood is also the origin of al-Gama'at al-Islamiya—the Islamic Group—headed by Sheikh Omar Abdel-Rahman. Rahman, known as "the Blind Sheikh," is currently in a U.S. federal prison serving a life sentence for his involvement in a plot to blow up New York's Lincoln Tunnel. Although, luckily, the attack never came to fruition, Rahman was convicted on conspiracy charges.

His organization, al-Gama'at al-Islamiya, is tight with al-Qaeda. The Blind Sheikh's son, for instance, was a top Bin Laden official before he was killed in the American bombing of Afghanistan after 9-11. It was in this world that Qaradawi, the man I was trying to stop from preaching on U.S. soil, was a major player.

I can hear the chorus now: Isn't that an accusation of guilt by association? You be the judge.

Quaradawi had been hosted for more than a decade by numerous radical Islamic organizations in the United States and had been invited to various conferences as a featured speaker. One such conference was held in Toledo, Ohio, in 1995, by the Muslim Arab Youth Association, MAYA. There he delivered this speech:

> This is what is told in the Hadith [a narration about the statements of the Prophet Muhammad that is not from the Qur'ân] of Ibn-Omar and the Hadith of Abu-Hurairah: You shall continue to fight the Jews and they will fight you, until the Muslims will kill them. And the Jew will hide behind the stone and the tree, and the stone and the tree will say: "Oh, servant of Allah, oh Muslim, this is a Jew behind me. Come and kill him!" The resurrection will not come before this happens. . . . Our brothers in Hamas, in Palestine, the Islamic resistance, the Islamic Jihad [PIJ], after all the rest have given up and despaired, the movement of the Jihad brings us back our faith. . . . We can stand still for a while, get some rest, but the Jihad continues . . . until the Day of Resurrection.

So, another Muslim cleric hates Jews and Israel. What's the big deal? Muslims hate Jews, it's an old thing, there's not much you can do about it. Why should America deal with that?

To begin with, the groups for which Qaradawi has shown affinity are on the federal government's List of Foreign Terrorist Organizations, as defined by the secretary of state in 1995—that fact alone is enough to render Qaradawi excludable from the United States according to the Immigration and Naturalization Act.

But here's the icing on the cake. Qaradawi, in a *khutba*, sermon, that was delivered in 1996 and was available on Hamas's official Web site, stated that Hamas and Islamic Jihad suicide bombers were engaged not in terrorism, but rather in martyrdom, and that all members of Israeli society were valid targets for such attacks. Qaradawi, you see, was the first prominent Muslim cleric to state that barbaric suicide attacks—"martyrdom," in the most grotesque use of the word—are a legitimate weapon against civilians. He was the first to issue a fatwa endorsing and justifying such methods, making him the spiritual father of suicide attacks. In a way, he is to blame for 9-11 as much as Bin Laden himself. Qaradawi wasn't satisfied merely with endorsing Hamas and PIJ and didn't recommend jihad and suicide bombing just theoretically. He and his family were also major shareholders in Bank al-Taqwa, which after 9-11 was designated as an al-Qaeda supporter and whose assets were frozen by the U.S. government. Al-Taqwa, according to the Treasury Department, not only financed al-Qaeda, but also arranged shipments of guns for it.

This was the guy I was trying to keep out of the United States. Bad, bad girl.

Now, Farhan. The secretary-general of the Islamic Action Front, IAF. IAF served as the political wing of the Muslim Brotherhood movement in Jordan. It was tightly associated with Hamas, also an extension of the Muslim Brotherhood, and much like Hamas, it was opposed to the peace process in the Middle East.

But Farhan went beyond merely opposing the peace process. Nasser Hidmi, a Palestinian youth arrested in Israel in 1992 as he was attempting to detonate a bomb, exposed the role of the Hamas military wing in the United States, how this wing recruited new terrorists, and how Islamic conferences in America were used for the training of terrorists. These conferences were sponsored by both IAP and MAYA, Hidmi said, and Farhan played an integral role in them, not only as a speaker but also as a recruiter of Palestinian youth to partake in the activities of Hamas. In his statements to the Israelis, Hidmi said:

> At the Islamic Conference there were five thousand invited guests that stayed at hotels surrounding the center. . . . At the conference in Kansas City, Muhammad Salah gathered about twenty young men including

myself for a secret meeting of the activists of Hamas. . . . They informed us that all the young men that were present and were chosen for the secret meetings were from the Occupied Territories and were selected according to forms they filled out in the [refugee] camps. This was done in order that they will take part in activities that will support and strengthen the Intifadah within the framework of Hamas. . . . Among those that lectured to us was Ishaq Farhan who is a member of the Jordanian Parliament.

So Farhan is active with Hamas and talks in secret meetings, recruiting and instructing terrorists. But isn't Hamas Isreal's problem? No it's not. To imagine that is a tragic mistake. This faulty approach was adopted by the U.S. government, which for years treated Hamas and PIJ as a Middle Eastern problem. Officials completely misunderstood, or ignored, the fact that all these organizations are essentially one and the same, tentacles of the same creature—Islamic fundamentalism—and that their goal is identical: to kill, kill, kill. Hamas members were obtaining military training in Bin Laden's camps in Afghanistan. Richard Reid, the so-called shoe bomber, the al-Qaeda operative who tried to blow up American Airlines Flight 63 from Paris to New York, visited Israel a few months prior to 9-11. There he met a Hamas activist who once trained in Bin Laden's camps and who coached Reid in the tricks of the trade.

When 9-11 happened, the government's attitude changed, but by then it was too late.

Here's why Ishaq al-Farhan is definitely a problem for America. Between July 1995 and April 1997, an extradition trial of Musa Abu Marzook, the head of the political bureau of Hamas, took place in Manhattan. During that time the White House and the U.S. embassy in Amman, Jordan, received numerous requests for the release of Marzook. Farhan, as the secretary-general of the IAF, wrote letters demanding his release. In a letter dated May 13, 1996, Farhan calls "on all the governments of the Arab and Islamic Worlds and all defenders of human rights to raise their voices and demand the abolition of this decision and the release of Dr. Musa Abu Marzook, a prisoner of opinion and political struggle." Six months later, on November 10,

1996, the American embassy in Amman received this, regarding the release of Marzook:

> We demand that you immediately release Dr. Musa Abu Marzook and urge you not to hand him over to the Zionist enemy. . . . We warn you that if you do not release Dr. Musa Abu Marzook, and if you hand him over to the Jews, we will turn the ground upside down over your heads in Amman, Jerusalem, and the rest of the Arab countries and you will lament your dead just as we did to you in Lebanon in 1982 when we destroyed the Marine House with a booby-trapped car, and there are plenty of cars in our country. You also still remember the oil tanker with which we blew up your soldiers in Saudi Arabia.

The State Department translated the above threat, and an official there scrawled on the translation: "The Arabic fax bears the Islamic Action Front name." That fax was received from the offices of the IAF, headed by Farhan.

And thus, George and I prepared thick binders on these two characters, Qaradawi and Farhan, and sent them to Veronica. Frankly, neither of us believed this information, however airtight, would actually be put to good use.

For eight months I'd heard nothing about Qaradawi or Farhan. With the government, information travels only one way: to the government. As soon as you provide its agents with your findings, your information becomes classified, and even you cannot get your material back. The government will never even acknowledge getting it from you. All my work, all my contributions to national security, remain behind the scenes. I must not be revealed, and I never get credit for what I do. It's part of the game, and while I chafe sometimes at no one knowing it was me, anonymity ensures my safety. The bad guys don't even know that I'm there. Or at least they won't until this book is published. Still, being kept in the dark about the information that I'd provided in the first place can be frustrating. I give them smoking guns, they confiscate the guns and leave me with the smoke.

One morning Veronica finally called me and with urgency in her voice I'd never heard before, she told me to listen to the news.

All hell had broken loose. I'd created a diplomatic incident, no less. I almost felt guilty about it. Almost.

A *New York Times* article dated May 5, 2000, summarized that incident with Ishaq al-Farhan, taking a clear side on the issue: "Immigration officials at Kennedy International Airport detained a prominent moderate Islamist political leader from Jordan for a long interrogation and sent him home on the next flight, he said, prompting high-level protests to embarrassed American diplomats here today."

Moderate Islamist political leader. Right. The article, which then incorrectly called him a university president and senator—in fact he's a *retired* senator—said that the sixty-seven-year-old Farhan "arrived on Tuesday in New York on a Royal Jordanian Airways flight from Amman. He had planned to visit a son and daughter who live in the United States and to give talks to American Islamic groups. . . . Mr. Farhan's Jordanian diplomatic passport was stamped with a five-year multiple-entry visa valid until December 2003, the latest in a series of United States visas that he had since graduating with a doctorate from Columbia University four decades ago. On presenting his passport, Mr. Farhan said, he was taken to a room where officers from the Immigration and Naturalization Service told him that the State Department had revoked his visa and requested that he be interrogated. . . . After six hours of questioning, he said, he was ordered to buy a $2,000 one-way ticket on KLM flights back to Amman. . . . [Farhan] said the immigration officials had told him that he would not be allowed to re-enter the United States for at least five years."

Now here's what happened. The INS had taken the report George and I put together, researched the data, conducted its own investigation, verified the facts, and come to its own conclusions. INS then compiled *its* report and sent it to the State Department. The agency recommended that Farhan be added to the State Department's watch list.

The State Department then reviewed the INS data and report in great detail, crossed it with information from the U.S. embassy in Amman, checked other sources, and put the man's name on the list.

Only problem was that Farhan, as a former member of the Jordanian parliament, is in the State Department's eyes a diplomat. The proper procedure in cases like his is to inform the diplomat, through the relevant embassy, *before* he leaves his country of origin that he has to surrender his visa. The State Department failed to do that. Farhan arrived in New York, his name popped up in the INS computer, he was treated like a terrorist, searched, questioned, and then kicked out of the country. Before he was deported, though, Farhan made a call to the Jordanian ambassador to the United States, his longtime acquaintance. The news spread like wildfire. By the time Farhan returned to Jordan, there were massive rallies there and Muslim Brotherhood demonstrations condemning the United States, with thousands crying, "Death to America!" The Jordanian media was full of reports about the incident. The United States ambassador to Jordan, William Burns, called Farhan to "express his concern" about the incident. Later, Burns was summoned to the Jordanian foreign minister's office to provide an official explanation. By that time, King Abdallah had called President Clinton for an explanation. Clinton was apologetic. Upon State Department instructions, the American ambassador to Jordan personally apologized to Farhan for the incident. And Farhan was awarded an indefinite U.S. visa.

Was this my goal? Was this what I wanted? By no means. I felt that this whole incident was my fault. I originated the idea, I provided the information, I caused all this racket. I called Veronica and spoke to her. She too was upset, but not because she thought we'd done anything wrong. No way. She immediately told me, when we spoke, that this was not my fault. I did the right thing. One hundred percent. So did the INS counterterrorism unit. Absolutely. But the State Department messed everything up by failing to adhere to protocol. Then the State Department did something even worse to quiet things down: It chose politics over security. Although Farhan wasn't notified properly, he still was who he was. He still had no business receiving a formal apology from an American ambassador—or an unlimited U.S. visa.

Veronica was right. We were the good guys. Farhan was not.

The story of Qaradawi was much simpler. This happened a few

months after the Farhan incident. As with Farhan, the INS checked the evidence we provided them, made their own report, forwarded it to the State Department, and Qaradawi's name was added to the list. The State Department, for a change, did their job properly. Maybe they learned their lesson. When Qaradawi tried to renew his visa, he was summoned to the American embassy in Qatar and his ten-year multiple-entry visa was revoked. Straightforward, effective, as it should have happened with Farhan.

I didn't know that this had happened until I heard that Qaradawi had failed to show up for a conference in Baltimore, Maryland, at which he was on the bill. Finding out about his visa felt like a big victory for me. Qaradawi, and other Muslim clerics who abuse their power to preach for jihad, have no business coming here.

MORE THAN A YEAR after the Farhan incident, I heard that Sheikh Ikrima Sabri, the grand mufti of Jerusalem and Palestine, was scheduled to attend the 26th Annual Convention of the Islamic Circle of North America, ICNA, in July 2001. By now I'd been promoted yet again at work, had finally moved down to the third floor, and was overseeing a team of talented young researchers.

This mufti, top Islamic religious authority, is notorious for his calls for the annihilation of the United States and for his endorsement of jihad, suicide bombings, and child "sacrifices" through encouraging children to become martyrs. "The younger the martyr," he said, "the more I respect him." Appointed by Yasser Arafat himself to this distinguished position, Sabri spoke on the Voice of Palestine, the Palestinian Authority's official radio station, in 1997: "O Allah, destroy America as it is controlled by Zionist Jews. . . . Allah will paint the White House black. . . . The Muslims say to Britain, to France and to all the infidel nations that Jerusalem is Arab. . . . Allah will take revenge, in the name of his prophet, on the colonialist settlers who are the descendents of monkeys and pigs. Forgive us, O Muhammad, for the acts of these monkeys and pigs who wished to profane your holiness."

The mufti went on the official Palestinian Authority television station on August 24, 2001, a mere fortnight before 9-11, and delivered a *khutba* in which he said, "Allah, keep al-Aqsa safe. Allah, destroy the occupation and its helpers and agents. Destroy the U.S. and its helpers and its agents. Allah, destroy Britain and its helpers and its agents. . . . Allah, grant victory to Islam and the Muslims."

In the aftermath of 9-11, Israeli authorities arrested Sabri. He had just returned from an illegal visit to southern Lebanon, where he met with Hizballah officials. While in custody, Sabri told Israeli authorities that "the White House will turn black, with Allah's help, and that America, Britain, and Israel should be destroyed."

As a powerful Palestinian religious figure, Sabri's statements are, for all practical purposes, fatwas. When someone with the authority of Sabri, the Blind Sheikh, al-Hanooti, or Qaradawi calls for the destruction of America, it's not just rhetoric, and it's not freedom of speech, either. These men, while not holding the gun physically, are as responsible for terrorism as the terrorists themselves. Maybe even more so, because they ignite the flame that burns in the hearts of the terrorists. They make murder a religious mission. They use their tremendous influence to teach death instead of life, hate instead of peace, and martyrdom instead of hope.

As with Qaradawi and Farhan, keeping Sabri out of the United States was clearly the right thing to do. So my researchers and I prepared a report on the mufti, detailing his statements and proof of his support of terrorism and of his strong ties with Hamas. We sent it to Veronica. She called me a few days later and said that their report was already on its way to the State Department. "I see no reason why they won't block him," she told me. I too thought the evidence was strong enough that the State Department would happily deny this guy a visa.

A week later, Veronica was on the phone again. She was beyond furious. The State Department had refused to put Sabri's name on the watch list. The story was that when the State Department reviewed the file, some functionary noticed Sabri's formal title "the Grand Mufti of Jerusalem and all of Palestine." Seeing the title, that someone had gotten cold feet. Sabri's visa remained untouched. The title, not the man, was being evaluated. Again, politics 1, security 0. Veronica said Dan had tried to appeal the decision, but officials at the State Department hushed up the whole thing.

Sabri made it to the convention in Cleveland. There, he urged support of Hamas and of suicide attacks and continued to issue such statements as "The Jews do not dare to bother me, because they are the most cowardly creatures Allah has ever created," and "We tell them [the Jews]: In as much as you love life, the Muslim loves death and martyrdom."

With such incitement, no wonder that terrorists are willing to give their own lives as long as they can take others' with them.

To make things even worse, a year after 9-11 Dan Cadman accepted a position in Europe. He's off the counterterrorism beat.

Now that he's gone, who at the INS will help me stop terrorists from coming to America?

DESTINY. It had to be. Max's request to make a report on IAP. Like so many other times, the original report came to very little use. But my knowledge, my research, my ability to connect the small details and see the big picture, all these did not go to waste. I studied IAP, and with the information I obtained, I helped the government prevent Qaradawi from coming to the United States. Indirectly, I even caused a diplomatic incident with Jordan. And there was more.

Soon after I'd found it in *Ila-Falastine,* I gave copies of the ad with the Hamas charter—as well as many other excerpts from that publication—to various people and on different occasions. Years later, a judge in a civil lawsuit asked for the Justice Department's opinion on whether HLF was a front group for Hamas. The department, in support of its decision that it was, submitted documents to the court in April 2002. When I obtained these documents, I was amazed to find out that the ad with the charter, some other ads for HLF fund-raisers, and some Hamas communiqués that I'd collected from *Ila-Falastine* were all submitted by the Justice Department. My handwriting, the notes I'd scribbled in Hebrew, were clearly visible on some of these documents.

So the never-ending story of IAP did go a long way, after all. . . .

I started this business of IAP, Hamas, and these deportations with al-Hanooti. I'd also like to finish it with him. I'd learned that al-Hanooti was one of the main character witnesses in Marzook's trial in Manhattan; why, he even sang ballads in his praise at the trial. Then I learned that al-Hanooti was one of the unindicted conspirators in the 1993 World Trade Center bombing. He was in good company; Usama Bin Laden was named as an unindicted co-conspirator, too.

In mid-1999, as the turn of the millennium approached, I sat at my desk and thought about how the same names kept appearing, over and over again, in every investigation. They were always connected, one way or the other, and the distinction among PIJ, Hamas, Hizballah, and al-Qaeda became ever fuzzier.

I finally completed my file on al-Hanooti. Based on the imam's accomplishments and on the statements he made time and again at Dar al-Hijra, seasoned with my increasingly pessimistic view of the government's ability to protect us from the likes of him, I finished my report on al-Hanooti with this grim prediction: "As long as radical Islamic imams such as al-Hanooti hold key positions in major Islamic centers, it would not be at all surprising if something similar to the World Trade Center bombing would happen again, in an attempt of radicals to achieve their ultimate goal: Muslim world domination."

~~~~~~

CHAPTER 6

The Friday Sermon

WHETHER IT IS on purpose or not, the vast majority of large Muslim conferences in the United States coincide with major American holidays, such as Thanksgiving and Christmas. Is it just coincidental? Is it, perhaps, because American holidays often incorporate long weekends into the celebrations, thus easily accommodating three-day meetings? Or is it a statement about the patriotism and loyalties of the organizers and attendees of these conferences?

It was 1999, and as it does every year, the IAP conference took place in Chicago, Illinois, over the Thanksgiving weekend. I wanted to attend the conference, but I also wanted to spend the holiday with my family. Leo wanted to be in proximity, too, in case something went wrong with my undercover job or my pregnancy. As I hate flying, Leo and I decided that the whole family should make the thirteen-hour trip from New York to Chicago in our old minivan. He and the kids could have a little vacation while I worked, and we'd be together in the evenings.

Leo didn't mind doing all the driving, and I worked on my laptop most of the way. The boys behaved beautifully. They played their computer games and watched movies on the portable TV-VCR contraption we set up in back. They worried about me on the job— there's only so much you can hide from your kids—and they tried to help me by being very good.

However, by the time we got to Rosemont, a suburb of Chicago, they were ready to get to the hotel and shake their bones. We took a room not in the Ramada Plaza, site of the next day's conference, but in a nondescript hotel located a few blocks away. There was no way we could stay at the Ramada. Leo and the kids look nothing like Arabs, who mostly populate these conferences. One accidental meeting in an elevator, lobby, or a restaurant and my cover would be blown. At night, after work, we ate in restaurants a safe distance from the Ramada. Even so, I had a cramp in my neck from looking over my shoulder that weekend.

Before we went to bed, I arranged my Muslim disguise and recording equipment for the next morning. I did this in advance to avoid stress in the morning. I wanted to make sure the batteries were charged, the tapes blank, and the accessories in place. The boys needed to roughhouse a bit after the tedious ride, and they were jumping on the two queen-size beds. I didn't have the heart to ask them to stop, but all that childish glee jangled my nerves. When we finally turned in, the kids fell asleep almost immediately. I couldn't. I kept moving in bed and turning from side to side. I couldn't seem to find a comfortable position. At four in the morning, when I returned from one of numerous trips to the bathroom, I looked at Leo. He stared back at me, quietly, eyes wide open. He, too, stayed awake all night.

Just before dawn on Thanksgiving Day, I got up, took a hot shower, and washed off the remnants of the night and its worries. How ironic to be wearing a costume today, I thought as I dressed in my Muslim robes. Wasn't Halloween the time for scary costumes? I triple-checked myself: recording equipment securely attached, batteries full, tapes cued. I put extras of everything in my purse. I also carried my business cards—my alter ego is a professional seamstress; I chose that cover because I did, after all, know a thing or two about the clothing business—and a lot of cash. You never know what you could find at these conferences. I couldn't walk around with my credit cards; they had my real name. Ultimately I blessed the decision to take a good amount with me, because that morning I purchased my meals for the entire conference, and later that day, I paid for a martyr's son.

THE KIDS WERE still fast asleep when I finished dressing up. Leo went to get the car, and a few minutes later I went downstairs. It felt funny to be dressed like a Muslim woman in a Chicago hotel. It seemed to me that everyone was staring. Since I wasn't even who I pretended to be, I felt that much more awkward.

Afraid someone would notice that I emerged from a car driven not by a "brother," I had Leo drop me off some distance from the hotel drive. People were already streaming toward the Ramada's entrance. I joined them, walking hurriedly in the piercing cold, not looking back. I could feel Leo's worried gaze trailing me all the way to the lobby. I noticed that the cars circling around in search of parking spots had Illinois plates. Many were older models, which meant that they were not rental cars. So a good number of these people were locals; they'd likely know one another. I'd have to be very clearheaded about my cover story.

The clerk at the front desk directed me to the registration table in a far corner of the lobby. A queue had already formed there. As I joined it, I began to get jittery. This was an IAP conference. Islamic Association for Palestine. Many of the attendees, therefore, would be Palestinian. Any of them would recognize from my accent that I was an Iraqi. What if they asked me about it? What if they asked me other questions? What if I got tripped up on some detail of my story? The people at the registration table were very suspicious of anyone they didn't recognize or who didn't look Middle Eastern. They grilled several people standing in line. Some of the answers they approved, and those people they signed up. But just ahead of me in the line was a guy who didn't look Mediterranean. Nor did he speak Arabic. They asked him a few questions. He tried to explain himself, but the organizers weren't buying his story. They were polite—and very firm that he was not getting in.

The conference was for registered IAP members only, they told him, and they asked him to leave. When my turn came, they smiled at me. I smiled back, but my heart was pumping fast.

They didn't suspect anything. A Middle Eastern–looking woman, and a pregnant one at that—I had the perfect cover. I registered for the conference and paid the fee, and then they asked whether I was a member. I wasn't? Oh, well, they said, did I want to join? For only $30 more I'd regularly receive their publication, al-Zaytuna. I agreed immediately. My confidence was slowly returning. They asked me whether I was interested in purchasing meal tickets. I was, of course, because I was pregnant and hungry all the time, and the price seemed reasonable.

"So which way to breakfast?" I asked as my stomach growled. They pointed the direction for me. I walked until I found a large, beautiful dining hall. Elegant moldings, large crystal chandeliers, plenty of light. The buffet breakfast looked very promising. I didn't see too many other attendees eating, so I assumed it was still too early. I sat alone with my plate. The food was superb. I made three trips to the buffet. When I was about to leave, a waiter came by. I gave him my meal ticket and asked for some more coffee. He looked at me as if I were nuts. "What's that?" he asked.

"The coupon," I said. "For breakfast!"

Speaking to me as though I were a half-witted child, the waiter, who'd realized what happened, elucidated that the breakfast for the conference attendees was across the lobby, in the smaller dining room, where a tiny sign read "Third Annual IAP Conference."

I felt stupid, but my stomach was full. When satiety rules, such things seem only humorous. The waiter had me pay for my breakfast, which I found much less amusing, since it cost me more than what I'd paid for meals for the entire conference.

After breakfast, I returned to the lobby. The people at the IAP's registration desk showed me the way to the conference rooms, which were located in another part of the large hotel. Going there, I passed through a brightly lighted corridor decorated with large windows on both sides and overlooking a lovely patio. I had the impression that the other part of the hotel was a later addition to the structure rather than part of the original building. Beyond the corridor I found a large hall, with looming chandeliers, dark maroon-and-yellow-dotted heavy carpets, and the heavy smell so typical of conference rooms. It had the solid, characteristic appearance of a conference center, indistinguishable from many others I've seen throughout the country. To the left was a smaller hall in which a bazaar would later take place, where various tapes, books, and other artifacts would be sold. The main conference room was located outside the large hall, beyond two connecting doors.

It was still early, and people were just starting to set up their booths in the large hall. There was an IAP booth, naturally, and an HLF booth. Remember HLF? The charity that was designated after 9-11? There was also a booth for the Global Relief Foundation, GRF, another charity that was designated as a front for terrorism less than a year later; and a booth for the Benevolence International Foundation, BIF, which was designated a month after GRF. And there were some more charities, all linked to terrorism.

One booth stopped me in my tracks. Seeing the man who was putting it up, I felt a sudden spasm in my stomach. I had to overcome that feeling, because I had to meet him. It wasn't often that I got such an opportunity.

He was small, thin, nearly bald. Totally harmless looking. I approached, dragging my fake smile out of its hiding place with great difficulty. He introduced himself. Muhammad Salah, a Muslim human rights activist. He was giving out green pins and asking for donations. I gave him $10, and we started to talk.

His first question: Did I know who he was? No, I lied. "This is why these conferences are so important," he told me. "So that we can teach you about the oppression and the sufferings of Muslims in America and all over the world." He began telling me his story. He was a Palestinian, but he had American citizenship. He was a used-car salesman here in Chicago. He said that in the early 1990s he went to Israel to visit family and friends. And what happened to him? He was detained by the authorities and imprisoned for five years.

"Why?" I asked, trying to look horrified.

"I'll tell you why. Because the Israelis oppress innocent Palestinians," he said, full of indignation. "And do you know what is the most shocking part? When I returned to the U.S., after I was tortured and I thought I was going to die in that prison, the Americans placed me under investigation and froze my assets! Me, an innocent citizen, a car dealer, a family man, father of five!"

I really had to struggle now to be able to put on the show. "Of course! Now I remember," I exclaimed. "How could I have forgotten? You are a great hero. I've told your story to my three boys, and I hope it will motivate them to become mujahideen, *Insha-Allah!*" [Holy warriors, God willing.]

I told him how courageous and persistent he was, and how we Muslims should all learn from his example. He asked me to look for his wife, who was also at the conference, and talk with her. I promised that I would. We talked some more, and then I left. I didn't learn new facts, but the conversation with Salah was enlightening. Know the ways of your opponent. My motto.

Now here is the other side of this story. My side. Here's what I immediately saw when I laid eyes on the small, fragile man who claimed he'd been so cruelly treated. Salah was the head of the worldwide military wing of Hamas. He was arrested in Israel in early 1993 carrying nearly $100,000 in cash. The money, according to his own testimony, was intended for distribution to members of Hamas's military wing. Salah's trip to Israel was an effort to rebuild the shattered infrastructure of Hamas following Israel's deportation of most of the group's dangerous activists. While in prison, Salah revealed through conversations with other inmates and in a freely written confession in Arabic, thinking he was disclosing it to fellow top Hamas officials rather than to the Israelis, detailed information about Hamas's structure and funding. His testimony was later accepted as legitimate and used as evidence in the trial of Musa Abu Marzook in New York.

In his testimony Salah described how he was appointed to his esteemed position by Musa Abu Marzook—the man who was the head of Hamas's political bureau and whose extradition trial moved someone in the office of ex-Jordanian diplomat Ishaq al-Farhan's IAF to send threats to the U.S. embassy in Amman. Marzook, one of Hamas's most prominent leaders, had a close working relationship with Muhammad Salah. Salah disclosed that he'd been authorized by Marzook to recruit individuals for training in the uses of explosives to fight in the "holy war." In the United states, Salah began training ten such recruits, three of whom were chosen to carry out attacks. In addition to supervising the building of bombs, explosives, and remote detonation devices, Salah was instructed by Marzook to develop biological and chemical weapons for Hamas.

Nasser Hidmi, the Palestinian youth who was caught trying to detonate a bomb in Israel and who revealed how Ishaq al-Farhan participated in the recruitment of terrorists at a conference in Kansas, said that the man who actually cherry-picked these twenty potential terrorists was Muhammad Salah.

He the innocent citizen, used-car dealer, and family man.

There's one more thing to ponder. Marzook deputized Salah to negotiate the release of Hamas leaders from Israeli prisons. He gave him a bargaining chip to dangle before the Israelis: Salah knew where to find the body of an Israeli soldier who'd been kidnapped and murdered by Hamas. This soldier was brutally tortured, his eyes gouged out, his body mutilated. When I first laid eyes on Salah, putting the finishing touches to his booth, I couldn't help but imagine the torture and hear the screams of the victim. I just hope to God they killed him *before* doing what they did. . . .

I react badly to the idea of torture. I develop a strong physical reaction to it, with nausea, abdominal pain, and palpitations. Every time I think about it, I recall the old man who was tortured in prison with my father, the one who brought his letter. He told Mama in a few words about the brutality, the pulling of nails, the hanging on rotating ceiling fans. As he handed the letter to Mama, I could clearly see dozens of small scars from cigarette burns on his hand. My being pregnant made the reaction far worse this time, but I had to suppress all these feelings as I listened to Salah tell his hypocritical, vicious lies.

By now the HLF booth was up and running. I walked over to it and a man approached me at once and asked, in Arabic, whether I was familiar with his organization. Inside, a thundering laughter rolled through me. I probably knew more about them than they knew about themselves. On the outside, with great effort, I put on a naive face and confessed I knew very little. During the conversation, he asked why I, obviously an Iraqi, was showing interest in the Palestinian cause. I said that we were all brothers, that we were all Muslims, that jihad had no boundaries. He loved every word of it. Besides, I told him, my husband was a Palestinian. Poor Leo. The mere thought of him attending this conference was more than I could handle.

The chubby redhead speaking with me looked no more Palestinian than Leo. After giving me a short introduction about the HLF and the importance of sending money to Palestine, he told me that one of the group's most important projects was the child adoption program. He explained that for as little as $50 a month, I could "adopt," meaning sponsor, a Palestinian child of my choice. "Especially now that the holy month of Ramadan is just a few weeks away," he said, "the money can be used to purchase all kinds of treats for these children. They will be delighted to get these holiday packages, so if you choose to sponsor a child, now would be the best time to start."

I felt that something was cooking here. "Can you tell me a bit more about that?" I asked.

He was delighted. He told me that this was one of their most successful endeavors lately (to funnel money to Hamas, no doubt, I thought to myself). He pulled out a few large folders with pictures of children. Orphans. There were also descriptions of these children. Age, gender, place, and what event had transpired to make them parentless. I looked through some of these descriptions. A good number were children of *shuhada*. Martyrs! Suicide bombers and such! So this program was another incentive for anyone considering martyrdom as a path to paradise, because he could be assured that his kids would be provided for. I looked carefully through a few more pictures and descriptions.

"You know," I said to the redheaded guy, "sponsoring a Palestinian child is truly a noble cause. But if I am doing a good deed, I want to go all the way. I want to adopt a martyr's son." He looked very pleased, but then he knitted his eyebrows. "That may be a problem, dear Sister. You see, I don't have any available right now. Obviously, they go first. They are the hottest item on our list!"

I persisted. I said I had children of my own, and I knew how terrible being orphaned was; at least I wasn't lying about that part. I would feel so much better, I told him, if I knew my money went to the best cause, and what could be better than to support the son of a man who died for jihad?

It worked. He confirmed I was staying for the rest of the conference, and then he suggested that I stop by his booth the next day. He'd try to arrange something special, just for me.

Lunch was upon us, and I was hungry again. I followed the crowd, to make sure I went to the right place this time, and entered the hall with the other women. Women and children were in a large, dull-looking room, which had a connecting door to the men's dining room. The children sat with us, but some kept running back and forth between the two rooms. This separation from the men worked out beautifully for me; no one here would notice that I was alone at the conference.

The numerous tables in our dining room bore only plain white cloths. There was a long line for the steam-table buffet, which consisted of chicken, meatballs, rice, and salad. That was *it?* Not only was it bland, but the food servers were obviously under orders to dish out very small portions. Some women ahead of me in line asked for larger helpings and got yelled at. How *Oliver Twist,* I thought. I quietly took my gruel and went to sit at one of the tables.

The ten women there all knew immediately that I was not local, because they were acquainted with most of the people in their community. It was also obvious that I wasn't Palestinian. As a result, they showed great interest in me. They asked who I was and how I came to be here, and I rolled out my cover story casually. I said that my husband couldn't leave his work, that he was a government employee, and while he'd certainly attended conferences before, he felt uncomfortable coming to political events. As I rattled on, I had to take care not to slip up and say a word in Hebrew—those words and expressions that I use without second thought, the equivalents of "ya know" and "okay." I told them we figured that since I, the woman, was with the kids most of the time (as is expected of a Muslim woman), it was important for me to come to this event so that I could educate my children with the ideas and practices of Islam I'd learn here.

After lunch, I bumped into Salah again. This time he was with his wife, whom he deposited with me. We looked so much the same, she and I. Long dark dress, long white *hijab,* no nail polish or makeup. But there was a giant gap between us, of which she had no clue, and on account of which I was becoming increasingly edgy. I let her do most of the talking. These long conversations were getting too tedious and too risky. But I did flatter her on her bravery, on surviving with five kids without her husband for five long years. I asked her how she'd managed.

"Praise Allah," she said, "for our generous local Muslim community. Practically everyone here helped us, aware of the sufferings of my husband, and we were never short of anything. Our unity as Muslims is a very powerful weapon."

"This is very true," I told her, and I meant every word of it.

LEO WOKE ALL of us up early on Friday morning. The kids sprang like coils out of bed, even though they'd come back Thanksgiving night very tired from their adventures in the city of Chicago. As I was chitchatting with Muhammad Salah and trying to purchase a martyr's son at the HLF booth, they were walking the wide avenues of downtown Chicago, watching the city's Thanksgiving Day parade, where they literally bumped into the actor John Malkovich. The combination of the long drive and miles of walking in the brisk autumnal air had made the boys sleep like logs. I didn't understand their uncharacteristic morning liveliness until Leo confided that he'd promised them a whole day at DisneyQuest, Chicago's indoor interactive theme park.

The kids even beat me to it. When I was fastening my recording equipment, they were all ready and waiting. Not much was said. When I finished dressing, we went downstairs, separately, and off we drove to the Ramada.

Friday is a holy day for Muslims. Their day of rest. On Fridays, believers go to the mosque and listen to *Khutbat al-Jum'aa,* the Friday sermon. Back home, a million and one light-years away, Friday is where I love to have the traditional family dinner. Not this time, I thought. No real Thanksgiving meal, and no Friday meal, either. Just IAP and *Khutbat al-Jum'aa.*

By now I had a pretty good sense what the conference was all about. The main lectures took place in the large conference room, while satellite conferences and lectures were held in smaller meeting rooms sprawled throughout the hotel. I knew that today the sermon, not any of the lectures, would be the main event.

I watched as conference organizers shooed everyone from the room and applied duct tape to the floor in neat rows. According to tradition, worshippers should stand in perfectly straight lines during a prayer for it to have maximum potency.

Closer to the time of the sermon, the huge hall began filling up. It became more and more packed, and it seemed that every single Muslim and Palestinian in the Chicago area was coming to hear the sermon. I later found out that this was not far from the truth—many local imams told their parishioners that *salat,* prayers, for that Friday, would take place in the Ramada conference hall immediately after the sermon. So many of them came that there was hardly any room to stand. As people crushed up against me, I got panicky. The recording equipment could fail or, worse, be discovered.

The air in the room turned hot and dense with the body heat. Everyone was complaining about it as we were pushed ever closer to one another. Unlike the arrangement in the lectures, where we women sat on one side of the hall and the men on the other, during this sermon our place was behind them. The sermon was deemed important, thus the men were given the privilege of standing nearer to the imam so as to be able to listen more carefully. Men are far more equal in the Muslim world, even if they happen to reside in the West.

Dr. Salah Sultan was scheduled to deliver the sermon. Sultan was a medium-built, forty-year-old man with dark hair, dark beard, and very dark eyes radiating something sinister. He had recently established the Islamic American University in Southfield, Michigan. This university was endorsed by many leading Muslim organizations and a good number of distinguished Muslim scholars. One such intellectual was Yousef al-Qaradawi, the cleric who endorsed suicide attacks and who, owing to my work, was banned from entering the United States. Well, this distinguished scholar not only gave his blessing to Sultan's university, but he also served as president of the Islamic American University in Qatar. Tentacles, tentacles everywhere.

In spite of the terribly uncomfortable conditions in the hall, I was eager to listen to what the distinguished president of this Islamic university, Dr. Salah Sultan, would have to say. I knew very little about him then, and I hoped that, as a scholar, he would give a state-of-the-art talk about his vision of the Muslim issue in America and his perspectives on the theme of the conference, "A Century of Empowerment." He began talking, and as he spoke, I felt more and more uncomfortable. Here is some of what he said, translated from Arabic:

What does "the Cause" mean to you? And what does it mean to your children? . . . How much do they know about these tragedies? Did we mention to them that the Children of Zion over there cut open the wombs of mothers? As Khalid M. Khalid mentioned in 1992 when he visited Shamir [Yitzhak Shamir, Israel's prime minister at the time of the Gulf War] and saw on his desk a strange ashtray. He asked him, "What a strange ashtray is this?" Shamir told him that this was the skull of an embryo. The skull of an embryo! An Israeli soldier opened the womb of a Palestinian mother, took out the embryo, cut off his head, and gave it to him as a present. He gave it to him as a present! This is the method of the Jews. Killing a Muslim or any other non-Jew does not matter to them. Because their motto is, "The gentiles mean nothing to us." This is what the text of the Talmud says: "If you come across a non-Jew, kill him!"

The air grew unbearably thick as Sultan preached, and as he went on and on for nearly forty minutes, I found that breathing became more and more difficult. My *hijab* was growing heavier on me, weighing like lead. My head was about to explode. The recording equipment constricted me. Women on all sides squeezed me. When Sultan began talking about the soldiers and the women and the embryos, I felt queasy. I needed air. The large room began spinning around me. I had to get out of there, but there was no way I could get through the jammed hall. How could he say such things? There were women and young children here. How could they listen to this? Sultan continued:

> I want every child to sleep on the wound of Palestine and the actions of martyrdom. . . . I want to be a man who defends the land, who defends honor, who defends Holy Jerusalem. If this honor is violated, I want to give my life. The day will come when these peoples rise, carrying the banner of jihad. . . . The Zionist regime is a danger to the Jews, a danger to Christians, a danger to Americans. Israel will be your undoing, it will deprive you of your sovereignty for its own interest. They killed Americans in Lebanon in order to make the conflict explode ever the more. Those people could not care less who they destroy: "The gentiles mean nothing to us. Kill the non-Jews. If you find a non-Jew in distress, do not help him, but make things worse for him, because that is pleasing to the Lord."

Jihad, martyrdom, beheaded embryos . . . I was choking, and my head was spinning faster and faster.

Then, finally, the sermon ended, and the Friday prayer began. Unlike my first time in Dar al-Hijra, now I was a pro. I knew exactly how a good Muslim prays. Each time we bowed I felt the weight of my belly and the extreme effort of rising back up. To our knees, then farther down, our heads touching the floor, then back up again. I was carried on a giant wave in a stormy ocean of worshippers, and I was about to drown in it. I felt clammy with sweat and I was about to pass out. The women around me would rush to my aid and support me . . . and find something peculiar under my robes. Given Salah Sultan's speech, they would surely lynch me. Gasping for air, I bit my lower lip until I could feel the foul taste of blood. When the prayer was finally over, I crawled out with my last drops of vigor. I was truly suffocating. I had to breathe. I had to get out.

BACK IN THE HOTEL, I took a long shower. I lay down and let my tears roll. Had I finally let them get to me? Or was it the story with the embryo? That gruesome image evoked turbulent emotions in me about my own unborn child and the child I lost. It was so incongruous; Sultan used terms directly borrowed from his own cultural background. The barbaric acts of decapitation and amputation are common in some Arab and Muslim countries, such as Saudi Arabia or Afghanistan under the rule of the Taliban, and are considered a reasonable punishment by such governments. You wear the wrong kind of shoes, the Taliban executes you in broad daylight. You steal, the Saudis chop your hand off. You have an affair with a married man, they stone you to death. You have no husband and you get pregnant, your own father slits your throat. In public. You are a reporter for *The Wall Street Journal,* you are barbarically murdered, and someone makes sure the heinous act is videotaped and posted on the Internet. Examples for this disrespect for the value of life are countless.

As Ikrima Sabri, the mufti, preached, "the Muslim loves death and martyrdom. . . ." On Palestinian official television, kindergarten-age kids recited, with blood-filled eyes, "Beware of my fury, I will eat the flesh of my enemy. . . ." Muslim clerics, imams, sheikhs, and even a Saudi ambassador to Britain, Dr. Ghazi al-Gosabi, praise suicide bombing. Even after 9-11. Their use of the term *martyrdom* for murder is, in itself, sickening. Parents of such "martyrs" frequently praise their children and say they will encourage their other children to follow the same path. And the Saudis, for instance, publicly and shamelessly raised funds for "martyrdom." One hundred million dollars raised in one telethon. Maybe they should have called it the "barbarithon." Usama Bin Laden, asked about the scores of Muslims who perished in the attacks on the U.S. embassies in Kenya and Tanzania, replied, as if the questioner were an idiot, "They all went to heaven!"

The culture from which Sultan comes nurtures violence and has no respect for life or limb. How deep, dark, and inconceivable must be the hatred in the heart of the distinguished president of the Islamic American University to make him say what he did. How enormous must be the fury that motivates him to call for jihad and martyrdom. Will Sultan pass on this hatred to his students in Michigan, just as he did in his *khutba* today? And how many people here, in the audience at the Ramada Plaza, believed the story of Shamir and the embryo ashtray? How far would such believers go if they actually took that for a fact?

Rested and reassured, I called Leo and the kids. They were having the time of their lives. It made me feel much better. It helped me get some order in my brain.

In my line of work, I have to deal with hate. Often, and with plenty of it. I read loads of hateful statements and incitement for murder disseminated by religious clerics and other prominent Muslim leaders. I browse Web sites that glorify suicide bombings, take credit for them, show wills of suicide bombers, call for jihad, provide specific instructions for kidnapping and murder, and show disfigured bodies of martyrs as a means of propaganda and recruitment of mujahideen. I see photos and videos of murder and execution and torture and mutilation from all over the world, like the lynching of the soldiers in Ramallah or the murder of Daniel Pearl. I see videos of terrorists training to kill, and hijack, and destroy.

Yet in spite of the tremendous amount of hate I constantly encounter, my life and this book are *not* about hate. They're about love. My life is full of love—for Leo, our kids, Mama, my brothers and sister, my friends. And for Baba and Grandma, who are no longer here but who will always be here. When I deal with all that hate, I try to disconnect, to use my brain rather than my heart. Rationalize. Like a doctor at a cancer unit. At times such as Sultan's *khutba*, it's a very difficult task.

I FINALLY FELT I was ready to listen to the *khutba* again. I rewound the tape and hit play.

The tape was blank. As I feared, the recording went wrong.

In my frustration, I broke down and cried again. This couldn't be happening. After all I'd been through, I couldn't go home without that sermon. The sermon took place, I didn't make it up, and I had to obtain the tape so that I could prove it. The only way to stop such incitement in the future is to show that it exists. Make it public.

I vowed to myself that I wouldn't leave Chicago without it.

I went to the lobby, grabbed a quick bite, and took a cab back to the conference. I went directly to the IAP booth, the booth of the organizers, and told the people there that I'd just heard the sermon and that it was critical I get a tape of it. Try back later this evening, they said. Then I paid a visit to the HLF booth. I still had to buy a martyr's son.

Wasn't sponsoring a martyr's son a step too far? I thought. Even my symbolic contribution was promoting martyrdom. While some of the money might even go to that kid, some would definitely end up with Hamas, funding jihad. But I had to follow my instincts. I thought that the benefit outweighed the downside. Maybe, I thought, I was like an undercover DEA agent, who needed to use drugs in some instances to demonstrate credibility. This didn't make a drug addict out of him. It was one of the requirements of the job. I had to get myself a martyr's son. That wouldn't make me a supporter of terrorism.

The redheaded HLF guy was again manning the booth. He remembered me very well. "Guess what?" he said brightly. "We were able to find one. A son of a real *shahid*. Just for you!" I acted appropriately thrilled. They told me he was ten years old and had three brothers. They showed me his picture and told me his father was shot dead in Jerusalem "while fighting for the cause." I donated $100 for two months and left the address to which all my seamstress's mail goes so that I could continue to sponsor him for $50 on a monthly basis. My HLF friend promised that he'd send pictures of him as he grew up, as well as HLF's publications. One such publication led me to an important discovery. My donation didn't support terrorism; it ended up helping to stop it.

Content with my new acquisition, I went back to listen to a few more lectures. In one of the corridors, I saw Muhammad al-Hanooti, then still the powerful imam of Dar al-Hijra. Al-Hanooti was very close to many of the organizers of the conference. He was scheduled to give a lecture. For some time, trying to play the detective, I followed him. He met another imam, and they embraced, the long, hearty hug of two old friends. This man, Jamal Said, was the imam of a local Chicago mosque. He was also the man who recruited our pal Muhammad Salah to the ranks of the Muslim Brotherhood. I continued to shadow al-Hanooti, trying to see whom he met and to listen to his conversations. After a while, I thought, How ridiculous am I? Instead I simply went to hear him preach. As I sat there in his lecture, taping what he was saying, I thought how funny it was. I knew so much about him. Everything, practically. He, on the other hand, knew nothing about me. Didn't even know I existed—a fact that I'm sure will be adjusted in his head after this book is published. It resembled the scenario of a movie star and his fan. I sat and thought of all the long nights I'd spent trying to make a dossier on him. I was looking at him and telling myself, Well, this is he. The guy you spent so much time on.

After his lecture, I went back to the organizers. I asked about the tape of the Friday sermon. I was told that they still didn't have it and that I should try later. Again I told them how desperately I needed the material.

Then I met Nahla al-Arian, Sami's wife. He was here, too, with his wife and three younger children. I spoke with Nahla, told her that I'd seen her at previous gatherings, which was true. She and I talked about Mazen al-Najjar, her brother, who was among the founders of ICP and WISE. He was arrested in 1997 because of a decade-long illegal presence in the United States. He fought his deportation and was held, based on secret evidence, without bond. A judge later established that he was a threat to national security on account of his ties with PIJ, and he was later deported on visa violations. But at the time of the conference he was still imprisoned, and I told Nahla that her brother was a national hero for us Muslims. She and I spoke about how hard it was to be a Muslim in the United States, how we could not take pride in being who we were, and how we were persecuted by the government.

Sami al-Arian gave a lecture at the conference. During that lecture, which I also taped, they showed a film starring his brother-in-law. The film showed al-Najjar in prison, claiming that he had no idea why he was being held there. Then they showed his wife and poor children. The movie was very emotional, almost heartbreaking.

I went to the IAP organizer's booth again. I talked to the organizer of the conference himself, asking for the tape of the *khutba*. I knew there'd be an official recording; there always is at these conferences. The organizer pulled out from under the table a bunch of tapes and gave a set to me. I got it at last. I paid for the tape and rushed to my hotel without even waiting for my change.

MY FAMILY WAS BACK in the room when I got there. I wanted to listen to the tapes immediately, and I wanted to tell Leo what I'd been through. But I couldn't, not in front of the kids. Besides, they were starving. We went out for a nice Italian dinner. Felt strange without my *hijab*. . . . The kids didn't notice how tense I was, but Leo did. After we tucked the boys in, I rushed eagerly to play the tapes. I found the one with the sermon. I put it in the recorder and listened. It was blank. The damn thing was blank! Upset, I went to bed, forgetting to tell Leo about my adventures that day.

The next day—the last day and my last chance to get the sermon— I wasn't giving up. I approached the organizer again. Twice. I told him my sob story. I told him that I was a teacher. That I had kids of my own and kids I taught in school. I desperately wanted to teach my children the true ways of Islam. I would pay any price for the sermon. The sermon was the essence, the core, the whole meaning of Islam. It was absolutely essential for me to get the sermon so that I could play it to my kids, and *Insha-Allah,* they might become *shuhada* themselves one day. He seemed to believe me. At least I hoped he did.

In the evening came the closing ceremonies, culminating in the performance of schoolchildren on the stage. Young kids. The name of the play was *How I Became a Martyr.* On stage, in the Ramada Plaza hotel in Chicago, Illinois, the United States of America, in the last days of the twentieth century, young Arab Americans acted out how good Muslim boys engage in jihad, kill Jews, and become martyrs. It was a gruesome display.

I went back to the organizer, who was in the rear of the hall, busily taping the performance. I asked him for the tape, for the thousandth time. He gave me a long look, then bent down and pulled a tape from under his table. It was clear that this tape was not mass-produced like the others I'd been given previously. It wasn't even labeled. He handed it over to me and said, "Good luck."

"How much do I owe you?" I asked.

"Nothing, Sister," he replied. "From you I wouldn't even take a penny."

When I checked the tape later in the minivan, I realized that I finally had it. The whole *khutba,* unedited. The smoking gun.

A half hour later, when the show was over, I pestered him once more. I asked for the tapes he'd just recorded of the children's performance. He took my address, promised to send me the tape. A few weeks later, it arrived in the mail. The dancers were there, the music. But the kids were edited out, completely. *How I Became a Martyr* had been omitted from the conference's official tapes.

IN THE MARCH 2000 *Washington Report,* Raeed N. Tayeh wrote a short note on the conference, under the title "IAP Attracts 2,000 to Chicago Convention."

> Nearly 2,000 persons attended the third annual convention of the Islamic Association for Palestine (IAP), held over the four-day Thanksgiving weekend at the Ramada Plaza Hotel in Chicago. Speakers elaborated on the convention's theme, "A Century of Empowerment," by describing the roles that Muslims must play in order to achieve justice for themselves, for Palestine, and for Muslims worldwide. . . .
>
> After the conference, attendees expressed their satisfaction. "The speakers were great. I learned a lot of things that I never knew before," said [one of the attendees]. "I never knew that Muslims in America were so oppressed, like Muhammad Salah and Mazen al-Najjar. The IAP did a great service by holding this conference."
>
> The closing session included a fund-raising drive that brought in

more than $100,000 in pledges and donations. Following the fund-raising, the audience was treated to a performance by members of the Nujoom dance troupe.

The young men performed the traditional Arab folklore dance, the *debka,* while Nujoom musicians sang heart-pumping Islamic songs. After the dance performance, children performed a skit portraying the determination of the young generation of Palestinians to liberate Palestine. . . .

Great journalistic coverage. Now we know how many people attended the conference and how much money was raised by IAP, which, let me remind you, is a front group for Hamas. And we also know how terrible is the oppression of Muslims in America, as in the case of poor Muhammad Salah, a used-car dealer and a human rights activist. But most of all, I found perplexing the report of the skit in which the children showed "the determination of the young genera-tion of Palestinians to liberate Palestine." Through martyrdom and jihad, naturally. It's all in the way things are said. Same skit, different truths.

And one last note. Trying to learn how much money was actually raised in the IAP conference, I looked into the IAP's tax forms for 1999. I looked very, very carefully. No donation from that conference was ever mentioned on those forms.

CHAPTER 7

The Millennium Plot

FROM THE AIRPLANE WINDOW, the empty streets of the nation's capital seemed gray and gloomy on that early Saturday morning in January. As much as I dislike grays, the gray wintry mix coating the city didn't diminish its beauty in the least. I've traveled there frequently, especially in recent years, and in my many visits I've never stopped admiring the European-style architecture and the elegant serenity of that city. So different from New York . . . Washington's confident tranquility befitted a superpower's capital.

As our shuttle approached Reagan National Airport, the frozen Potomac River, the Capitol, and the towering obelisk of the Washington Monument in the heart of the National Mall revealed themselves to us in their splendor.

It was very cold outside. Even the short walk to the rental car lot sufficed to spread ice through my veins and joints. Or was there something else that made me feel like that? I could feel the frost penetrating right through my bones. But there had to be another reason I was trembling so badly. After all, I was pretty well dressed, a few thick layers under a heavy coat. And the car heater, as I started to drive, was blowing dense, hot air with all its might. So why was I so cold?

On the way out of the airport, we stopped at the Federal Express office to pick up a box that was supposed to have been sent to us from California. It was there, as promised. My heart pumped wildly as I looked at it. Was the answer in it? It had to be. Otherwise our meeting wouldn't be the success it should—and I'd make a fool out of myself. Not good for a first impression. Not good at all, considering where we were heading.

I'd never been there before, in the White House. None of us had—not on official business, anyway. My traveling companions, Max and two researchers from our office—Bruce and Neil—were anxious about going to the White House. So was I, bent over the steering wheel, and I wasn't giving much thought to the slippery roads, or the sparse traffic, or even the traffic lights, for that matter; after a sleepless night and a morning flight to D.C., the only things on my mind were the scheduled meeting, the package I was carrying for that meeting, and how I got this package.

Neil was trying to guide me using the directions from the Internet, but we had little time left—we *had* to look at the contents of that box before the meeting—and my winter driving wasn't helping our nerves as we fishtailed around Pierre L'Enfant's beautiful, impossible maze of ceremonial spaces and diagonal avenues, searching for the White House and a parking spot. By the time we skidded to a stop on Pennsylvania Avenue, we had not even a minute to look at the contents of our package. We rushed out of the car into the blustery cold and hurried to the gates. The gates to the executive offices of the White House.

We entered a long corridor covered with an ugly gray carpet. No security outside, at the gates. This has changed since my first visit there; after 9-11, the security booth was relocated to the front of the building. We presented our IDs at the security booth at the end of the corridor. The guard called the person with whom we were meeting and suggested we sit in the adjacent waiting room. We practically ran there, pulled together two large, wooden benches, tore open the FedEx package, and spread out its contents on one of the benches.

The box contained a large file on an organization called Charity Without Borders. These documents had been sent to us by the state of California. More than two hundred pages of names, projects, and employee time sheets, provided to the state by the directors of this tax-exempt charity. We were frantically looking through these documents for a name . . . and there it was! Yes! Yes! The name I wanted. Joseph J. Adams. That was it. I'd known all along it would be there.

I noticed that I wasn't so cold anymore. I looked up. The ceiling was very high. So were the windows. Huge windows, very impressive. The room we were in was minimally decorated, but it still looked very welcoming. What could be more welcoming than my current situation? There I was, an escapee from Iraq, a new immigrant to America, waiting for an appointment with a top official in the White House to brief him on national security. In how many places in the world can that happen? In how many lifetimes?

The man we were meeting was quite high up in the administration. His assistant, Peter, who came to get us, was of medium height, with thin blond hair and a smiling face. At that point my face was smiling, too. I was no longer anxious or tired. The smoking gun in the package gave me confidence.

Peter escorted us to the next security point. We all passed through the metal detectors and entered a very large hall filled with people, dressed casually yet busy with activity. The floor of the hall was decorated in beautiful black-and-white mosaic tiles, like a giant chessboard. The government must really be on edge, I thought, to have so many people here on a weekend.

We made our way through the massive building, Peter all the while giving us the official spiel on this hallway's history, that painting's provenance.

The official we'd come to meet at the National Security Council came out himself, in his pullover sweater, to show us in; his secretary, naturally, had the day off. As he opened the door to his office, my heart missed a beat. The door, which looked like a plain old wooden door, was at least two feet thick and made of metal. It seemed more suitable for a giant vault than for the small office we found behind it. The office, albeit tiny, was adorned with high-tech screens on which maps of America were blinking with colorful beads of light.

We sat at a conference table, Peter and his boss at each end, the four of us from the office in the middle. After we went around the table introducing ourselves, the official told us that Peter was leaving the next day, heading for the Persian Gulf. He said they were interested in seeing the material we had on this 501(c) nonprofit, Charity Without Borders.

Before Peter came to collect us from the waiting room, right after we'd found Adams's name, everyone decided that I would lead the presentation. "Why me?" I asked. "Your English is so much better." But Max, Bruce, and Neil knew I could recite that stuff in my sleep. So I thought about the material and the research we'd done in the past few days. It was all new information, very fresh in my head, and it was sizzling. I was ready to begin.

A FEW DAYS BEFORE the meeting in the White House, everything in our New York office was calm. Every year around that time, most things in the city slow down to a stupefied crawl. Even here, in the financial nerve center of the world, the combination of the holiday season and the cold weather proves more powerful than the endless bustle of the nuclear reactor nicknamed New York City. That year, though, there was a twist: It was the countdown to the millennium, just days before the year 2000, Y2K. Everyone, even the sworn skeptics, was concerned with Y2K. Everyone tried to show that he or she was absolutely confident that no disaster would come to pass, but many secretly decided to let a few days go by before they flew or used elevators again. "Just in case, y'know," they'd tell their closest friends. "Not that I'm worried or anything like that."

Meanwhile, in the government, things were far from relaxed. While some were busy trying to prevent Y2K bug problems, others were worried about much more dangerous bugs.

The first warning sign had come early in December. Ahmed Ressam, an Algerian trying to enter Washington State from Canada as a tourist, was discovered at the border driving a car loaded with a petrifying quantity of explosives. Nitroglycerin-based bombs, probably homemade, similar to the type of explosives used in the 1993 World Trade Center bombing. The U.S. Customs officer who caught Ressam had received no alerts from the federal government that terrorists might try to enter the country. She noticed that Ressam was acting strangely, and followed her hunch.

Shortly thereafter, Ressam's apartment in Montreal was searched and his plot was uncovered. He was carrying the stuff in his trunk in hopes of offering his idea of a New Year's gift to the American people, compliments of a cave-dwelling, deranged murderer posing as a holy man: Usama Bin Laden. Ressam, hoping to become a holy man himself, planned to contribute to the millennial fireworks display by blowing up Los Angeles's international airport, LAX.

Around the time of Ressam's arrest, several other terrorists, including some al-Qaeda members, were picked up in locations around the world. In the White House, the concept that no foreigner would be so bold as to launch a terrorist attack on U.S. soil was beginning to crumble.

The first visible seam in the wall of confidence occurred after the World Trade Center bombing. But then came the Murrah Federal Building bombing in Oklahoma City; once the government ascertained that Oklahoma was the work of American Timothy McVeigh, officials again dismissed the idea that Islamic terrorists could strike us at home. The few warnings of such danger were suppressed. Again the old FBI line resurfaced: The World Trade Center bombing was a once-in-a-lifetime event perpetrated by the lunatic fringe.

But the message of the explosives Ressam carried in the trunk of his car was too real to be ignored. In the waning days of 1999, experts were looking very carefully at the vast number of threats and leads regarding potential attacks against American targets in the country and abroad during New Year's festivities. Serious threats were evaluated regarding American embassies, including the one in Amman, Jordan, and other targets abroad. As a result, U.S. embassies went on highest alert.

On December 17, 1999, Jordan's secret service arranged for the extradition of Khalil al-Deek from Pakistan. Al-Deek, a Jordanian of Palestinian descent, was suspected of being the mastermind of the terrorist cell that was planning to strike Western targets in Jordan, including the American embassy and the Radisson Hotel in Amman, and the Allenby and Sheikh Hussein Bridges.

In the United States, al-Deek was wanted for his ties to al-Qaeda. A computer specialist, he was responsible for digitizing a large number of al-Qaeda documents, including al-Qaeda ideology and the *Encyclopedia of Jihad*. He posted many of these documents on the Internet as a means to recruit mujahideen. Based on intelligence reports, U.S. officials believed that he was a key to the financing of al-Qaeda attacks planned for the millennium celebrations. Because al-Deek's name and numbers were found in Ressam's telephone book, it was thought that al-Deek's money might have fed Ressam's Canadian cell, the one in charge of the plot to blow up LAX.

I learned of al-Deek's extradition from Jordanian newspapers in Arabic, which reported it before the U.S. press did. The stories noted that al-Deek was an American citizen, which piqued my interest. I decided to look him up. Why, you may ask? Why bother researching someone already in custody? Shouldn't I have concentrated on other things, while the U.S. and Jordanian intelligence communities were celebrating their success in closing that file?

The answer to that lies in the understanding of the al-Qaeda network and its modus operandi. Al-Qaeda operatives and members never work alone. Instead, they operate in small cells. While cells may be spread over several countries, many times the operatives in these cells live close to one another; working together becomes easier that way. Those who worked with Ressam, for example, lived in the same apartment with him.

Al-Deek funded Ressam's cell, but also several others. Thus, I assumed, he didn't belong to any cell, but rather coordinated and funded others' cells. He still had to have accomplices; operations like these are rarely run by one person. Although al-Deek was in custody, his collaborators might have posed a real danger to America. Since al-Deek was a U.S. citizen, I thought, the best place to be looking for his colleagues would be his address in America.

And so Bruce, Neil, and I started to look for traces of al-Deek in the United States. It's so much easier when a few people work as a team than when one person is trying to do it alone. In a team, each person can take a few databases and search engines and work on those. The information can then be cross-referenced, verified, and compiled in one file.

Public record databases can yield enormous amounts of information. One such database that we often use, for instance, provides the following on any given name that we search: AKAs, with Social Security numbers (SSNs). Other names associated with these SSNs. Driver's licenses. Addresses associated with the name. Phone listings for these addresses (if it is an apartment building, all numbers at that address will show up, too). Vehicles registered to the addresses. Others who used that address. Real-property ownership, business affiliations, relatives, criminal history . . . The list goes on and on. With a few mouse clicks, a trained researcher can get (almost) anything on any person. Some of these searches yield twenty, thirty, or even more pages filled with such data.

Doing such searches on al-Deek, we found some interesting pieces of information. One, that he used an alias, Joseph J. Adams. Another, that he became a naturalized U.S. citizen after a fictitious marriage in Texas to a woman who had a healthy business serially marrying Muslim men in order to qualify them for American citizenship. I don't know what she got paid, but in all she married four of them.

Following his marriage, al-Deek moved to California, where he lived in an apartment complex on W. Winston Road in Anaheim. Some of the neighbors must have been in on al-Deek's ventures, I thought, and others may have known of his activities, even if they weren't his collaborators. I knew that his Anaheim address was worth looking into.

Our search yielded scores of telephone numbers associated with the names al-Deek and Adams. Some numbers were directly related to these two names, others were numbers of neighbors and associates. While Bruce and Neil kept looking for more information on the address itself, I began calling, one by one, the numbers that were linked directly with al-Deek's address. Some numbers were disconnected. Others were clearly unassociated.

I tried one of these numbers.

"*A'-Salamu Aley'kum.*" (May peace be with you.) I began with the customary Muslim greeting.

"*Wa-Aley'kum as-Salam.*" (And peace to you too.) The man spoke Arabic well.

I continued in his language, presenting myself as Fatma, a reporter from *al-Hayat,* the renowned London-based Arabic newspaper. I was delighted to speak Arabic with him. After all, Arabic is my mother's tongue.

"I am doing an investigative piece for our newspaper," I said, "and I've been hearing that some people in your neighborhood have been harassed by the authorities."

"*Na'am, Ukhti!*" (Yes, my sister!) "You wouldn't believe what they did."

He was right. I didn't. Even for the FBI, it sounded too fantastic.

"Very early in the morning," he said, "they knocked on my door. Two agents in dark suits and bright red ties. They asked me a few questions, and then they asked whether I knew Usama Bin Laden."

"What?"

I wasn't sure whether this man was pulling my leg. What agent in his right mind would ask such a question? Did they expect a terrorist on whose door they'd knocked to say, "Oh, sure, I just returned from Bin Laden's military training camp in Afghanistan?"

He continued. "They asked me whether I knew Ahmed Ressam or anyone who was tied to him. They said he was a terrorist who planned to plant a bomb in Los Angeles's airport."

He then complained bitterly about how hard being a Muslim in America was, how every time someone wanted to blow up something, everyone immediately blamed the entire Muslim community for it.

"Write about it, Sister," he said. "The world needs to know how we are being treated here."

I kept calling other people. They repeated the same story, how early one morning FBI agents knocked on their doors and asked whether they knew Usama Bin Laden or Ahmed Ressam. Some said that the agents showed them pictures of Bin Laden and asked them what their ties were to him.

So I learned that the FBI, like Bruce, Neil, and me, had showed great interest in the W. Winston address. I also realized that the agents were obviously not making any progress. The FBI approached this as they would any criminal probe: Ask questions, show photos, did anyone hear or see anything? But their efforts were random and ineffective rather than targeted and rational.

One of the people I talked to, a woman who didn't speak Arabic, mentioned that the FBI kept interrogating her even though she told them she was working for a Muslim charity. Charity? That word doesn't go by me unnoticed. "What charity?" I asked her.

"Ah . . . I'm not sure I'm allowed to tell you. Do you mind giving me a call in a couple of hours, after I speak with my boss about it?"

I took her numbers, including the cell phone, and before we hung up, before she could take the call, I used another line to call her cell phone. This message greeted me: "This is Life for Relief and Development. We can't get to the phone right now, but your call is important to us. . . ."

We ran a search on that charity. Most of its money went to fund relief efforts in Iraq. Some was sent to Jordan, too, but I couldn't find a specific link to al-Deek.

After a few hours of telephone calls like this—interesting but leading nowhere—I dialed a number I had tried and couldn't reach before, one that was listed as al-Deek's. A nice old lady answered the phone.

Unable to say even one word in English, the old lady was nonetheless quite talkative. Her accent was Egyptian. I presented myself as Fatma again.

"*A'-Salamu Aley'kum.* May I talk to Khalil?" I tried.

"Khalil who, my soul?" she replied, using an expression in Arabic that means something akin to "my precious."

"Khalil al-Deek," I didn't give up.

"I don't know anyone by that name."

I believed her. "How about Joseph Adams, do you know him?" I asked, trying al-Deek's alias.

In an apologetic tone, she said, "You know, I don't know all my son's friends too well. I am only here visiting him from Egypt."

"And your son's name is?"

"Hisham Diab, that's who my son is."

"Has your son been living at that address for a while now?"

"Oh, yes, he has been living here for a few years already."

"And how long has he been in the U.S.?" I pressed her. "Is he an American citizen?"

"No, not yet," she said. "But he told me he would become one soon."

"And you never heard him mention Khalil's name?"

"No, my eyes," she said, using another expression in Arabic that means something like "my dear."

She was really cute, that old lady. She was bored and happy to talk to anyone on the phone. About anything. Unfortunately for her, I had no time to waste.

"So may I speak with your son, then?" I asked.

"*Mish Mowjood,* [he's not here,] my soul. I think maybe you should try after five."

Five in California means eight in the evening in New York. But I couldn't do this from home. I'd have to use the office's secure telephone system. I might be onto something here.

Meanwhile, we ran a search on Hisham Diab. He was associated with a charitable organization. That by itself, in the context of al-Deek, was enough to raise my index of suspicion, given my experience with Islamic charities and their links to terror organizations. The charity's name was Charity Without Borders, and it was a 501(c)(3)—a tax-exempt, nonprofit organization. Perfect name. No borders. An officer of such a borderless organization would have to travel around the world, right? Besides, the name betrayed not even a hint of a Muslim connection.

Around five o'clock Pacific time, I tried again. This time, Diab himself picked up the phone. Naturally, the conversation took place in Arabic. I wasn't so loquacious now—I didn't want to risk making a mistake in my cover story. I told him my name, title, and credentials, and again I claimed to be working on an article describing discrimination against Muslims in the United States. I mentioned al-Deek, an American citizen, as an example of yet another Muslim who was wrongfully arrested. I told Diab that I'd been informed that he used to live with al-Deek.

Diab was as reticent as his mother was chatty. He was defensive, even. He mumbled something about hardly knowing al-Deek, claimed that he'd met him perhaps once or twice. When I asked him about his charity, he told me that what they did was aimed mainly at "benefiting the general public." That was about all I got out of him. Yet I learned crucial information from that conversation. I knew now that Diab *did* know al-Deek. Very peculiar, claiming that he'd hardly known al-Deek but having shared the same telephone number with him. This might be a coincidence, but it seemed less likely now.

There was also something fishy about Charity Without Borders. While there's no law that says a Muslim can't run a charity "benefiting the general public," Diab's brief explanation about his operation was outright bizarre. It seemed to me that Diab had something to hide. I knew I needed to look very carefully into him and that charity of his.

Through public records, Bruce, Neil, and I obtained basic information about the charity's finances. Thursday evening we called the pertinent department in the government of the state of California, told the people we spoke to there that this was a real emergency, and asked for additional records. We needed the charity's 990s, its articles of incorporation, and a few other documents. The state clerks on the other end of the line promised to fax whatever they could the next day—Friday—and to FedEx the rest.

Sure enough, the forms were faxed to us on Friday afternoon.

Looking through them, we found that Hisham Diab was Charity Without Borders's chief executive officer in 1997 and its chief financial officer in 1998. According to its 990 for 1997, the charity reported $75,257 in reimbursable expenses for running a program that informed Californians about how to recycle motor oil. That program was subsidized by the California Integrated Waste Management Board. So this charity, in addition to avoiding any taxes, received a reimbursement from the state in return for this service. Something smelled very bad there, and it clearly wasn't the recycled oil. But we still didn't have *proof* that al-Deek was associated with Diab or that he was directly involved with the charity. We had to wait for the FedEx package. I knew we'd find our answer there.

Meanwhile, Bruce and Neil's research had turned up more than one hundred names affiliated with al-Deek's address, names of people who'd lived there and of their neighbors. We couldn't possibly study them all, so we limited our research to the specific time frame when al-Deek was there, and this still gave us more than thirty names. We continued to search the public records on each and every one of these names and obtained even more leads.

For example, we found that in the same apartment building where al-Deek had lived, his brother Tawfiq al-Deek had lived also. Living in big communes is a tradition in Arab societies. They call them *hamula,* and such a household, or clan, can include family members from four generations or more. Much like my grandfather's harem in al-Basrah. But in this case, the custom might have had another twist to it; it could enhance the collaboration among operatives. We ran a search on Tawfiq al-Deek and discovered that he presented himself as IAP's spokesman in California. IAP! The Hamas front in America! IAP was fresh in my mind; only a few weeks before, I'd attended the IAP conference in Chicago. This was no coincidence, I knew, and the FBI had missed a big lead. The W. Winston address was hot.

Bruce, Neil, and I found that the apartment complex on W. Winston Road was made up of twelve units and was owned by an immigrant from Czechoslovakia. We learned that Khalil and Tawfiq al-Deek and Hisham Diab all lived there at the same time. This confirmed for me that Diab knew Khalil al-Deek better than he claimed he did. We ran searches on other names listed at that address. Most were dead ends. One of them, though, Khalid Ashour, who'd lived there two years before, was also linked to a certain address in Tucson, Arizona. The second I saw that address, I cried out, "Holy s———!" As far as I was concerned, that was it. That was my answer right there. The information wasn't hot anymore. Now it was burning in my hands.

We began studying Khalid Ashour carefully. We found that he was a former resident of Qatar. Like al-Deek, he was of Palestinian descent. He too was associated with IAP. Ashour left Qatar for the United States in August 1985 to seek an American university education. He enrolled in the fine arts/graphic design school at Pima Community College in Tucson. While there, Ashour became heavily involved with the Islamic Center of Tucson. From September 1992 through January 1993, his listed address was that of the center, 901 E. First Street.

At that point in my professional life I'd already accumulated an enormous amount of knowledge about the Islamic Center of Tucson. At this point in the book, however, it's premature to discuss it; I promise I'll share some of what I know about the center in the next chapter, where this story belongs. What's relevant here is that the Islamic Center was a place where, in the late 1980s, the IAP had a strong presence. And that the Islamic Center of Tucson was also the first base in America for yet another organization:

Al-Qaeda.

As soon as I learned that Ashour was involved with the Islamic Center, I knew he was my man; he was the one I needed to investigate. Doing some more research on him, we found out that in 1991 he was arrested at the Blaine, Washington, border crossing, trying to enter the United States with a fake ID. In his car were paramilitary magazines—meaning, in plain English, handbooks of explosives and bombs—as well as IAP literature. He admitted to U.S. officials that he was associated with IAP, and while he was initially held as a security risk, a few days later he was allowed to return to Canada. Somehow, he later returned to the United States.

Ashour resided in that same apartment complex in Anaheim for some time, starting in late 1993, and then he moved to another place only a few blocks away. Another address that was listed in Ashour's public records was in Phoenix, Arizona: the address for American Express CapitaFinance, LLC, a financial services company. Ashour must have used the company's address to satisfy an IRS requirement: whenever more than $10,000 is transferred as a single transaction, tax law requires the person moving the money to fill out a form with his or her personal information, including an address. We later found out that Ashour moved close to a half-million dollars out of the country in 1999 alone. Now, where would a person making $600 a week get that kind of money? Very frugal, that guy must be, to save so much on such a salary. Also, why should anyone go to so much trouble and travel so far—from California to Arizona—for such a financial service? There are American Express CapitaFinance branches everywhere!

We were building an ever stronger case on Ashour and Diab. But we still didn't have a direct link to al-Deek besides the fact that they all lived at the same address. Then Max showed up in our office and asked whether we had a strong enough case to present.

"To present to whom?" I asked.

"To the White House. They just called."

Al-Deek's extradition from Pakistan and the information about his plans, combined with the fortuitous capture of Ressam at the Canadian border, had left the White House unsettled. The FBI, on the other hand, was running around in circles, coming up with no substantial leads in the al-Deek and al-Qaeda investigations. So someone at the National Security Council decided to call Max, albeit a "civilian," to see what we knew.

"What time is it, Max?" I asked, not even looking up from the pile of papers on my desk.

"Around two."

"Let us work on it a bit more, and I'll tell you."

Our investigation on al-Deek was far from over, but we were getting closer. Al-Deek's brother was tied to IAP. One of his neighbors headed a charity that received large tax reimbursements from the state of California. Another neighbor was tied to the Islamic Center of

Tucson and was transferring large sums of money. I didn't yet know where that money was going, but I had a good idea where it could have gone. Around five that Friday afternoon, we finished analyzing the information about the charity. I briefed Max on our investigation and told him that I suspected Charity Without Borders was a key to al-Deek's dealings in the United States.

Max left for dinner and returned two hours later. He said that as soon as he'd told the people at the National Security Council, NSC, about the 501(c) that al-Deek's neighbor was running, they asked to meet us in the White House the next morning.

"You still have all evening and all night," Max said. "Do you think you can do it?"

"Time's not the only problem," I replied. "We're also waiting for some documents from California."

"Ask them to FedEx them overnight directly to the airport in Washington," Max said. "If they can do it, we'll all go down there on the shuttle in the morning."

The folks in California agreed to FedEx the material to us for Saturday morning.

Now I had only a few hours to prove that al-Deek was directly tied to Charity Without Borders. Max said we needed to concentrate our efforts on Diab, as he was the head of the charity, and that's what we were going to talk about in our meeting with the NSC officials. I said that we didn't have time for everything and that we should work on Ashour. We argued, and he started to raise his voice.

I blew a fuse. "Stay out of this," I yelled, "and let us do our investigation. We'll let you know what we found when we've found it. You go set up the meeting for tomorrow."

Max looked surprised, then turned on his heel and left. I was a bit surprised myself. This wasn't like me. Then I realized that it was dinnertime and that I hadn't eaten anything all day long. Fasting isn't a good idea when you're pregnant.

While I was on the phone with an official from the state of California, Berta stuck her head in my office and said that I had another call.

"Not now, Berta. Take a message."

"But—"

"Let them call me again in half an hour."

"But it's Gil," she said. "He says you promised to be home by seven."

I looked at the clock on the wall. It was ten past seven. I'd promised my family that morning that after the traditional Sabbath dinner we'd go out, watch a movie, spend the evening together. What movie? What dinner? I asked Berta to apologize on my behalf and to tell Gil I'd call home in a few minutes. "Tell them I'll be there soon, I promise."

Now I was not only hungry, I was ashamed too. All that week I'd been working very hard and coming home late at night. I'd vowed to my kids that Friday I'd be there in time for family dinner.

A few minutes later, Max came and announced that Berta had gotten us tickets for the first morning flight to D.C. There was very little time left, and although we had a lot of information, we had to tie everything together and prepare a cogent presentation.

Leo was on the phone. I'd forgotten to call them back! It was almost ten P.M. I'd had no idea it was so late. I apologized up and down to Leo. Without making too much fuss over it, he let me understand that neither he nor the kids were pleased with my disappearance that evening. I broke a promise.

"I hope you've at least eaten something. You can't abuse yourself or the baby." I could hear the competing disgruntlement and concern in his voice.

"Yes, of course, Leo. I've eaten," I lied. "I'm fine, don't worry."

"Obviously you're busy. I'll call you later." Leo hung up. The hurt in his tone was painful to me, but I didn't know what else to do. I had to finish the work.

We began to prepare the charts depicting the ties among Khalil al-Deek, Tawfiq al-Deek, Ashour, Diab, and Charity Without Borders. We photocopied documents we had on file regarding the Islamic Center of Tucson. The center would be one of the main topics in our presentation. We photocopied old newspaper clips. Tomorrow's talk was looking better and better as time passed.

The phone rang; it was Leo again. He wasn't at all happy. I asked him to put the kids on. There was an incredulous silence on the other end of the line. "They went to bed. A long time ago."

To bed? I looked at the clock, and my heart missed a beat. It was *two o'clock in the morning.* I needed to start wrapping things up, but I had to make sure that we didn't seem like amateurs tomorrow in Washington. There's only one first time at the White House. We had to make it perfect. We all certainly did our best to make it just that. At three A.M., Max showed up. He looked at the presentation, reviewed the charts, and nitpicked. I was too tired to even get mad.

"These are the charts for tomorrow. Period," I said.

Finally, at three-thirty in the morning, the four of us left the office. Outside, the streets were covered with snow. When I finally got home, Leo was awake, waiting. As soon as I was home safe, he could finally fall asleep. But I couldn't. I ate for the first time in twenty hours. Adrenaline was still coursing through me, and information was ricocheting around in my head as I at last got into bed. Then the baby started moving around in my belly, and I was tossing and turning until six in the morning. Time to get up and go. I did my hair and dressed for the occasion. Part of the presentation was to look respectable enough for it. I only wished we didn't have to fly. . . .

In the waiting room at the White House, we'd looked anxiously through the files sent from California. There, we finally found the proof of al-Deek's connection to Charity Without Borders. Using his alias, Joseph J. Adams, he'd listed as his personal address P.O. Box 4035, Garden Grove, California. That address was, in fact, that of the charity. No coincidences, no mistakes. Everything was falling into place. What we saw was that Joseph J. Adams was not only linked to Charity Without Borders through an address and a telephone number, he was also one of the crew leaders on its motor oil–recycling project. For his work on that project, al-Deek drew hourly wages, with benefits even, from the state of California! While he was billing California for teaching its residents the dos and don'ts of oil recycling, he was actually abroad for more than two years, according to his brother. During that time he was running around the Middle East and Pakistan, trying to blow up various places. His brother Tawfiq was paid consulting fees for his work as an environmental engineer on the recycling project. I wondered how the residents of California would feel if they knew that their tax dollars were being used to reimburse a charity whose CFO had ties to an al-Qaeda operative suspected of funding attacks against Americans.

THE MEETING WITH the NSC officials at the White House was going well. For a first briefing there, it was actually going extremely well. I showed them al-Deek's ties to Charity Without Borders. I explained his background and his arrest in Jordan. I shared everything that we'd learned about the charity and the meticulous process by which we learned and verified it.

"Do you know what the FBI has on that?" asked the official we'd come to see. This question was addressed to Peter rather than to me.

"As far as I know, they don't have any of this," Peter replied.

"How come the FBI was unable to come up with that information?" the official continued.

"Maybe they know things they aren't sharing. Even when they do have something, they hardly ever share it with anyone else anyway," said Peter.

Hearing this statement for the first time, I thought I misunderstood what was said. I didn't. It did shock me at first, but I've gotten used to it since. I later heard it from countless government agents, and I gradually learned that this was the rule, not the exception: The FBI just doesn't share information. The FBI gets leads and information from other sources and agencies, including the NSC, INS, and Treasury. Sometimes even as part of a joint task force. But the Bureau doesn't share anything with these agencies in return. Not just the information it has, but even what it has been doing with the material it was given by the others.

"How did you get all that information?" Now the official *was* addressing me.

"Public records. You just have to know what you're looking for," I said.

I didn't know what to make of his look. It could have been disbelief at what I'd just told him. That without leaving our office, we'd obtained information that the FBI, investigating on location, had been unable to produce. Or perhaps the look reflected a sudden urge to find the FBI agents responsible for the investigation of al-Deek and slap them senseless.

"This is as far as I can go," I continued. "I don't have access to intelligence resources, and I don't have any authority to obtain what's beyond public records. I do think, however, that the FBI should take it from here and look into Ashour's and Diab's files."

Of course, I was thinking, How could those FBI agents find anything in al-Deek's neighborhood with the methods they used? *Knock-knock.* "Do you know Usama Bin Laden?" Instead of learning the material as my colleagues and I did, the FBI agents conducted the investigation of al-Deek's address in that *très* bizarre manner. That was why for them, the neighbors they questioned were just that. Neighbors. For us, they were Ashour and Diab and Charity Without Borders.

The good news was that my notions about how Islamic charities were being used to fund terrorism weren't altogether new to the NSC officials. This was one of the reasons they were so interested in meeting us and learning about Charity Without Borders. I learned later that the purpose of Peter's trip to the Persian Gulf was to get intelligence on some of these charities. But like me, these people at the NSC had found it hard to convince the Treasury that this was an urgent problem that should have been addressed, perhaps, by some legislative changes.

To me, the greatest indignity of the Charity Without Borders story was that it was actually collecting money from the U.S. government. We then discussed with the NSC guys an even more egregious example of which they were well aware: the Islamic African Relief Agency, IARA, which had ties to the government of Sudan—the government that for years had harbored Bin Laden. USAID, the United States Agency for International Development, is, according to its own literature, "an independent agency that provides economic development and humanitarian assistance around the world in support of the foreign policy goals of the United States." IARA was getting matching funds from USAID until it was established that it was tied to terrorism.

USAID funding to IARA was then cut off, for "reasons of national security." Yet IARA is still active, and still tax-exempt, in America.

"That's exactly why we're trying to put together a watch list of charities that may have ties to terrorism," Peter said.

That gave me an idea.

VERONICA AND I were having lunch. It was mid-2000. The weather was awful, thunderstorms and heavy rain. It didn't reflect how I felt, though. For me—both at home and at work—things were better than ever. I was busy at work. Good busy, not overstressed. For quite some time I had been thinking of telling Veronica about the idea I'd come up with regarding the watch list, but we had worked on other projects and I'd never come round to it. Our lunch together was a perfect opportunity to discuss my idea.

By now, my working relationship with the White House had intensified. I was going down there about once a month. I usually tried to combine these trips with other activities, like going to mosques or rallies or meeting other government officials. After Peter returned from the Persian Gulf, I asked him about the watch list. Obviously, he said, he couldn't tell me which organizations were on it. "But you don't need me to. You know perfectly well which charities need to be monitored."

He did tell me at one of our meetings, though, that when Jordanian secret service agents discovered the cache of explosives intended for the millennium-timed attacks on Western and strategic targets in Jordan, the one that was funded by al-Deek, they were terrified by the amount accumulated there. Someone said that there were enough explosives there "to blow up the entire Middle East."

As Veronica and I were sitting in an Indian restaurant not far from the INS building, I began telling her about my idea.

"Regarding that watch list of charities that the FBI and the White House are putting together for the State Department," I began.

"Yes?" Veronica said. She had a strange look on her face.

"You obviously know about that list, right?"

Obviously, she didn't.

Mysterious are the ways of the government.

That list was for the State Department's use. INS was at that time operating under the authority of the State Department. Veronica and Dan Cadman should have known about the list! That list was intended to help the State Department differentiate between legitimate charities and those that were linked to terrorism. It seemed only natural that the State Department would notify the INS's National Security Unit—the official name of the unit then—about the list.

The State Department didn't. The first time Veronica heard of the list was from me.

I told Veronica that I didn't know for sure which charities would be on that list, but that I had a pretty good idea. I then told her that she had to get that list, and that in the meantime I'd tell her what I thought would be on it and give her background information on these organizations.

Then, before I conveyed my idea to her, I gave her the necessary background about charities in general. I explained that some charities not only raise funds for terrorism, but they also use their resources to help their supporters meet and hold conferences where hate speeches are delivered as part of a recruiting strategy. Moreover, these charities sponsor U.S. visas for all sorts of dubious characters hiding behind the veil of religious purposes and charitable work. They're tax-exempt and altruistic seeming, and their inherent internationalism dovetails nicely with worldwide money transfers. Above all, these charities often use the magic words *relief work* as a cover. As a "relief worker," I told Veronica, anyone could travel practically anywhere as frequently as he wanted and carry large amounts of money without raising any suspicions. No one would doubt a "relief worker" on his way to help the unfortunate, sick, and hungry.

One such charity was Help Africa People, founded and headed by a man named Wadih al-Hage. In his spare time, al-Hage also served as a personal secretary to . . . Usama Bin Laden! Eventually, al-Hage was convicted of plotting the embassy bombings in Kenya and Tanzania. Help Africa People allowed him to move about freely and fund these bombings.

Another relief worker was an Egyptian pediatrician who visited the United States in 1995 as a representative of the Kuwaiti Red Crescent. His name? Ayman al-Zawahiri. His day job? Bin Laden's chief deputy, personal doctor, and the ideological architect of al-Qaeda. Al-Zawahiri has been indicted in the United States for the American embassy bombings in East Africa, and he's been sentenced to death in absentia by an Egyptian military court for his pivotal role in the Egyptian Islamic Jihad terrorist group. Meanwhile, as recently as 1995 he traveled freely in America. He arrived here from Afghanistan and conducted a fundraising tour for what he claimed was to benefit widows and orphans, on which he collected close to half-a-million dollars. He probably forgot to mention that these widows and orphans were those he was planning to *create* with that money, which was used for the charitable cause of bombing the Egyptian embassy in Pakistan that same year. Such is this pediatrician's idea of relief work.

I finally told Veronica my idea. "What the State Department should do is check people whose U.S. visa was sponsored by the charities on the watch list. It should go over visa applications of people who use these charities, and conferences arranged by these charities, as their reasons for wanting to travel in the United States. If their visa applications say their intent is to work for these charities, the applications should be double-, triple-, and even quadruple-checked."

Veronica loved the idea. She asked me to give her the list that I'd put together. She assumed that it would be pretty close to the formal list, and she wanted to start familiarizing herself with it while she tried to get the official list from the FBI. A few days later, I sent her my roster of charities, accompanied by thick binders on each charity and its activists. Two days later I called her to ask whether she'd gotten the formal list. I could help her get it faster through my other government sources if she needed me to.

Veronica told me that she'd put in a formal request to see the formal list, but her request had been formally denied. Veronica was formally shocked.

I couldn't believe it, either. It didn't make any sense to me that the FBI and the State Department would refuse to let an agent from the

INS's National Security Unit see such a list. I was certainly accustomed to such prohibitions. I was used to hearing, "You can't get that, see that, know about that." But I wasn't working for the government. How could the FBI refuse to collaborate with the INS? What good is that list, anyway, if the INS, Customs, and other agencies charged with protecting our borders aren't getting to look at a definitive list of whom they shouldn't allow into the country?

Furious, I called the White House. Peter had been promoted to another department, but the guy who'd taken his place knew who I was, and he took my call. I told him what had happened to Veronica.

"Let me call the FBI and see what's going on," he said.

He called me less than an hour later.

"It's taken care of," he said. "I spoke with Steve, from the FBI. I told him about you and your idea and explained why the list needed to be shared with the INS. He said he'd like to talk to Veronica, and I told him she'd call him. I suggested that you and he talk. You may find you'd like to collaborate with him in the future." He gave me Steve's number.

I called Steve later that day. He was politely dismissive. "So what was it exactly that you wanted?" he asked. I gave him a detailed explanation. I told him who I was, who Veronica was, my ideas about the government's list. He said that Veronica should call him.

She did, almost immediately. Five minutes later she called me. "Guess what?" she said.

"Was mine close?" I blurted excitedly. I was sure she was calling to tell me that the two lists were almost identical.

"How would I know?" she replied. "Steve told me that the list was confidential and that I didn't have the clearance to get it."

"You're joking."

"I wish I were. He refused to give it to me. I asked if the White House official had called him, and he said yes and that he *still* wouldn't give me the list!" Veronica lamented. "I suggested that he talk to my boss. He said that talking to him would change nothing."

I called the White House and spoke with the NSC official again. Now he thought *I* was joking. When he realized I wasn't kidding, he blew a fuse. He called Veronica, asked about her talk with Steve. The next thing he did was to send the list to Veronica directly, although this was not what's considered the proper channels.

I then suggested that since they already knew about one another, maybe the INS and the White House people should meet and discuss ways to collaborate on that list or other mutual interests. Hearing that, Veronica almost fainted.

"Are you crazy? We and they aren't on the same level. No one will ever allow such a meeting to take place."

So the White House's National Security Council is supposed to fight terrorism. As is the INS's National Security Unit. They're all on the same side, right? Yet these entities are not allowed to meet and not allowed to collaborate? In a communist country, or in a tyrannical dictatorship such as the one I'd escaped as a child, too much collaboration can be dangerous. Close working relationships among high officials in such regimes can lead to conspiracy. The rulers of these regimes must divide and conquer to maintain their power. But in the greatest democracy of all time, government agencies aren't allowed to collaborate on the issue of stopping terrorism? This was incredible to me. Were al-Qaeda, Hamas, PIJ, and all their front groups and charities also going through proper channels as they plotted to destroy the West? Obviously not. So while the terrorists were humming along, sharing lists of potential American targets and funding one another, the U.S.'s counterterrorism agents were busy untangling themselves from miles of red tape. Meanwhile, their so-called collaborators in the FBI wouldn't share information with them. If not for me, Veronica would never have even known about the watch list.

When I met with Attorney General John Ashcroft after 9-11, I brought up the story of Veronica and the list and the issue in general. "How can one expect the government to fight terrorism when its various branches aren't allowed to meet, communicate, or share information?" I asked him. How can we get anywhere if the FBI sits on information even after it's been instructed by the White House to share it?

Luckily, I don't work for the government. I don't have to play by the government's rules, and I can do the right thing without worrying about jeopardizing my promotion or blemishing my official record. I can meet any official I want, whenever I want.

ONE DAY AT WORK, I was reading the HLF's quarterly newsletter, which I was getting regularly as a result of sponsoring my *shahid*'s son. Given that the HLF should have been one of the first charities on that watch list, I was quite surprised by what I read in its publication. The organization was proud to announce that it finally had been approved for USAID dollars!

The State Department was yet again showing its incompetence. A watch list had been devised for them, HLF was definitely on that list, yet State had approved it for USAID anyway. I immediately called the White House. What was the point of the list, I asked, if entities on it were eligible for U.S. funding, which would undoubtedly be used to finance terrorism? My contact at the White House couldn't believe it, either. He asked me to fax him the page from the HLF publication that crowed about receiving USAID dollars. A few days later he called me again. The State Department had acknowledged its blunder and denied HLF its USAID eligibility, he said. The mistake had been rectified.

Had I not read its newsletter, HLF—a group that George W. Bush in late 2001 designated as a terror organization—would have received money from the U.S. government. The government would have been literally funding terrorists who attack its citizens.

So why wasn't anyone else—say, the FBI, who so desperately clings to information, never sharing it with anyone else—able to notice that "mistake"?

THE INFORMATION I'd provided at that first briefing at the White House was forwarded to the FBI. What did they do with it? I'd asked Peter about it several times, and he always said that he'd never heard back from the FBI. He assumed that the agency was probably just sitting on the material.

He assumed correctly.

Was this an exception? Does the FBI usually follow things through, or is its sitting on files for years a recurring pattern?

Here's a story. Robert G. Wright was an FBI agent in Chicago. His work led to the seizure in 1998 of $1.7 million in the bank accounts of Muhammad Salah, the used-car salesman cum Hamas operative I'd met at the IAP conference in Chicago. Wright's superb 1998 affidavit on Salah showed that he'd recruited terrorists and funded terrorism. The FBI agent also showed that Salah's funding was linked to a wealthy Saudi businessman named Yassin Qadi. Qadi funneled money to Hamas through a New Jersey company called Beit Maal Investment (BMI). After 9-11 the U.S. government designated Qadi as a financial backer of Usama Bin Laden.

So how, you may wonder, did the FBI reward Wright for his excellent work? By suspending him from the investigation on harassment allegations, how else?

In the course of his work on Salah and Qadi, Wright became associated with a fellow FBI agent, a Muslim by the name of Gamal Abdel Hafiz. Hafiz maintained a close relationship with BMI's accountant, who at the time was seeking to get a job as a translator with the FBI.

Wright, who was aware of attempts by Hamas members to penetrate the FBI, asked Hafiz to wear a wire to a meeting with BMI's president, who at the time was under grand jury investigation. Hafiz refused. When Wright brought up the subject with his supervisors, Hafiz was again asked to wear the wire. Again he refused to allow the conversation to be recorded in any form unless the man he met was notified of the recording. He said he didn't trust the FBI to protect him (let me remind you that Hafiz *was* an FBI agent). More important, Hafiz said, "A Muslim does not record another Muslim." It turned out that Hafiz had declined to do similar undercover work in the past.

Wright complained about the incident: he reasoned that he, a Catholic, never took religious consideration into account when he investigated terrorism. Hafiz in turn filed a complaint against Wright, alleging harassment based on religious and ethnic discrimination. Instead of closely examining where Hafiz's loyalties lay, the FBI suspended Wright from the investigation. Hafiz, meanwhile, was promoted by the FBI. He now serves as the FBI liaison in . . . Saudi Arabia.

After 9-11, when Yassin Qadi was designated, it had nothing to do with the FBI's investigation; ever since Wright was suspended, not one bit of progress was made by the Bureau on the investigation. Salah is still free in Chicago, where he works as a human rights activist. Qadi continues to claim that he was never involved with terrorism. Had Qadi been designated when Wright filed his affidavit in 1997, maybe he and other rich Saudi businessmen would have thought twice before giving money to terrorist organizations.

And Wright? Oh, yes, his suspension was terminated a little over a year after 9-11. But he was also prohibited from having any contact with the BMI and Qadi investigation.

He doesn't even have access to his own files from when he was on the case.

True, the world was a different place before 9-11. But did anything change after the tragedy? Do government agencies work closer together now? Did the FBI retool itself to more efficiently and effectively hunt down the terrorists in our midst, after it became widely known that the lack of collaboration among agencies was a major reason for the 9-11 intelligence failure?

The public is led to believe that there are those who worry about its safety, obtain information, share it with others, do everything to ensure terrorists couldn't strike again.

Is this really so?

You be the judge.

In March 2002, I received an e-mail from Dan Cadman, saying that he'd gotten a phone call from an INS immigration attorney he knew, named Loraine. Loraine told him that she was assigned to Sami al-Arian's case by the INS's commissioner. After reviewing the information, she told Dan, it seemed to her that there wasn't enough evidence to deport Sami. She was planning to dismiss the case. Dan asked her to talk to me before she made up her mind. We agreed to meet in New York, at an INS building downtown.

So I went down there with some of my Sami files. I wasn't sure what, exactly, it was that she needed; after all, the FBI had been working on Sami's case for several years. Mike, a young lawyer who'd just joined our office, came along to help me carry. We needed two folding grocery carts to haul the material. When we walked in, Loraine looked at us, and at the stuff we were carting, and she was stunned.

"What's that?" she asked.

"You did want a briefing on Sami, didn't you?"

Before I could start, I had to know what Loraine had and where her investigation stood. There was no point in going over what she knew already.

"I guess I know everything there is to be known. I've reviewed all the information," she said, "and there isn't enough to convince any judge." She added that she was meeting with me at Dan Cadman's urging only. "I respect him, so here I am."

"And what information did you review?" I asked. "Most of it is with the FBI, in Tampa, you know. You can't dismiss the case before you see what they have."

I knew what the FBI had, though they certainly weren't letting *me* see it. Several rooms were dedicated to evidence on Sami al-Arian. The FBI had thousands of documents, hundreds of tapes that were translated and transcribed, an enormous amount of information.

"Well, I've been in Tampa," Loraine said, "and I've seen what the FBI has. I reviewed it thoroughly."

"When was it that you said you were assigned to this investigation?" I asked. There was no way she'd seen all the FBI's evidence. It would take an expert on Sami, someone like John Canfield, months to get through the FBI's material.

"For almost two weeks now."

I thought as much. Something in her story didn't make sense.

"I went down there," she said. "They were obnoxious, but I'm already used to that. They're always like that. A guy put me in a room and gave me two carton boxes." She gestured about one foot square. "He said that he knew nothing about what I was investigating but that he'd been told to give me the material and say that this was what they'd prepared for me. In these boxes I found a videotape, a letter Sami wrote, and a few documents. It took me a few hours to study them carefully, though it would probably have taken me half that time if there was someone there who could've answered my questions."

The FBI had a mountain of evidence, yet they'd given Loraine two boxes and no one to explain what was inside them. No wonder she wanted to halt the investigation.

So I started from scratch. Since Loraine knew next to nothing, I went all the way back, to the beginning. ICP, WISE, Ramadan Abdallah Shallah, Bashir Nafi, *al-Mukhtar al-Islami, a-Taliya al-Islamiya.* Everything I talked about with John Canfield that first time we'd met, and more. Practically a rerun of that show, only then I was speaking with people who knew a lot about Sami and had been following him for years. Now I was talking to someone who'd just joined this investigation and knew very little.

I talked and talked, pulled out documents and explained, and pulled out more documents. After a few hours, Loraine asked me to stop. She'd reached her saturation point. Late in the afternoon she said that she was convinced and that she thought any judge would be, too. Then I told her that the FBI had everything I'd showed her and much more. Not only had the FBI hidden the material from her, the information wasn't even theirs to begin with! The original search warrant, I told Loraine, the one that led to the raid on ICP and WISE and yielded most of the information now in the FBI's possession, was an INS warrant. If this information belonged to anyone, it belonged to the INS.

On the way back to the office, Mike told me that he, an attorney, would never have believed that story had he not witnessed it himself. "The FBI approach is not just inconceivable," he said, "it's freakin' scary."

Thus, after 9-11, the FBI continues to hide information.

This attitude reminds me of my young daughter, who grabs things that don't necessarily belong to her and states: "It's mine." Sometimes it requires a significant effort to get these things back from her. The FBI behaves like her in that respect. "It's mine," the FBI says, "and that's it." And no one else can have it, even if the FBI isn't using it.

Like my daughter's logic for not sharing, the agency's reasoning is infantile selfishness. If the FBI shared with other agencies, you see, perhaps those agencies would use that information to lead an investigation that might deflect some of the glory away from the FBI. Even when this approach endangers America, the FBI still doesn't deviate from it. My toddler will soon grow out of this behavior. But will the FBI?

One day in early 2002 I received a phone call from a pleasant woman who presented herself as an assistant U.S. attorney in California. She told me that shortly after 9-11, Governor Gray Davis summoned the federal prosecutors in her division and told them that he wanted to switch gears and focus on counterterrorism. He said he couldn't allow a disaster like 9-11 to happen in California. So she and many others were reassigned and were now beginning to learn about terrorism. Somehow, she'd been referred to me. "I need your help with some information on HLF and other terrorism connections in California," she said.

"Why, if I may ask, do you need me for that?" I didn't understand. The president had just designated HLF as a terrorist organization. "As far as I know, the Justice Department has at least two thousand documents on it. Why don't you get the information from them?"

"Don't think that I didn't try," she said with a bitter laugh. "They told me I didn't have clearance."

After I'd learned so much about the FBI, I was no longer surprised by such stories. "Just let me tell you," I said, "that even the FBI's fifty-page report on HLF was declassified after HLF was designated. Much of this stuff is public records."

I promised her I'd send her some information on HLF and other terrorist organizations in her state, and a few days later I mailed her a box filled with documents on HLF, al-Deek, IAP, and al-Qaeda in California.

I'd given her what her own employer, the Justice Department, would not.

She e-mailed me a few days later. "Got it. Read it. Fascinating. Could I please come meet you and get a briefing on this?"

Okay, so the FBI doesn't share its information with others.

But does it share it with itself?!

An FBI agent from California called me around the same time that the assistant U.S. attorney from there did, about four months after 9-11. He was looking for investigative leads relating to al-Qaeda in California. I told him about al-Deek, Diab, Ashour, and Charity Without Borders. He'd never heard of any of them, so I told him the whole story, which he loved. He asked what kinds of documents I had. I told him that among the documents I'd received from the state of California more than two years ago were the charity's canceled checks. "Ah, those could be very helpful," he said; with them the FBI could subpoena bank accounts and learn what had happened with the charity's money. He asked me to send him whatever I thought was important.

I sent him a large box with documents that Bruce, Neil, and I had compiled while preparing for our first White House visit. They included names, addresses, and companies that were affiliated with al-Deek and Diab, partners they'd had in these companies, lists of the charity's employees, and copies of the charity's checks. A few days after I sent him the material, he called again.

"The case," he told me, "is *very* strong. I went through the files we have on these people, and I read your stuff. Your documents are superb, and I want to go all the way with this investigation."

I knew the people at the NSC had understood the importance of the information we'd given them and that they'd immediately forwarded it to the FBI. It was now obvious, as the agent was picking up the investigation, that nothing happened with it during those two years.

But there's more to this story. Petrifying stuff.

"When I looked at our file on al-Deek," the FBI agent said, "it seemed that al-Deek and others had been running military training camps in Southern California in the early nineties." I later learned that these camps trained, among others, the followers of the Blind Sheikh, who tried to blow up the Lincoln Tunnel in New York.

I freaked out. "Oh my God. How long has this information been sitting there?"

"Years."

"And even this discovery wasn't enough to investigate? Why was nothing done to try to stop these people?"

"Intel information. Unusable," he said.

So in addition to sitting on my information on al-Deek and his associates for years, the FBI had learned that al-Deek was running military training camps for al-Qaeda in California and was planning to blow up various American targets. And the agency let these people go about their business undisturbed.

While al-Deek was in custody in Jordan in late 1999, Ashour, who'd requested asylum in America, could have been easily located, investigated, and if necessary, denied asylum and deported. As I write this, he is roaming the West Coast of the United States, a free man. And Diab, well, around 9-11 he flew off to Pakistan. By the time the FBI agent called me, it was too late. Diab was long gone.

The FBI, which had the information, did not follow it through, claiming that the way this information had been obtained would have made it unacceptable in court.

Go tell that to victims of terrorist attacks and their families.

But at that point in time, I had an enthusiastic FBI agent calling me; it seemed that maybe after 9-11, things were finally improving. Moreover, he was experienced in the field. He'd been involved in previous counterterrorism investigations and arrests of members of al-Gama'at al-Islamiya, the group headed by the Blind Sheikh and tied to al-Qaeda. It seemed that now, finally, something was happening out in California.

The agent registered his investigation, according to the Bureau's protocol, so that it would be known that he was on it, and so that anyone with leads on this investigation could contact him.

A few days later he called me and said that he'd been taken off the case. It seemed that the Anaheim office of the Bureau had noted that al-Deek's address was within their jurisdiction. They'd take it from there.

An agent from the Anaheim office did eventually call me. He was quite unpleasant. He asked me to send him the documents I'd sent my first California FBI agent. He said he'd work on them and then call me back.

Again I mailed a giant box of material to the West Coast.

But I never heard from him again.

WHY, YOU MAY ASK, didn't the FBI investigate al-Deek, Diab, Ashour, and Charity Without Borders, even after I'd given the White House all the leads about them? Why didn't the FBI do anything about all this merry company when there were more than enough reasons to investigate these people?

The answer to that is simple. The FBI couldn't, because it was quite diligently investigating someone else.

The FBI was busy investigating me.

CHAPTER 8

Face of a Monster

After many centuries of internal disputes and fighting came a time when young men from many Arab countries began to unite in a single movement. Until then, the Arab and Muslim worlds had been divided into sects, tribes, nations. But when the Soviets invaded Afghanistan in the late 1970s, Sunni Muslims and Shi'a Muslims, Jordanians, Palestinians, Iraqis, Saudis, Algerians, Moroccans, Syrians, Lebanese, and Egyptians all rushed to join that unified movement of jihad.

Such joining of forces under one banner, a pan-Arab movement of that magnitude, was the first of its kind since the days of the Prophet Muhammad himself.

Starting as a small, local conflict in Afghanistan, this movement would soon change the face of American history.

The driving force, the reason for that movement, was one charismatic and extraordinary individual.

A man named Abdallah Azzam.

———

THE PAIN IN my lower back had become intolerable. I'd been suffering for three days now, and it was so intense that I couldn't walk anymore. I decided to call my obstetrician.

I'd had pregnancies before, but none were like this. This time it was different—or perhaps I was different. At first, I couldn't believe that I was having a girl; even after I saw the baby on ultrasound, even after I'd gotten the chromosomal analysis from the amniocentesis. Until the very end I was still convinced that I was having a boy. As in my other pregnancies, I'd continued to work the whole nine months, I'd lagged behind on the weight gain charts, and my baby refused to come out on the due date. But this time my hormones were different, I knew, because my libido was working overtime. This had never happened to me before.

Neither had such horrific pain. During my previous pregnancy I'd arrived at the hospital only when I was having regular contractions every three minutes. Twenty minutes later I had a baby. But now I had no contractions, just pain.

On the phone, my obstetrician told me it was probably due to pressure of the baby's head on my pelvis. "It's time for the baby to come out," she said. "Tell me when you'd like to go to the delivery room—today, tomorrow, the sooner the better."

I wasn't used to that at all. Scheduled delivery? Until now, I'd had no say in these matters; my babies chose their birth dates. "Anytime I choose, and you'll deliver?"

"Sure. You're a week past your due date. Come in, we'll induce you and get your baby out in no time!"

Tomorrow wasn't good; we still had to sign the contract on the house we'd just bought. The day after tomorrow, a Wednesday? Yes, Wednesday was good. School was almost over. Jordan was graduating, with honors, from middle school on Thursday, so I'd go to the hospital and deliver the baby, and then Leo would be able to attend Jordan's ceremony.

"Agreed," the obstetrician said. "We'll see you then."

And so I went, two days later, to deliver my baby.

WHAT DOES ONE TAKE to a delivery room? Some personal hygiene items, obviously. A toothbrush, of course. Makeup, an absolute necessity. A few things to read, perhaps, such as magazines and a book or two.

Could I take any of my binders into the delivery room? Hardly. They're too heavy, and besides, if a nurse happened to read any of the material . . . The best option was to take only Arabic reading material.

On my way to the hospital, I stopped by the office, grabbed a few old magazines—my favorite reading material—and a couple of books I'd been meaning to get to for some time. The few days at the hospital could be a good opportunity to go over these items on my "to do" list, I thought.

Only when Shirley was born did I finally believe that she was a girl. I took her in my arms and kissed her. Overwhelmed with happiness, I started to cry. Shirley was the most beautiful thing I'd ever seen.

She fell asleep as soon as I finished breast-feeding her. I burped her gently and carefully put her in her bassinet. She lay there, so tiny, so adorable. I couldn't be happier. Looking at her, I felt blessed. She, the boys, Leo, the new house, my job—everything in my life was perfect.

Leo had stayed with me overnight. In the morning he'd gone home to help the boys get organized for their last days of school. Tonight was a big night for them. Jordan and Charlie had an important recital in the evening. And afterward, Jordan was delivering a speech at his graduation ceremony. Three hundred of his classmates had applied to give the four commencement addresses, and Jordan's speech was among the four chosen. So Leo had to take the boys to the recital in the city and then drive them back to Jordan's school.

I was tired, but at the same time I was excited. I couldn't sleep. Maybe I should have a quick look at the reading material, I thought. That would bore me just enough to send me yawning into the kingdom of dreams.

But first I turned on my cell phone and called Leo. He'd been awake with me all night, and he must have been as excited as I was.

"How's everything?" I asked.

"Couldn't be better, dear. The kids are home from school. Jordan read me his speech. It's beautiful! I'll tape him reading it at the graduation for you. We'll all go to the hospital directly after the ceremony. How's the baby? How are you? Do you need anything?"

I'd done a meticulous job in packing for this planned delivery, and I said we both were just fine. I told him how beautiful Shirley looked in her sleep, and I could feel how happy that made him.

Leo and I had grown much closer since we'd moved to the United States. Maybe this was because we were now so far from everyone else, our family and friends. Here we only had each other. And the kids, sure, but some things you can't share with them. Leo and I are true soul mates. We agree on all the major issues in our lives. But in the beginning, back in Israel, we quarreled a lot. In Israel people tend to be emotional and to get into useless and petty fights over the most trivial things. Maybe it's the stress of the political situation, or a Middle Eastern temperament, or just a part of the rough ride every young nation has to go through before it comes to maturation. But when we came to the United States, Leo and I noticed that our quarrels became infrequent. Our bond grew stronger, and after Shirley came, it intensified further still.

As soon as Leo hung up, I stuck a hand into the bag I'd parked in the stuffed armchair beside my bed. I put the cell phone in and pulled something out. It was a book, not a magazine. So, not even photos— I'd probably fall asleep in ten minutes.

The book was published by Adel Abdul Jalil Batterjee, a name I knew. I'd first stumbled upon Batterjee in 1999, when I was studying the Benevolence International Foundation, BIF, as part of my quest for dirty charities. I'd seen BIF around. It always worked in collaboration with the Global Relief Fund, GRF, and with the HLF. At the Muslim conferences I attended, I noticed that whenever one of these charities had a booth, the others were nearby. Many a time I was notified, via e-mail or snail mail, about joint fund-raisers involving BIF and GRF, or GRF and HLF. Since I knew exactly what HLF was, I was pretty confident that GRF and BIF were involved, too. I obtained BIF's 990s and saw that it had raised millions of dollars every year and sent most of the money to Afghanistan, Pakistan, Bosnia, and Chechnya, never detailing what was actually done with the money. All these places were strongholds of al-Qaeda and Bin Laden. Although BIF was supposedly based in Chicago, I discovered that its headquarters were in fact in Saudi Arabia. When I looked at BIF's articles of incorporation, I discerned that the charity had three founders: Adel Abdul Jalil Batterjee, his cousin Shahir Abdulraoof Batterjee, and Mazin M. S. Bahareth. Each of these respectable gentlemen listed his address in Jedda, Saudi Arabia.

The Saudi link immediately set off my alarm bells. Too many times I've encountered Saudi-funded charities that are linked to terrorism. So I studied these three men carefully. My investigation of two of the three led nowhere. That had happened to me countless times; I'd go down several wrong research avenues until I'd finally find the right one. But Adel Batterjee was not a dead end; I found that in addition to BIF, he headed WAMY. According to an FBI communiqué, WAMY, the World Assembly of Muslim Youth, is a suspected terrorist organization. I remembered that WAMY publications had been found in the luggage of Ahmed Ajaj, the man who'd planned with Ramzi Yousef to bomb the World Trade Center in 1993. Like BIF, WAMY's headquarters is in Saudi Arabia. Its main office in the United States is in Falls Church, Virginia. WAMY's director in the United States, Abdallah Bin Laden, is Usama's half brother. As for BIF, after 9-11 it was designated by the government as an al-Qaeda financier. Its director in the United States is in an American prison as these lines are being written. So I knew that I should keep an eye on Batterjee and BIF. I could feel it in my bones: Batterjee would turn out to be very important.

Lying in bed in the delivery room, I looked at Batterjee's book. On the bright red cover were two fists raised against each other. On the left fist was stamped the Soviet symbol, the hammer and sickle. On the right fist was tattooed a sentence in Arabic, *La ilaha il Allah* (There's no God but Allah). The right fist, Muslims; the left, Russia. Pretty militant, that cover. Pretty promising. Of course, I'd read so many books that appeared promising but were nothing but a big drag.

The name of the book was *al-Ansar al-Arab fi Afghanistan* (*The Arab*

Volunteers in Afghanistan). A small logo on the corner of the cover—two hands stretched out toward each other with the globe in the background—was nearly identical to the BIF logo.

A short paragraph on the back cover talked about the Soviet-Afghan war. "This is the Jihad in Afghanistan," it said. "The Arab people are the stream that feeds the Jihad river." There was also a note that the book had been published by BIF and WAMY. I opened the book and started to read the introduction. It explained how the war against the invading Russians became a critical turning point in the way Muslims and Arabs perceived the West. The war, which started as a mission of jihad to liberate Afghanistan, turned out to be a crushing defeat for the Soviet Union, the superpower. The glorious victory, said the introduction, opened the eyes of many young Muslims. They felt that they were strong. Their unity made them feel invincible. Victory gave them a taste for more. If they could beat the Soviets, they reasoned, they could easily overcome the decadent West.

Jihad, their new jihad, could lead to Muslim world domination.

I looked over at my little angel. She was asleep, her pink cheeks made for kisses. Speaking of pink, it occurred to me, I'd finally be able to shop in the pink sections of the children's clothing shops and the toy stores. Until she came, everything had had to be in blue. I imagined braiding her hair someday, the way Grandma used to do mine. It would be a while before that would happen, though. Shirley arrived in this world nearly bald.

I returned to the book. The introduction went on to talk about Abdallah Azzam. Not a surprise, considering that practically any material on the Soviet-Afghan war from an Arab or Muslim perspective talked about the man who'd succeeded in doing what no other Muslim before him had done, not since the early days of Islam: convincing Arabs and Muslims from all sects and countries alike to join forces in jihad. As a Palestinian, Azzam had great interest in Palestine and its liberation, but he realized early on, in the beginning of the 1980s, that Afghanistan was fertile ground for an international jihad movement. He traveled from one Arab country to another, preaching, lecturing, talking, and convincing, and he began to recruit warriors for his cause: jihad to liberate the Muslim world from the infidels' grip.

None of this was new to me. Everyone in my field knows these facts about Azzam and the war in Afghanistan. This book will get me nothing but a good nap, I thought. A few more pages should do it, and I'll be out like a light.

The ringing of my cell phone cut harshly through the quiet. Shirley stirred in her bassinet. I grabbed the telephone as fast as I could, cursing under my breath for not having turned it off after speaking with Leo.

"Hello?" I said in a low tone.

"Are you in the middle of something?" asked the familiar voice. It was John Canfield.

"Hi, John!" I didn't at all mind getting a call from him. "What's up?"

"I have good news, and I have bad news. We were able to change the date, like you'd suggested, and now we have a new one. Hopefully, this time it's final. It's set for late September."

John was talking about the Tampa task force's scheduled trip to Israel. John and a number of FBI agents were supposed to go to collect information on Sami and PIJ. The trip had been postponed so many times that I was skeptical it'd ever take place. Finally, a few weeks prior to my delivering Shirley, John had called with the news that they were actually going . . . in August.

"The state of Israel goes on vacation in August," I told him. "Most people won't even be in the country when your delegation arrives."

John took my advice, and now he was telling me that the date of the trip had been changed again.

"Good," I said. "So what's the bad news?"

"Well, it looks like a good number of the meetings the FBI was hoping to arrange aren't going to happen," he said. "We've got no one good to meet over there. Maybe you have some ideas for us? Who do you think we could meet?" He sounded miserable.

"Oh, is that it? Don't worry, John, there's still plenty of time," I said.

"I'll give you all the names and contacts you need. Relax, and leave everything to me. I can't do anything right now—I'm out of the office for a few days—but as soon as I get back, I'll start working on it. I promise."

Relieved and having gotten what he called for, John joked with me, "And who let *you* out of the office for so long? Where are you?"

Men! Any woman would have guessed immediately. John knew I was nine months pregnant, but he didn't make the connection.

"I'm in the delivery room. I have a new baby."

A punch from Mike Tyson couldn't have been delivered more effectively.

"No, really, where are you? You're kidding me, right?"

"No. I'm in the delivery room."

"You are crazy, do you know that? You're completely out of your mind. I never wanna talk to you again! You just gave birth, and you're discussing work with me? You should rest, think about your daughter, do anything—but don't think about work!"

"Relax, I had her a few hours ago, she's asleep right here next to me, and I'm fine. I was reading a book when you called. About Afghanistan."

"You're nuts. That's all I can say." Then, trying to lighten things up a bit, he asked, "Do you still look the same? I mean, as good as ever?"

I didn't think about it until he asked. How *did* I look? During the pregnancy I was very active. I'd gained only sixteen pounds, and my obstetrician was pretty worried about it. Naturally, my breasts were engorged and my tummy large; but I had no edema, and only hours after delivery I already felt that I had lost most of the weight I'd gained in nine months.

"I look about the same, I guess," I replied.

"Your husband is a lucky devil. That's all I can say. Now go get some rest, would ya? And most important, congratulations!"

"Talk to you later." This time I did turn my cell phone off.

I love talking to John. He's one of the good guys.

I was now wide awake. I took Batterjee's book again and hoped that this time it would do its job and put me to sleep. I flipped through the pages of the preface, foreword, introduction . . . all repeated the same old stuff about Azzam. How he went to Afghanistan in the early 1980s, how he began to recruit mujahideen for the war there. Boring, boring, boring.

The first chapter went on to tell stories of a few of the people who'd been there, in Afghanistan, gathered around Azzam, listening to him preach. "One of the men who led the Arab Afghan Jihad forces," it said on page twenty-six, "came from one of the wealthiest Saudi families; influenced by the Afghan struggle, he would live with them and sacrifice everything for the Afghani Jihad. This man was a young, tall man who followed Dr. Abdallah Azzam to fight in Afghanistan."

My blood ran cold.

I read these lines again. And again. It couldn't be, but there it was. Black Arabic print on yellowing paper. The book I was holding in my hand was a treasure far greater than King Solomon's mines and Ali Baba's cave combined. Incredible as these few sentences were, I immediately realized what story they were recounting and how important the book had to be. It was about Bin Laden. The book was actually telling the story of Usama Bin Laden's first steps during the war in Afghanistan.

Trembling, I continued to read. I tried to swallow the entire text, dashing through it, turning pages frantically, yet at the same time I read each and every word carefully, trying to memorize and absorb this one-of-a-kind document.

"In 1979, the Abu Abdallah was not more than 22-years-old, and he was hardly 70 kilos. He was very thin," the book said. Abu Abdallah was Usama Bin Laden's nom de guerre. Many of the Arab warriors who fought in Afghanistan adopted such aliases. "He was 180 centimeters tall, but Usama who was a graduate from the economic faculty from Abdulaziz al-Malik [King Abdulaziz] University in Jedda, held a huge responsibility in running, together with his nine brothers, their father's properties."

From there the book continued to tell the story in Abu Abdallah's own words: "In 1399 [A.H., After Hijra—the Muslim year that corresponds to 1978], I remember I heard while I was in Jedda that the Russian forces entered Afghanistan. This influenced me very much and I decided that I had to join my mujahideen brothers in Pakistan. It took me about two weeks to prepare myself and to collect some financing from my family and my brothers."

The account later describes Bin Laden's fears during his first years there. "Until the first quarter of the year 1984, Bin Laden used to frequently visit [officers of] the Jama'at-e Islami [Party] in Lahore to hand over donations. But Usama remained scared to visit the battlefront or even to travel beyond Lahore, Islamabad and Peshawar."

So he was a big coward, I thought. His fellow mujahideen died fighting the Russians while he watched them from a safe distance, from across the Pakistani border. Bin Laden relates of those days: "Until 1984 I was under the spell of a reluctance to join physically . . . unfortunately I continued like this—now I regret bitterly—until the month of Rajab of 1984, when for the first time I ventured into the interior to the battlefronts and jihad."

This change of mind, when Bin Laden seemed to be leaving his fear behind, came through the influence of Azzam. This charismatic man, Bin Laden's mentor and spiritual leader, instructed him "to go to Jaji where Sheikh Sayyaf is."

The book continued: "In Jaji, close to the border separating Afghanistan from Pakistan, Sheikh Sayyaf, who was then head of the Union [of the mujahideen parties], had established a camp in the liberated areas. . . . Here Sheikh Sayyaf maintained several tents, one of which was reserved for Usama Bin Laden when he set foot for the first time in Afghanistan. Here Bin Laden was able to observe the conditions of the jihad and mujahideen closely. He summed up his reaction by saying: 'I was shocked to see the extremely miserable conditions and the lack of facilities for everything: weapons, roads, trenches. Asking Allah the almighty for forgiveness, I felt guilty for having listened to the advice of some Brothers, and sheikhs, and relatives, who told me not to go to the interior, as that would be a security risk for me. I felt that this delay of four years could only be remedied by martyrdom in the path of Allah.' " So this is where it all started, I thought. It was

there that Bin Laden decided to use his wealth and expertise in construction to create the infrastructure and build the fortified facilities for
the warriors of jihad. There, in Jaji, near the Pakistani border, Bin
Laden later established his first base in Afghanistan, his first training
camp for Arabs swarming into Afghanistan to join jihad. This camp,
and Bin Laden's newly formed group, became known by the name al-
Masada, or "the Lion's Den."

I LOOKED OVER at Shirley. Still asleep. I continued to read and
reached the place where Azzam in his own words describes how he got
involved in the war. "I looked at the state of affairs on Earth and felt
that strong yearning for jihad which I had always felt. I saw that there
was jihad going on in Yemen, between the Islamic Movement and the
communists, as well as jihad in Afghanistan. Therefore, I decided to go
to one of those two places. I signed a contract with the King Abdulaziz
University in Jedda and taught there for one semester." That was
where Azzam met Bin Laden. "God Almighty might have looked into
our hearts and, on noticing the longing for jihad, granted our wish and
paved the way for us."

The book then revealed one more astonishing story. It told of
another rich Saudi, a man named Wa'el Julaidan. Julaidan would
become the third element in the triumvirate that shook the world
nearly twenty years later.

In a U.S. university, in the State of Kentucky, Abul-Hasan [an alias for
Julaidan] was attentively following lectures on "Human Civilization."
The professor tried to convert the hall of scientific research into a
forum for the spread of ideological conflict and methodological confusion. But the disciple turned against the master, the poisoned arrow
turned into a boomerang. Abul-Hasan relates: "In the summer of
1980, a Jewish professor by the name of Godson concentrated on
Islamic civilization. . . . The professor continued talking about
Islamic Jihad, warning against its danger by telling the students that it
was the basis for the destruction of all human civilization. He said
that the remnants of Greek civilization were destroyed in the name of

Islamic Jihad and that Byzantine civilization fell under the onslaught of Islam, that the Persian civilization ended for the same reason, and also the Pharaonic civilization. The professor concluded by saying that 'Western civilization, which we are enjoying in the 20th century, will also go under in the name of Islamic Jihad. . . . Once this Jihad sets into motion, it will reach Moscow and will take over Russia. At that point a Third World War will break out in the name of Islamic Jihad, and this will signal the end of the human civilization which we presently relish in the West.' At that moment I understood, as a young Muslim, that there was great hope connected with the Jihad in Afghanistan. It is the enemy who is telling this, before even the friends. It is the ones who are conspiring against it who say so, before even those who support the Jihad. From that moment on I was determined to get to the battlefield."

I knew that Julaidan was a key player in al-Qaeda. But until I read Batterjee's book, I had no idea *how* key.

The book went on to describe, in painstaking detail, the first years of the war in Afghanistan. How Azzam, Bin Laden, and Julaidan established Maktab al-Khidamat, "the Services Office," and the Arab military training camps in Afghanistan. Maktab al-Khidamat was established in 1984 to assist the mujahideen and the refugees from the Soviet-Afghan war. The book lists a large number of Arab fighters—jihadists—including Americans, who fought close to Bin Laden. Some of these people would later be convicted for their roles in the embassy bombings or indicted for supporting al-Qaeda. One such man was Enaam Arnaout, director of the Chicago-based BIF (the charity that co-published Batterjee's book), who in February 2000, under a plea deal, pleaded guilty to a racketeering conspiracy count as the government dropped a charge accusing him of supporting al-Qaeda. Many others mentioned in the book decorate the FBI's "most wanted" lists. Many of these names I knew; some of these events I also knew; but there was nothing like that book to put everything in order, organize loose bits of information, and clear parts that were obscure to me (and to everyone else).

The book, Batterjee's book, was not only the most fascinating book

I'd ever read pertaining to Islamic terrorism, but also an amazing primary source of information about Bin Laden's first years as the most heinous terrorist of all time. It told his story, from the earliest days, and the stories of those who surrounded him then. It was a unique, firsthand account of one of the biggest enigmas in the field of counterterrorism: the origins of al-Qaeda. No other book or publication has done that.

The book also cleared up yet another crucial point for me: Bin Laden had a small group of loyal men, whom he could trust, who started out together in al-Masada and then scattered all over the world to form al-Qaeda bases—in the United States, in Spain, in Germany, in Bosnia, in Saudi Arabia. Al-Qaeda became a truly global organization. The book, an astounding combination of textbook and memoir, completed in my mind the picture, the entire saga that should have been titled *Al-Qaeda: The Birth of a Monster.*

The thought scared me, and I stopped reading for a moment. I looked at Shirley. She was awake now, not making a sound but looking intently at me. I wasn't going crazy. She was really staring at me. I picked her up and talked to her, and after a few moments she began losing her patience. She was hungry. I arranged her on me so that I could read while she nursed.

"This way Bin Laden diagnosed the real wound," the book continued. "He was now fully convinced that the methods of dispatching supplies used hitherto did not make things reach the war fronts and had to be changed. With his specialization and the expertise he had gained working with his brothers in building the famous tunnels of Mecca he now began to toy with the idea of applying his expertise to the mountains of Jaji. The thought did not take long to crystallize in his mind. . . ."

The owner of a giant construction company, the rich businessman, had finally found a place to use his resources. In these mountains he'd construct impenetrable fortresses. In the years ahead, after 9-11, he'd find refuge in these bunkers as U.S. Special Forces and fighters from the Afghan Northern Alliance would hunt him down.

I made sure that Shirley was comfortable, and I went on:

As Bin Laden tells the writer: "The Mujahideen need tunnels to store their arms and to maintain hospitals, as well as resting places for the people. When I say people I mean the good ones who love jihad and Islam. The infidels, the Russians and the Americans, have so much impacted the minds of Muslims, making them believe that they [the infidels] are indefatigable superpowers, that they have all kinds of gadgets and intelligence and stuff of that type. Most of that is inflated and far from true."

So here was the proof that he hated us even then, I thought. Even then, in the very beginning, when the United States, through the CIA and its Pakistani counterpart, the Inter-Services Intelligence, was funding him and training him and hoping to use him against the Russians. In his earliest days, when we still considered him an ally, he already hated us and everything that we stand for.

Even today most officials believe that Bin Laden turned against us only after the Gulf War, supposedly because he felt that the presence of American troops on Arabian soil desecrated his holy land. Batterjee's book proves otherwise. Bin Laden merely used the Gulf War as an excuse for his propaganda. The book shows, in Bin Laden's own words, that his plans to destroy us were baking in his twisted, evil, monstrous brain nearly a decade before Operation Desert Storm.

I looked at Shirley, who was so small and innocent. Large tears fell on my cheeks as I put the book on the dresser beside the bed.

Shirley, unperturbed, continued to suckle.

ONE HOT, CLEAR DAY early in August 1998, I was heading to the office. I'd been working there for a good number of months already, and I was still learning a lot every passing day. As always, I was listening to the news on my way. I follow the news religiously, print as well as broadcast and electronic media. I have to be the first to know and the most informed.

Around eight, I heard the breaking news about an attack on American embassies in Kenya and Tanzania. The magnitude of the devastation was soon evident. I was shaken by the number of dead and wounded, and by the cunning with which the bombings were executed. I also understood, as soon as the name al-Qaeda was uttered in relation to the bombings, that I was behind. Way behind. I'd been studying PIJ and Hamas thoroughly, but I didn't know enough about al-Qaeda.

I can't be blamed for that, really. Until then, everyone discounted al-Qaeda as an insignificant nuisance.

Take the American public, for example. Back in 1998, the bombings in East Africa were in the news for a while—and then the media's interest in them subsided. We humans are local patriots: we worry first about what's closest to us. The loss of life in Africa was tragic, but the attack was not on U.S. soil, and most of those who died were not Americans. What we told ourselves was that those U.S. citizens who did perish knew that they were taking jobs in a risky part of the world. For the vast majority of Americans, al-Qaeda wasn't even on the radar screen.

The problem was that the U.S. government was as cavalier about al-Qaeda as was the American public, and this should never have happened. The government should have taken al-Qaeda much more seriously, years before the embassy bombings.

Immediately after the bombings I began to study al-Qaeda. I knew then, as everyone else did, that the organization started sometime during the days of the Soviet-Afghan war. It was also common knowledge in the mid- to late 1990s that the United States had supported Bin Laden in his early days. This may have seemed like a good idea at the time, at least from a tactical point of view. Strategically, it was a disaster. Surprising? Hardly. Supporting terrorism, whatever the justification, always backfires.

What was the thing, I thought as I began my research on al-Qaeda, that transpired in Bin Laden's mind, the thing that made him transform from an ally to a bitter foe?

As I always do, I tried to get to the bottom of things and to understand how and why al-Qaeda does what it does. I knew that in this case I couldn't do any undercover work. All I could do was collect publicly available information. I had to look for published material, the old papers and books that described those obscure days in Afghanistan.

I began collecting old copies of al-Jihad from every corner of the earth. This periodical was written by Abdallah Azzam and other Arab warriors in Afghanistan and published by Azzam's Maktab al-Khidamat. I obtained books that Azzam had written. I laid my hands on *al-Binyan al-Marsous,* the *Solid Foundation,* a Pakistani-based publication in Arabic that detailed the Soviet-Afghan war from the perspective of the Arab fighters.

I read in these publications that during the war against the Soviets, there was no terrorist organization named al-Qaeda. There was Abdallah Azzam, who succeeded in uniting the Arab world in jihad and, like the Pied Piper of Hamelin, to convince numerous young Arabs to come and fight in Afghanistan. Nationalism, heretofore the motivating force for many of these young warriors, was completely set aside at that point; the burning issue was Afghanistan. I learned that Azzam, Bin Laden, and Julaidan established Maktab al-Khidamat not as a terrorist group, but rather as a charitable organization.

So this, I thought, was the germ of the idea to use charities for terrorism. Charity, refugees, funds, mujahideen, jihad . . . brilliant. The more I read, the clearer it all became. I understood how the idea evolved. During the Soviet-Afghan war, one of the difficulties the mujahideen had was to smuggle guns and arms across the Pakistani border. On the one hand, the Pakistanis were giving them trouble. On the other, many Afghans, who strongly opposed the presence and activities of the Arab fighters, were also standing in the way of these shipments. That's when Bin Laden and his men began using charities. You haul a layer of supplies for refugees, and underneath you smuggle the real merchandise, your toys of war. One such charity that was actively involved in this operation was the Saudi Red Crescent, headed by none other than Wa'el Julaidan.

In time I obtained nearly every issue of *al-Jihad* and *al-Binyan al-Marsous.* In them I discovered some very interesting things.

For one, Maktab al-Khidamat had established centers in various countries in Europe, Asia, and America. In America, Maktab al-Khidamat, "the Services Office," was given a name more suitable to its "charitable" orientation: al-Kifah, "the Refugees Office." Indeed, it did raise funds for what it called relief work, such as for Afghan orphans who were available for sponsorship. Much like HLF, I thought. Even the brochures of Maktab and HLF looked similar. The sponsorship application I filled out at the IAP conference was practically indistinguishable from Maktab's forms.

Then I discovered a crucial point: Both *al-Jihad* and *al-Binyan al-Marsous* listed their addresses as that of the Islamic Center of Tucson, Arizona. The center in Tucson, then, served as Maktab's first branch in America.

I decided to do some research on the center. I ordered its annual reports, all of them public records, my specialty. I saw that in 1983, Wa'el Julaidan was the president of the center. Like Usama Bin Laden, he heard Abdallah Azzam speak, got hooked, and left everything behind to dedicate his life to jihad. The more I looked into Julaidan, the more I understood how important he was to al-Qaeda. But in my numerous briefings to officials from the FBI, NSC, Treasury, and INS, no one, not even one agent, knew who Julaidan was. On several occasions I gave government officials material, trying to interest them in him. One such time was during my briefing on Khalil al-Deek at the White House, during the millennium investigation. I brought up Julaidan's name because we were discussing al-Qaeda, and I wanted to let the officials know how important a figure he was in that organization. I brought with me a thick dossier that included his picture in *al-Jihad,* proof of his ties to the Islamic Center in Tucson and of his connections to the Saudi charities linked to Bin Laden, and even newspaper interviews in which Azzam and Bin Laden talked about him as a brother in their jihad. Yet no action was taken by the United States against Julaidan until a year after 9-11.

As a founder of Maktab, Julaidan used the Islamic Center in Tucson as his contact in the United States after he left it in 1984, through which he continued to distribute Maktab's publications. The center was also used for recruitment of mujahideen. Wadih al-Hage, Bin Laden's personal secretary, who was convicted for his role in the embassy bombings in Africa, had learned about Maktab and began his way in jihad in the center. Julaidan continued to use the Tucson mosque for a few years, until Maktab's headquarters were established in New York in late 1987. Soon thereafter, Maktab had spread at least twenty branches in cities across the United States, including offices in New York, Chicago, Boston, and Tucson.

The New York office of Maktab was heavily involved in several terrorist attacks and plots in New York City: the murder of Rabbi Meir Kahane in 1990 by al-Sayyid A. Nossair, the 1993 World Trade Center bombing, and the foiled plot to blow up New York's Lincoln Tunnel. Maktab operatives participated in these operations; Maktab funded and provided the explosives for the attacks.

The FBI dismissed all these attacks as isolated incidents. Why worry about the Kahane murder, thought the FBI, since it's only one fanatic Muslim who killed one crazy Jew? The FBI made a deadly mistake. Nossair, while in prison, helped Maktab operatives to plan the attack on the Lincoln Tunnel.

When FBI agents raided Nossair's house shortly after he assassinated Kahane, they found thousands of manuals, some of which were published by Maktab, in Arabic, in which there were comprehensive descriptions of assassination techniques, of kidnapping techniques, of hijacking methods, and of selecting enemy targets. These manuals were only translated three years later, after the World Trade Center bombing. Not even that, however, convinced the FBI that there was a plot, a conspiracy, a network of murderous terrorists involved in the bombing, working together, plotting future attacks. Even after translating these manuals the FBI continued to deem the 1993 World Trade Center bombing the work of madmen and was unaware of Maktab's role in it. But the 1993 World Trade Center bombing could never have taken place without Maktab's support.

The FBI in these investigations took the same approach I've seen it take in many other terrorism-related probes, such as those of PIJ and Hamas. Just as its agents had never bothered to study *al-Mukhtar,* the publication PIJ used, or Hamas's *Ila-Falastine,* the FBI failed to study *al-Jihad,* Azzam's publication. The FBI never took an in-depth look at Maktab. But I did.

Amazingly enough, the FBI and I reached the same conclusion

about the 1993 World Trade Center bombing. We agreed that it wasn't perpetrated by Maktab.

The FBI said it was a lunatic who did it.

I said it was al-Qaeda.

HOW, THEN, was al-Qaeda involved in all this?

After a few years together in Afghanistan, Bin Laden began to disagree with the way Azzam envisioned jihad. Bin Laden knew that Azzam and Maktab were supporting the fight, but he began to feel that military training was more important than the other services provided by Azzam's organization. Azzam opposed that idea. Mentor and student argued over the issue of Afghanistan. While Azzam saw in it just a stepping-stone for further activities, Bin Laden saw it as the future base for worldwide jihad. Thus, in late 1985, together with some fifty Arab warriors loyal to him, Bin Laden finally parted from Azzam and established al-Masada, a military training camp in the outskirts of Jaji, where he hoped to train the best mujahideen, the most ferocious warriors in the entire world. From there these warriors could be dispatched for jihad, wherever it was needed, anywhere around the globe.

Azzam met his death in Peshawar, Pakistan, in 1989, in a car bomb explosion. One popular theory is that Bin Laden eliminated his onetime mentor turned competitor. But was that what really happened?

Batterjee's book, published two years after Azzam was killed, tells of the argument and parting between Azzam and Bin Laden. They didn't speak for almost a year, but then Azzam visited al-Masada, fell in love with the way the camp was run, and couldn't praise Bin Laden's operation enough. He stayed with Bin Laden a few weeks, during which he sat and taught the warriors Qur'ân in the mornings before they'd go out for their military training. At the time of his death, not only was there no rivalry between them, but Azzam was enthusiastically supporting Bin Laden.

As I read Batterjee's book, I remembered how years ago I'd come across, in *al-Jihad,* an article written by Azzam in 1988. In it he described his new vision of jihad in the final days of the ten-year-long

Soviet-Afghan war: "Islamic society cannot be established without an Islamic movement going through the fire of tests. Its members need to mature in the fire of trials. This movement will represent the spark that ignites the potential of the *Ummah*. It will carry out a jihad in which the Islamic movement will provide the leadership."

After describing what could only mean military training as he'd seen at Bin Laden's al-Masada, he concluded: "We have now understood the importance of this base which has been trained in Islam, from its earliest infancy on brought up in the Islamic mission." Thus Azzam himself explained that his early disapproval of Bin Laden's training base had transformed into full support. Bin Laden understood that message well and held no grudge against Azzam.

Azzam's article, describing his change of heart after he saw al-Masada, was titled *"al-Qaeda al-Saliba,"* "The Solid Base." In Arabic, *al-qaeda* means "base," as in headquarters or military base.

Azzam, the intellectual architect of worldwide jihad, gave his disciple a parting gift before he was blown into oblivion. Azzam was the first to call Bin Laden's operation al-Qaeda, and the name stuck.

FOR A FEW YEARS, al-Qaeda and Maktab worked in close collaboration. Maktab would recruit men as potential mujahideen. These men came from the four corners of the earth to Pakistan, and there they were hosted in *beyth al-ansaar,* "guest houses." From there they were sent to wage jihad, while their belongings and documents remained in these guest houses. The *beyth al-ansaar* were financed, at least in part, by the Muslim World League, MWL, a Saudi-based organization that serves as an umbrella for a large number of charities. Wa'el Julaidan, who left Maktab with Bin Laden and became one of the highest-ranking officers of al-Qaeda, also headed MWL's office in Pakistan. The best trainees sent from the guest houses, the most ferocious and brave, would be dispatched to al-Masada, Bin Laden's camp.

Yet Maktab gradually disintegrated in the early 1990s, around the time of the World Trade Center bombing. First, its legendary leader, Azzam, was killed. Then, Mustafa Shalabi, the head of Maktab in the United States, was assassinated in his New York office. It was believed that this was the result of either internal rivalries within Maktab or disputes with the Blind Sheikh, Omar Abdel-Rahman. And then the Blind Sheikh was arrested and convicted. Maktab's operatives and branches seemed simply to vanish into thin air.

It bothered me greatly, and I asked government officials, including some in the White House, about this phenomenon. Where did all these numerous Maktab operatives go? It couldn't be that suddenly all of them retired and went to work as car dealers or bankers. They must have found another way to continue their efforts to fulfill Azzam's vision of Muslim world domination.

Wadih al-Hage was the prime candidate to take over after Mustafa Shalabi's murder as head of Maktab in the United States. Instead, he ended up becoming Bin Laden's personal secretary and one of the men who blew up the embassies in East Africa. Enaam M. Arnaout, BIF's director, was a Maktab activist. He made a plea bargain with the government in February 2000, pleading guilty to funding rebels in Chechnya and troops in Bosnia, and his charity, BIF, was designated as an al-Qaeda front. Rabih Haddad, president and treasurer of GRF, was involved with Maktab. Haddad was, as of this writing, in jail, and his charity, like BIF, was designated as a front for al-Qaeda. Many others from Maktab found themselves on similar paths.

So this is where some of them went, I thought. Arnaout, al-Hage, Haddad, and many other Maktab operatives understood that charities had tremendous power, and that they could raise funds and pay for jihad. So these men founded their own charities. The more of these charities they established, the less they needed Maktab.

And out of Maktab sprang one more offshoot, one more haven for its members: al-Qaeda.

The government didn't watch these people carefully, and they went about their business undisturbed. Even worse: The government never really understood that Nossair, Yousef, Ajaj, and the rest of the gang that blew up the World Trade Center in 1993 had worked closely with Maktab, the Blind Sheikh, and al-Qaeda.

Worse still, while Bin Laden is one of the unindicted conspirators in the 1993 World Trade Center bombing, the government has never accused al-Qaeda of that attack. Not even after 9-11 has the FBI acknowledged this mistake.

But that's not even the worst part. That would be, beyond question, the fact that the government, and particularly the FBI, repeatedly missed clues and evidence in its dealings with al-Qaeda. To date, law enforcement agents admit that they don't know when, why, or how al-Qaeda began. Regarding al-Qaeda, the FBI left a trail of clumsiness at best, or criminal negligence, depending on one's point of view, all the way from the World Trade Center bombing in 1993 to September 11, 2001.

AS SOON AS I LAID eyes on the booklet, the inscription came at me like a raging bull. I looked at it again, and my throat dried up. There it was, in plain Arabic, all over the booklet. I immediately called Max to tell him about it. To say that he was surprised would be the understatement of the year. Then I called a friend of mine, a Muslim scholar, to tell him about it. I wanted to make sure that I wasn't making a mistake. Next I called Andy McCarthy, the lead prosecutor in the World Trade Center bombing. When I told him what I saw, what name was on the booklet, he was thunderstruck. He asked me to fax it over to him, which I immediately did.

I called him again a week later, to follow up, but I never heard from him again.

Then again, what could he have told me about it?

The sequence of events began in September 1992, when one Ramzi Ahmed Yousef boarded a Pakistani International Airlines flight from Pakistan to the United States. Traveling with him on that flight was Ahmed Ajaj. These two characters met in a training camp in Afghanistan in the early nineties. The Soviet-Afghan war was over, but the training camps were running stronger than ever, and Bin Laden had used the best construction techniques and materials to build bunkers and tunnels in the desolate hills of Afghanistan. He declared war on America, and Ajaj and Yousef enlisted. On the flight from Pakistan, Yousef cut out the picture from the fake Iraqi passport he'd just purchased in Peshawar's black market for $100. Ajaj, who'd previously traveled to the United States, didn't show the same respect for the abilities of the immigration authorities by trying to make his passport look authentic. He left his fake British passport as it was.

The immigration authorities, to Ajaj's great disappointment, did apprehend him in the airport, mainly because he didn't even remotely resemble the picture in his passport, but also because for someone with a British passport, his English was inexplicably poor. Seeing that his accomplice had been seized, Yousef made a quick decision. He turned himself in to the INS—and asked for political asylum. He knew that carrying an Iraqi passport would render him eligible for asylum. Sure enough, the INS let him go and instructed him to report in a few months and check on his application. In these short months, Yousef, with a little help from his friends, had managed to detonate a bomb in the bowels of the World Trade Center.

At the time of his arrest, Ajaj had in his possession some manuals. Thousands of pages of manuals. Two suitcases full of them, to be exact.

Some of these manuals discussed the use of coded language. The FBI translated them and used them as exhibits during the World Trade Center trial.

One of these manuals was wrapped in an official WAMY envelope. On the envelope was an emblem: a globe emphasizing the Middle East and a hand holding a sword that pierces that globe. The inscription on the emblem said: "Military Studies in Jihad Against the Tyrants." These manuals were a detailed course in hijacking, bombing, and assassinating techniques, as well as in methods for mujahideen to mingle in the West and become inconspicuous. Cynically using Western views on human rights, the manuals detailed how captured operatives should immediately claim that they were tortured and that their confessions were forced out of them. The manuals also listed methods of selecting targets. American embassies ranked very high on that list.

One of these manuals said on its third and fourth pages:

Islamic governments have never been and will never be established through peaceful solutions and cooperative councils. They are established as they [always] have been—

by pen and gun—

by word and bullet—

by tongue and teeth

in the name of Allah, the merciful and compassionate.

Belongs to the "guest house"—

Please do not remove without permission.

Also found in Ajaj's possession was a paramilitary manual that dealt with effective ways to stop a Russian tank.

That manual had a name, and that name appeared on its cover as well as on each and every one of its pages.

The FBI translator translated the name of the booklet as *The First Element*.

The name of the manual, the name that was found in the suitcase of a man who was headed to blow up the World Trade Center, the name that the FBI translator interpreted as the First Element, the name that appeared on the cover and on each page of the booklet, the name that shook me so when I first saw it, that name was—

al-Qaeda.

IN THE FIRST WEEK of 1995, the police in Manila, the Philippines, on heightened alert a few days before the visit of Pope John Paul II, raided a small apartment shortly after a fire started in the building. The police found loads of evidence of a terrorist conspiracy, including an improvised bomb factory—chemistry textbooks, a large amount of chemicals including nitrobenzene, pipe bombs, wires, and digital Casio watches. They also found, among the numerous items seized, priests' robes, detailed maps of the pope's planned tour, passports, and a computer on which were saved some of the terrorists' plans. These included the simultaneous bombing of twelve jetliners over the Pacific Ocean. The code name for that operation was Bojinka, after the

Serbo-Croatian word for "explosion." On the computer were found numerous files detailing airplane schedules.

Although the conspirators fled the apartment as soon as the fire started, one of them, Abdel Hakim Murad, was soon apprehended. Another conspirator, Ramzi Yousef, who fled the United States immediately after the World Trade Center bombing, managed, again, to escape from the Philippines, but a few months later he was finally arrested in one of Bin Laden's guest houses in Pakistan.

From the interrogations of these two men, a blood-chilling picture emerged.

Yousef gave an affidavit that was obtained in part on the flight on which he was extradited from Pakistan to the United States. He revealed how he planned and executed the bombing in the World Trade Center. To test-run his little gadgets and handiwork before the big game, he first bombed a movie theater in Manila, and then he bombed a Philippines Airlines plane, killing one passenger. He was particularly proud of that feat because he assembled the explosives on the plane and used a Casio watch as a timer to detonate the bomb after he got off the plane. He detailed his cell's plans to assassinate the pope by bombing a tunnel as the pontiff was traveling through it, and he told of the group's plans to assassinate President Clinton. He disclosed to investigators some of the ways in which he acquired information. His knowledge of airport security, including the workings of new, sophisticated devices, he maintained, came from a special report on CNN.

Although some things he refused to disclose so that other al-Qaeda operatives would be able to employ those techniques in the future, and although some of what he said was designed to throw the investigators off track, Yousef's affidavit revealed some terrifying details. His specific choice of the World Trade Center, for instance, was inspired by his desire to topple one tower onto the other and cause a total of 250,000 civilian deaths. That number, he noted, was the number of casualties that resulted from the U.S. atomic bombing of Hiroshima and Nagasaki during World War II. He told the FBI that since the World Trade Center bombing, he had been busy instructing others in training camps in Pakistan near the Afghan border in the use of explosives. Finally, he told the story of Murad, his friend since childhood, who'd traveled to the United States in 1992 to continue his training as a pilot, a regimen Murad began in Qatar.

Murad, too, gave a statement. He said that when Yousef found out that he was planning to visit the United States, he'd encouraged him to scout out potential targets during that 1992 trip. This is exactly what Murad did; he drove from Florida to California, from Texas to Washington, D.C., and eventually he came up with a list. That list included a large number of bridges and nuclear facilities—and, of course, the World Trade Center, where Murad made sure to take some photos for his scrapbook. Before there was nothing left to photograph.

So Murad would choose the targets, and Yousef would blow them up. They rendezvoused in Pakistan shortly after the World Trade Center bombing in 1993, and after planning future activities, they decided to go to the Philippines. They, and Yousef's uncle, the third arm of that al-Qaeda cell, a man named Khalid Sheikh Mohammed. There, in the Philippines, these three men came up with the Bojinka plan. And then they thought of something even more outrageous.

FBI agents summarized the interview with Murad: "What the subject [Murad] had in his mind is that he will board any American commercial aircraft pretending to be an ordinary passenger. Then he will hijack said aircraft, control its cockpit and dive it into the CIA headquarters. There will be no bomb or any explosive that he will use in the execution of the plan. It is simply a suicidal mission that he is very much willing to execute."

Sounds horrifically familiar, doesn't it? Murad planned to break into the cockpit, and with the flying skills he'd acquired in the United States, he'd crash the jet into the CIA building. The FBI knew, six years before 9-11, that this idea was in the heads of the terrorists who already tried once to topple the World Trade Center.

Murad was in custody in 1995. Later that year, Yousef was arrested, too. But Khalid Sheikh Mohammed, the third conspirator, was never found, and he never forgot the plans he discussed with his comrades, either. While the FBI buried any official concerns about those plans—

good old ostrich technique again—Khalid Sheikh Mohammed, currently the most wanted al-Qaeda member save for Bin Laden himself, revitalized and improved the original idea, making it a reality in the shape of the 9-11 disaster.

IN 1996, the FBI initiated, for the first time ever, an investigation of al-Qaeda. Whether it was triggered by Bin Laden's expulsion from Sudan and his move to Afghanistan that year, or the arrest of the Philippines cell the year before, or other reasons, the Bureau had finally decided to take action against the terrorist organization. That year, the Bureau began following Wadih al-Hage as a suspect in the al-Qaeda investigation. Indeed, he was a most reasonable choice.

Al-Hage was a Lebanese Christian who converted to Islam and married April Ray, an American citizen from Arizona. She, too, was a convert. They met through a newspaper ad, and her mother arranged their wedding. After they wedded, al-Hage moved to Arizona, where he became a member of the Islamic Center in Tucson. He spent a considerable amount of time traveling to Pakistan, Afghanistan, and the Sudan. He also grew increasingly involved with Maktab, and with al-Qaeda. In 1992, al-Hage took the position of Bin Laden's personal secretary in the Sudan.

In 1994, al-Hage moved from Sudan to Nairobi, Kenya. Within two years the FBI began following him, suspecting that his ties to Bin Laden were more than just "legitimate business." His phone lines were tapped and he was put under constant surveillance. His wife, who knew that al-Hage worked for Bin Laden, had suspected that their phones were bugged. While on the phone, al-Hage used to speak to her in codes. One time he asked her to send "ten green papers."

"Green papers?" she wondered. "You mean money?"

An upset al-Hage replied sarcastically, "Thank you very much. That's only for you. Nobody else is listening."

One time Ray was under the impression that she overheard voices coming out of their TV set, saying, "This is it. This is the line. . . . Yes, yes, is he Arab or English?" She attributed this incident to a careless wiretapping job.

In early 1997, in a joint operation with local authorities, the FBI raided al-Hage's house in Kenya, a short time after he returned from a meeting with Bin Laden in Afghanistan. Among the items the FBI confiscated were telephone books, letters, and computers. The telephone books revealed that al-Hage was up close and personal with a very large number of people who turned out, at one point or another, to be involved in terrorist activities, including one man who had contact with members of the al-Qaeda Hamburg cell that carried out the 9-11 attacks.

One of the letters found in al-Hage's house was marked "Top Secret." It was supposedly a report sent to "the officials in the administration," the latter meaning the chiefs of al-Qaeda. The first bullet in this report, titled "Abdel-Sabbur brings to light the new policy," talked about "the status of the young men and the Hajj and that they were fine and he received from him the trusts. . . . The new policy is . . . to prepare 300 activists before the arrival of the guest."

Abdel-Sabbur was al-Hage's alias. The Hajj: Bin Laden. The trusts: Money. The new policy: Revival of the military activism in Somalia. The guest: Local authorities and the FBI. As for the FBI, Bin Laden and his deputies called it "the Food and Beverage Industry." How ironic.

The moment I laid eyes on that letter I realized it was coded. The FBI, too, was supposed to be well aware of the existence of coded language. In fact, some of these translations were actually used as government exhibits in al-Hage's trial a few years later. After the 1993 World Trade Center bombing, the FBI reviewed telephone conversations that were recorded between Yousef and the imprisoned Ajaj. The two had used cooking and various names of vegetables as codes while planning the 1993 attack. The FBI knew for years that foods and cooking were codes for explosives and even presented these codes as exhibits in the World Trade Center bombing trial in 1995. But the FBI didn't make the connection between the 1993 World Trade Center bombing, al-Qaeda, and the plot to bomb the U.S. embassies in East Africa. The lesson the FBI learned about the codes was long forgotten less than four years after it was learned.

The report continued to talk about engineers (experts in demolition), communication (explosives), and "the best ways to go to the regions lower of Jubbah, south of Kenya," meaning potential routes of entry into Dar es-Salaam from Kenya or Somalia. The terrorists, it was discovered after the fact, tried out these routes several times before they traveled them with the explosives. Then the letter detailed the expenses in purchasing the "food" (explosives) for the planned bombing. Even I, a novice in encrypted messages, could see that the letter showed that something big was "cooking."

The letter wasn't the only thing the FBI had obtained from the raid on al-Hage's house.

On al-Hage's hard drive the FBI had found an e-mail that mentioned Bin Laden's declaration of war on America. The e-mail talked about "the agency" (al-Qaeda) rearranging for the future, meaning militarizing the Africa cell; this was the main message al-Hage brought back with him from his meeting with "the director," Usama Bin Laden, in Afghanistan.

The six-page, single-spaced e-mail continued: "The fact of these matters and others leave us no choice but to ask ourselves are we ready for that big clandestine battle? Did we take the necessary measures to avoid having one of us fall in the trap? Knowing we were counting on Allah's blessing with our limited resources."

Oh my God, how more obvious could things get? I thought. How could anyone have missed that? They were preparing for the "big clandestine battle," in so many words!

Then, toward the end of the e-mail: "Brother, I completed the first and second barakah [blessing], but since we agreed to keep in touch through discs, I typed you the most important items—the third and the last. Lastly, my regards to all the engineers. . . ."

Blessing: Specific stages of the planned attack. Two down, two to go. Chilling.

The e-mail, found by the FBI on al-Hage's personal computer in 1997, is now believed by the Bureau to have been written by Haroun Fazil, the man who orchestrated the embassy bombing. Fazil is currently on the FBI's "most wanted" list for his role in the embassy bombings, charged with twelve counts of murder, one for each American killed in the attack.

In 1997, after his house in Kenya was raided, al-Hage returned to the United States, to Arlington, Texas, with his wife and their seven children. The FBI continued to monitor him very carefully there, including wiretapping his phone and maintaining round-the-clock surveillance on him. Shortly after his move to the United States, on September 24, 1997, he was summoned to testify before a grand jury regarding his ties to Bin Laden.

In 1998, a year after al-Hage's house in Kenya was raided, two massive explosions in Kenya and Tanzania shook these East African states and took 224 innocent lives.

Wadih al-Hage was convicted for the embassy bombings on more counts than any of the other terrorists in that plot. The material used to convict him included evidence that the FBI obtained by surveillance, as well as the items raided in al-Hage's Kenya house. Such as the letter and the e-mail.

Material that the FBI held on to without action for a year.

Material that was sufficient to convict the murderer in court, yet was deemed insufficient by the Bureau to act preemptively against the plotters they were keeping under surveillance. In spite of the massive amount of clues, some of which cried, loud and clear, "Beware of an attack!" the tragedy was not prevented.

There was even more to it. The FBI knew, from Yousef's affidavit, that after the World Trade Center bombing he went to Pakistan and gave ten-day basic courses and twenty-day "expert" courses in the use of explosives. Yousef said that in the month before he arrived, sixty men were trained there; during his stay, he taught seventy others; and some sixty others were scheduled for the next course. Imagine how many experts in destruction were trained there. . . . Where did all of them go? Did they, too, become car dealers? Where are they now, and what are they up to these days? Shouldn't the FBI have made that calculation when they received that information from Yousef, and shouldn't they have considered doing something about it?

There were many other warning signs. That same year, 1998, Bin

Laden issued a fatwa stating that he had declared war on America. Then an intelligence tip was given to the CIA about certain terrorist plans of a charity linked to Bin Laden, the al-Haramain Foundation. Nine Arab suspects were arrested and the charity's offices in Kenya were raided. Since the material found in the foundation's files did not include a bomb plot, the CIA didn't even interview the suspects and dropped the investigation.

So the FBI starts a comprehensive investigation into Bin Laden in 1996. Good move. The agency chooses a suspect, Wadih al-Hage. Better move still. The suspect, as it turns out after the bombing, is indeed their man and therefore the perfect choice for surveillance. Great move. The FBI follows him very closely, and then agents raid his house and confiscate material that convicts the terrorist for his crime. A near perfect move. But then the FBI runs out of moves.

The information was there. The calls, the meetings with Bin Laden, the letters, the e-mails, the frequent trips, the coded language. All the hints and clues and signs and evidence that were needed.

One thing was missing, though, for the FBI agents to be able to make their final move and put their hands on the terrorists.

The crime was not yet committed.

When the embassies *were* attacked, as soon as the crime *was* committed, the FBI moved swiftly, arrested al-Hage, and brought him and some of the other guilty parties—the ones the agents could locate, at least—to justice. With all the evidence, the FBI could easily enable federal prosecutors to prove al-Hage's role in the bombing, in spite of the defense's claims that al-Hage's loyalties lay with America, not with Bin Laden.

But nothing was done—or, putting the best face on it, not enough was done—to prevent the loss of life in Kenya and Tanzania.

The FBI, as was its policy, refused to act before the crime was committed. It failed to properly use the information that could have been used to stop the murderers before they embarked on their deadly mission.

AS THE EMBASSY BOMBING TRIAL proceeded in New York, I followed its transcripts daily. In February 2001 I read that the government presented manuals as part of its exhibits. These were found in the Manchester, England, home of Khalid al-Fawwaz, one of the terrorists who was indicted for the bombings. On these manuals were drawings of a globe pierced by a sword.

The government presented these manuals as "never before seen."

But I knew I'd seen them before. Such an emblem is not easily forgotten. I went to my folders on the 1993 World Trade Center bombing, and sure enough, they were the same Maktab manuals that were found in Ajaj's luggage.

The same manuals that the government didn't take seriously for five years. Not after the 1993 World Trade Center bombing, not after the 1995 plot in Manila, not even after the 1998 bombing of the embassies did the government make the connection.

During the embassy bombings trial I learned another interesting fact. The name Tariq Hamdi came up in regard to a certain satellite phone. I recognized Hamdi's name at once, from the PIJ investigation. Yes, Sami al-Arian again. Hamdi was on the board of trustees for the Islamic Community of Tampa Bay, a mosque in Florida that was run by Sami, his brother-in-law Mazen al-Najjar, and Ramadan Abdallah Shallah, the current secretary-general of PIJ. Hamdi was also heavily involved with WISE and ICP. In 1990, he and Sami even shared the same post office box in Tampa.

At the trial, an employee of O'Gara Satellite Networks testified that an American citizen named Ziyad Khalil purchased a $7,500 INMARSAT satellite phone in March 1998. Khalil returned in May of that year to buy some accessories for the phone. This time, however, he asked O'Gara to send his purchase to a Mr. Tariq Hamdi at 933 Park Avenue, Herndon, Virginia.

What was the deal with that phone? It turned out that ABC News was seeking a personal interview with Bin Laden in 1998. They contacted Khalid al-Fawwaz, Bin Laden's aide in Britain. Al-Fawwaz referred them to a Mr. Tariq Hamdi in Washington. ABC then wrote a letter addressed to Mohammed Atef—Bin Laden's senior military commander—as a follow-up request for the interview. The letter referred to their previous communications through Hamdi, whom

Atef, it seemed, knew well. When the interview was set up, Hamdi traveled with the ABC News crew to Afghanistan. On May 17, 1998, upon his arrival in Pakistan, Hamdi faxed a personal message to al-Fawwaz telling him that they'd arrived safely and that things were going according to plan. *What* plan? Ziyad Khalil bought the phone. It was a special purchase for Usama Bin Laden himself. He then bought the battery, but there was a problem getting it easily to Afghanistan. What better way to do so than to have ABC News arrange—and *pay for*—Hamdi's trip, enabling him to deliver this battery personally?

So what's the big deal? you may ask. So what if Hamdi delivered some battery to Bin Laden?

The big deal is that this specific battery powered the satellite phone Bin Laden used to personally give the order to blow up the embassies in Kenya and Tanzania.

The big deal is that a man who worked with Sami al-Arian made the embassy bombings possible, with an able assist from ABC News.

IN THE DELIVERY ROOM, I wiped the milk off Shirley's tiny lips and put her in her bassinet. If she continued to be like this, I thought, bringing her up would be a piece of cake. Leo and I would soon learn that her first few days, when she only ate and slept, were nothing but a cunning deception. Soon she'd become her mother's daughter—and make me finally understand how my mother must have felt when she was chasing a young me around the house.

I began wondering why Leo and the kids hadn't arrived yet. It was past eleven P.M., and according to my calculations they should have been here by now. I looked at Batterjee's book, but I couldn't bring myself to pick it up again. It was too powerful, sinister, and disturbing. I knew that if I started reading it again, I'd never be able to fall asleep that night. I needed the rest, almost twenty hours after the delivery, and I decided to leave the book till after I'd slept.

I couldn't help but worry why they weren't here yet. Such is a mother's destiny; any minuscule thing out of the ordinary and all the alarm bells immediately go off. Maybe they were simply stuck in traffic? While waiting, I decided to call Max and tell him about my discovery. Batterjee's book would star in many an investigation, I knew, and I wanted to share my enthusiasm with my boss.

When I looked at my phone, I realized why Leo hadn't called me to tell me they were running late. After I'd hung up with John Canfield, I'd turned it off and forgotten to turn it back on. Indeed, there was a message from Leo. He said that the graduation went longer than planned and that they were on their way. According to his message, they were due any minute now. I called Max. He warmly congratulated me, we spoke a little, and then I told him all about the book.

He didn't see why I was making such a big deal out of it.

"But Max, can't you understand? This is a one of a kind! It's Bin Laden, in his own words, and it tells the whole al-Qaeda story from the beginning! Everyone's there, him, Azzam, Julaidan, Khalifa, all of them! Their beginning, their biographies! Max, it's big, it's enormous!"

He still didn't get why I thought this book was so great.

He wasn't the only one who didn't get it, either. Shortly after I returned to the office, a few days after the delivery, I called the White House and told them about the book. I explained what a crucial piece of evidence it was. Told them it was written in 1991, by the Saudis, when Bin Laden wasn't a dirty word yet, and it was aimed at recruiting more mujahideen. But the White House people showed very little interest. I didn't give up. I translated important parts of the book and gave it to them again. Again, nothing. When I inquired, they said they'd forwarded it but didn't know what had become of it.

After 9-11, after BIF (which together with WAMY published Batterjee's *The Arab Volunteers in Afghanistan*) was raided and its head, Arnaout, indicted and arrested, I was finally called by the Justice Department and asked to give them my copy of the book. Suddenly someone remembered it again, the book that had the detailed histories of Arnaout and his many associates. Like Mohammed Bayazid, whom the government accused of trying to obtain uranium to develop nuclear weapons for Bin Laden. Or Mohammed Jamal Khalifa, Bin Laden's brother-in-law, who was linked to the 1993 World Trade Center bombing and the Bojinka plan. Abu Talha, al-Qaeda's financier in Europe, who is believed to have helped pay for 9-11 and was arrested in Spain a few months after the attack. And many, many others, including Arnaout himself. All of them, the hard core of al-Qaeda, the fighters from the days of al-Masada. The book was practically the *Who's Who of al-Qaeda*. Yet the government took interest in the book only after 9-11, two years after I'd first discovered it and offered it to them. No wonder that government agents told me I knew more about al-Qaeda than they did.

Leo and the kids still hadn't arrived, and at that point I was really worried. What was taking them so long? An uneasy thought began creeping into my head, and the harder I tried to shake it off, the more unsettled I became.

I remembered how years ago, back in Israel, Leo was on his way from work; I was expecting him to come home and take the kids to their music lessons. He was late, and I knew something was wrong, and then I got a call from the hospital. He'd been in an accident, they told me, and they wanted me to come. Although I knew he was alive, I didn't know what to think as I was speeding toward the hospital.

We only learned what happened a few days later, from the police investigation. Leo himself couldn't remember any of it; a decade later, he still doesn't. It was nighttime and raining, and a truck driver who had just finished stealing boxloads of oranges from an orchard tried to sneak his loaded truck, headlights turned off, right onto the highway. Leo must not have seen it at all, coming over a small hill, when he crashed into the truck. The big American car he so insisted on driving saved his life, but he didn't escape unharmed. When I entered his room in the hospital, my heart pounding, I looked at him lying on the bed, a young doctor by his side. I was relieved, grateful, because he looked fine to me, and then he turned his head. I couldn't hold in the shriek that leapt from my throat. The left side of his face was battered, black-and-blue and covered with torn flesh and blood, and its dimensions were of a good-size watermelon. His left eye protruded like that of those terribly ugly goldfish. Leo's face was the face of a monster.

It took months of patience and surgical procedures and dental work for Leo to look like his old self again. It was also evident from his CT scan and MRI that he had major bleeding in his brain. The doctors didn't know what effect this would have, but I could tell he was different after the accident.

I never stopped loving him through all of that. He was always my husband, the father of my children, my love. And although his face was distorted, his soul was unchanged.

This dark cloud of thoughts was immediately blown away by the heartwarming breeze of their arrival. Leo and the boys rushed in on their toes, kissed and hugged me, and inspected Shirley as if she were some present sent to them from heaven. They told me of their tremendous success at the recital. Then Jordan and Leo told me about Jordan's speech. The school, children and parents, had been riveted by it; they'd laughed and clapped and wiped away tears. In his speech Jordan summarized the three years in which he'd transformed from a foreigner and an outsider to one of the most popular kids in school. When he finished, when the applauding audience finally sat down, his principal told everyone how Jordan had had a busy day, hurrying from the recital in the museum to the graduation, nearly missing it. Then Jordan took the microphone again and said:

"Oh, yeah, and also my baby sister was born early this morning. . . ."

The crowd went crazy.

This was a terrific year in all respects. The boys were prospering in every possible way. They'd been on TV for their piano playing, even performing with Billy Joel and other stars. Leo and I felt like teenagers, falling in love all over again. We were both doing well in our jobs. We'd bought a house, and now we had a baby. That night, my hospital room was filled with enough love and joy for ten large families to use for ten years.

Leo took the kids home. I began to fall asleep, and thoughts raced through my head. It all swirled around: the delivery, the recital, Leo's accident, the World Trade Center, the embassies, the FBI, Batterjee's book . . .

As my head was growing heavier, I thought of Leo and the monstrous face he wore for a few months, and then his face blended with that of the young, tall, soft-spoken Saudi man, sitting with his long beard and his turban, making plans to confront the infidels. Then my thoughts wafted to the other bearded men in *kuffiyehs,* gathered around the tall man in al-Masada, and then it was the imams, and the Muslim scholars, and the Saudi bankers, and the charities, and before I succumbed to a sweet, rescuing sleep, it suddenly cleared up, and I knew.

These mild-mannered, rich men, hiding behind the veil of charitable work, sitting in a fancy office in Virginia or a palace in Saudi Arabia while inciting jihad and paying for it—

They are the face of the monster.

‹‹‹

CHAPTER 9

Campaign Money

AS PART OF its investigation, the Tampa task force working on
Sami al-Arian and the Palestinian Islamic Jihad, PIJ, decided to go to
Israel to collect evidence. The missing data were to be the last pieces in
the PIJ puzzle: the money trail from the United States to PIJ and its
activists in the Middle East.

To prevent terrorists from easily moving funds into the country,
Israel scrutinizes all the money coming into the state as well as the
West Bank and Gaza. Therefore, terrorist organizations such as PIJ
cannot open and maintain bank accounts in Israel or in the Territories.
They have to devise methods to breach Israel's blockade. One way is
through foreign bank accounts. Fat'hi Shikaki, the head of PIJ who
was assassinated in Malta, maintained a bank account in Switzerland.
So did Sami's charity, ICP. The Tampa task force going to Israel hoped
to learn how these accounts were used to transfer funds and whether
they were interconnected.

There were other methods; one was rather ingenious. It was pio-
neered in the late 1990s by Hamas, which founded a bank named al-

Aqsa and opened branches of it throughout the Middle East. Al-Aqsa made an affiliation agreement with an American bank that had a branch in Tel Aviv: Citibank. Money could be deposited in any al-Aqsa branch, and anyone could withdraw that money from the Citibank branch in the heart of Israel. A simple and brilliant way to bypass the Israelis. And then there always was the good old system of couriers. Risky, but it worked most of the time.

The task force knew that Sami raised funds for PIJ. In 1995, a few days after a double suicide bombing by PIJ that killed eighteen people, he wrote a fund-raising letter referring to "two Mujahideen martyred for the sake of Allah" and requested donations "so that operations such as these can continue." What the task force wanted to find out was the route the money traveled from the United States to the hands of PIJ activists in the Middle East. The group therefore decided to go to Israel and talk to experts in the Israeli intelligence and academic communities.

This was the trip that John Canfield had called me about in the hospital, but I'd been hearing about it since before I was even pregnant with Shirley. It had been delayed repeatedly. First the Justice Department wouldn't approve the trip. Then it wouldn't approve the date. Another time it wouldn't approve either. Almost two years after it was conceived, the trip was authorized for August, but following my advice to John it was postponed again, this time until late September.

A few days after I had Shirley I was back in the office. The first thing I started to work on was John's itinerary. I could never have imagined that the trip, which I hoped would close the lid on Sami's investigation, would instead cause a crisis in my relationship with John and result in his removal from the case, in his near sacking, and in his transfer to another country. Not even in my worst nightmares had I imagined that the trip, planned to be the ultimate information-gathering tool for building a case against Sami in court, would cause tremendous harm to the investigation.

John told me that the FBI had scheduled meetings for the task force and asked whether I could help him arrange additional meetings with people I considered experts in the field. I immediately began making phone calls. To the Israeli Department of Justice, to intelligence and terrorism experts, to journalists, to high-ranking police officials, to academic experts—including some of my old professors at Tel Aviv University. Because of the time zone difference between the two countries, many of the calls took place either very early in the morning or late at night. I'd wake three or four times a night to nurse Shirley, and in between I'd make phone calls to Israel.

I then spent hours telling John about the people and organizations I was arranging for the task force to meet. I briefed him on each and every one of them and told him what they knew and what information he needed to extract from them. One such man, for example, a journalist who'd retired from the intelligence services, published a book in which he wrote a detailed report on the role of PIJ's Tampa cell. I translated the pertinent chapter for John and told him what information this author could add to the investigation. I gave him a list of questions for each of the people the task force planned to meet.

Four days after I'd started to work on the trip, the itinerary was jam-packed with meetings from early morning until late at night. Had these arrangements been undertaken through bureaucratic channels, they would never have been done on time. Had John tried to get the Department of Justice to make formal requests for each of these meetings—requests that would then be sent to Justice's Israeli counterpart—and then waited for approval and official coordination of the requests, nobody would have met anyone. Each of those formal requests takes months to get approved. So I made the initial contact with the experts in Israel. After the Israelis agreed to see the task force, John set dates for meetings with them. Only then did he send the formal requests through the proper channels, with the date, time, and the fax number in Israel attached to the request, so that the approvals could be immediately communicated to—and rubber-stamped by— the Israelis who'd already preapproved the meetings. John delivered a finished itinerary of the trip to the Department of Justice on a silver platter.

A formal letter was sent from the Israeli Department of Justice confirming that its officials were expecting "the delegation headed by

John Canfield." To me, that was obvious. John *was* the head of that delegation. Within the U.S. government, only John and one other agent knew Sami and PIJ inside and out. That other expert was Barry Carmody, the FBI agent who'd come to our office that first time with John. Barry had been part of the Tampa task force and he'd worked with John for years. But Barry, who had reached retirement age around the time Sami's organizations were first raided in the mid-1990s, had been taken off the investigation—and off payroll—just as the investigation was reaching its peak. Several new FBI agents were put on the case instead, and naturally they knew absolutely nothing about Sami or PIJ. So as far as I was concerned, John was indeed the head of the delegation. The FBI, however, thought otherwise.

A couple of months before the trip, the Bureau decided to increase its presence in the investigation—and on the trip. The FBI felt that the investigation was gaining momentum and getting closer to a court filing: John and Barry had drafted indictments already. The FBI decided it was time to take over. The Bureau assigned a new director to the task force, a man who knew nothing about PIJ, and added a good number of agents to the trip to Israel. According to protocol, the FBI office in Tel Aviv, located in the American embassy there, was in charge of coordinating the trip and the meetings with the Israelis. The Tel Aviv office did coordinate some of the meetings, but when its agents heard that the delegation was referred to as "John Canfield's," they hit the roof. Their colleagues back here were furious, too.

Then they realized that I, a civilian, was involved in the planning of the trip. My name kept coming up in each meeting between the task force and the Israelis. The FBI went berserk. The agents in the Tel Aviv office refused to give the task force, meaning Canfield, any relevant information.

It didn't help that some of the meetings were a disaster, too. While John was off on a side trip to Jordan to visit some experts there, the FBI agents stayed in Israel and asked some of the experts I'd lined up to meet with them again. In these meetings, in John's absence, the FBI agents quickly revealed their ignorance.

Some of the Israelis called me, outraged. One such expert, Gad, who'd shared information with John and then sat again for hours with the FBI agents upon their request, called me.

"What the hell is going on? Why are these agents you sent me so ignorant?"

Although I knew what he was talking about, I asked, "What do you mean?"

"It's this bunch of rookies that came to see me after we'd met with John," he said. "I sat there for hours, explaining everything to them like a kindergarten teacher!" I'd never known Gad to react like that.

"They asked me who Bashir Nafi was. Nafi! Who is assigned to investigate PIJ and doesn't know who Nafi is? They were so clueless! What's the deal with John? Why aren't his colleagues people who know something about this?"

I had no answer. In fact, at that point I didn't know how bad things really were.

A few days after the delegation returned from Israel, Jerry, the new FBI man assigned to lead the investigation, summoned John to his office. Abruptly, he told him, "The FBI has officially taken over this investigation. This is not a task force anymore. This is now my investigation. From now on, you are assigned to me. You will report directly to me. You will do exactly what I tell you to do. You will no longer embark on any individual investigation relating to Sami. At this point, as you are with Customs, you will only deal with PIJ finances, nothing else. On that matter, too, you will report to me and me alone." John just looked at him. Why should he—the only remaining government expert on Sami—report to this greenhorn? So he replied, in the most direct manner, "F— you."

He wadded up the pile of paper that Jerry had given him, threw it in his face, and walked out of the office.

Shortly thereafter, John's superior from Customs called him. He knew his employee well. He realized how much John knew about Sami and how good he was at what he did.

"There isn't much I can do, John," he told him. "They've taken over the investigation. Completely. There's no way we can fight it—

this is counterterrorism, and that's their field. They want a report from you on everything you've found in the course of the investigation, and you've got to surrender it to them. There's no choice."

The FBI assigned some twenty new agents to the investigation, none of whom knew the subject. And at the point when the indictments John and Barry drafted were ready to go, the FBI set the investigation back years, flushing almost seven years of hard work down the drain.

The Israelis were furious. They blamed this turnover in agents for hampering the investigation. They said the information they'd shared should have been more than sufficient to secure a conviction—wielded correctly, that is. While John Canfield went to Israel to deepen his already comprehensive knowledge of Sami's dealings and advance the investigation, the FBI went to Israel to learn everything from scratch—and to take over the investigation.

The investigation on Sami is, formally speaking, "ongoing." In effect, the FBI's pathetic quest for fame and prestige caused it to regress to its starting point.

The trip to Israel proved that the road to hell (for John and me) is paved with good intentions.

But that wasn't the end of the story.

IN THE MONTH after his face-off with Jerry, John and I continued to work together and talk as usual. John said he wasn't going to take that conversation too seriously. He still wanted to work, promote the investigation, and nail Sami al-Arian.

One day I paged him and he didn't call back. That was a bit unusual, as he'd ordinarily respond promptly, but I didn't think much of it. I assumed he was busy with an investigation, or a course, or in training, something to that effect. A week later, another page. Again, no response. I still didn't think anything was amiss. I called his office and left a message. Then I sent an e-mail. Two months passed, and still no reply. He must be really busy at work, I thought.

One day Gad, the Israeli expert who'd complained about the ignorance of the FBI agents he met, called me to ask my opinion on something. During the conversation he asked me what I thought of "poor John."

"What do you mean? What happened?" I asked. I should have known something was wrong! How could I sit for two months and take John's silence lightheartedly?

"Why, I thought you knew. Haven't you heard?"

"No, what are you talking about?" I got really scared.

"He was thrown out of the investigation altogether. He's off the case."

This couldn't be happening. I paged John immediately. And again, and a few more times that day and the following.

Nothing.

Now I knew for certain that he was avoiding me. I thought that he was depressed, or even ashamed—we'd worked so hard on the investigation, and just as he was about to succeed, he was kicked off.

I kept trying to reach him. I wanted to talk to him, to try to make things easier for him.

After a few weeks of no contact, I decided to call him at home.

His wife picked up the phone.

"How is he?" I asked. "Is he okay?"

"Well, he could be better," she said kindly, "but he's hanging in there."

"Is he depressed?" I asked.

"He is not happy with the new situation, no doubt."

"Please tell him not to worry. Things always happen for a reason, even if we don't know it as they do. Things will turn out for the better."

"I hope so."

"Is he home? I was really worried, and I've been trying to reach him for quite some time now. Can I talk to him now?"

"Well . . . he's, ah, unavailable right now."

"So when could I talk to him?"

"I'm sorry, he really can't talk to you now. But please, you've got to understand that he'll call you as soon as he'll be able to."

So he'd call me as soon as his mood improved.

For someone with my ability to read between the lines, I was being remarkably thick. One Friday, not long after I'd spoken to John's wife, Eli, an Israeli investigator who worked with him on the Sami al-Arian investigation, called me. He said that he and some of his colleagues were planning to come to the United States in a few days and asked whether I was interested in meeting and exchanging information.

"Yeah, sounds like a good idea." I added, "I only wish John were in a better mental state; otherwise he'd come meet you too."

"Mental state? There's nothing wrong with his mental state."

I couldn't be more perplexed. "How d'you know?"

"Well, I spoke with him two days ago. Cheerful as ever, he is."

"But," I sputtered, "I've been trying to reach him for ages, and he never called me back!"

"I thought you knew," Eli said. "He's not allowed to talk to you."

"Not allowed?" I *still* didn't understand. "His wife said that?"

"Not his wife!" Eli must have thought that I was losing it. "The jerks from the FBI! They forbade him from speaking with you. Not only about Sami, but in general. John's under investigation because of what happened between you two."

"*What?*"

"Yeah, they are questioning whether he gave you classified material."

"What are you talking about?"

"As far as I know, some country—not Israel—contacted the FBI, and the next thing the FBI did was to find out where you'd obtained certain information. They think John gave it to you. So they forbade him to speak to you."

Only then, after two long months, did it finally come to me. I'd refused to see the obvious. But now it was as clear as the Manhattan skyline on a bright, sunny, winter day.

IN MID-2000, a few months after my briefing on the Khalil al-Deek case at the White House, I faxed my contacts in Jordan and told them about the investigation and my findings. I asked whether they were interested.

They were. They really were. They asked for anything I could give them. So I e-mailed them, told them about Charity Without Borders, about Hisham Diab, about Ashour, and explained why I had reason to believe that large sums of money had been transferred to Jordan, and why and how these transfers might have been linked to terrorist activities. As al-Deek was in their custody, the Jordanians were thrilled to get that information. I told them that this was as far as I had been able to go with my investigation, but I said that the American government might have more information. I suggested that they contact the U.S. authorities.

They did.

They contacted the FBI.

As soon as the formal Jordanian request was submitted, someone in the FBI headquarters flew off the handle. My name was on the Jordanian fax. The FBI couldn't understand how I had information on al-Deek, Diab, and Ashour that it didn't. The agency assumed that the information had leaked from the government to me. The FBI just couldn't accept that I—a civilian, a nobody in their eyes—could give the Jordanians such superb leads. They couldn't understand the main point: that I'd obtained such information from public records and that I'd given information to the government—to John Canfield, in this case—and not the other way around. For the FBI, it was inconceivable that I could obtain important information without access to their vast "intel."

Worse yet, my name was already known at FBI headquarters. Some of the FBI agents who were reassigned to the Tampa task force came from the Washington, D.C., headquarters. They'd heard my name countless times during their trip to Israel. They heard from Eli that I knew more about Sami than anyone else; while briefing them, Eli urged them to collaborate with me on Sami's investigation. The FBI also knew that John and I had worked on putting the trip together. By the time the Jordanians, at my suggestion, called them, they'd heard my name one time too many. After the FBI agents were briefed in Israel, the Bureau realized that it had a great case on Sami and decided to take over the investigation of him. It now saw a golden opportunity to get rid of two obstacles in one shot: John Canfield and me.

When I'd first learned from Eli about the investigation, I panicked. How *was* the FBI investigating me? I knew its techniques. Phone tapping, surveillance, questioning . . . they don't go to databases, they don't read old newspapers. Was I being followed? Listened to? Could I safely use my phone without them listening? Maybe my office phones were also tapped? The bastards! Terrorists and criminals are running around unimpeded, and the FBI is investigating me! I've never asked for anything in return for my information. Not money, not documents, nothing. All I did was share, free of charge or obligation, my expertise and knowledge, because I wanted to stop terrorism. It infuriated me that while I was being investigated by the FBI, the good old boys from my millennium investigation, Ashour and Diab, were free as birds.

Not only was the FBI unable to find any of the leads that I'd found on Charity Without Borders; not only did it fail to possess one-thousandth of my knowledge on the relevant issues, such as the Islamic Center of Tucson; not only did the FBI knock on doors in Anaheim, California, and ask the residents if they knew Bin Laden, even after I'd given the White House information that would have allowed the agents to hone their investigation—the only terrorists in this plot that the Bureau could manage to investigate were John Canfield and me!

After the request for information and collaboration came from Jordanian intelligence, the FBI should have taken their hats off, acknowledged the potential of obtaining help from me, called, and asked to meet with me—just as the White House and dozens of other government agencies did, and do. Moreover, the Bureau should have jumped on the opportunity to work in collaboration with the Jordanians, who would have shed additional light on the investigation.

Instead, the FBI immediately destroyed any chance of collaboration with a friendly country. It also destroyed my ties with the Jordanians. After this, I e-mailed the Jordanians a few times, but they never replied. They'd probably gotten from the FBI the same instructions that John did.

Suddenly one day, John called.

I was stunned.

"John!" I almost screamed, "What, is it over? Can we talk again? Are they done with the investigation?" I was so relieved!

"Heck, no, nothing's over," John said. "I'm still not allowed to talk to you. As far as I know, they'll never tell me that it's over and I can talk to you again. They only let you know when they put you under investigation; they never bother to tell you when it's over. So to all of them who're listening now, and I know they do, I say, Screw you. I'm sick and tired of it. As far as they're concerned, they'd want us never to talk again. So they can go to hell."

I was surprised, but he made perfect sense. "Aren't you worried?" I asked.

"What else could they do to me, ha? Kick me out? Too late, they already kicked me out of the biggest investigation I was ever involved with. What else could they do to me—put me in jail?"

"John, whatever happens, happens for the best," I told him. "I really believe in that. One day you'll see that you only benefited from this dirty affair. And as for the FBI, there's a saying in Arabic, *Kul kalb yijji yoomo.* Meaning, 'Each dog's day will come.' "

We spoke for almost two hours. We had so much to catch up on.

"What about the wiretapping?" I asked him.

"What about it? That's the most pathetic part about this whole FBI investigation. They're listening to us, but what can they do with it? Do you think a judge gave them a warrant for that tapping? They're listening in—right, you freaks?—but it's intel information. And you know what they'll do with that."

I knew exactly. They'd do absolutely nothing.

"So tell these farts anything you want," John said. "All they can do is choke on it."

Not long afterward the FBI accused John of giving information to other civilians. One such accusation came after Gad wrote an article in which he talked about Iran's support of terrorist organizations. He mentioned a document, found in the raids on WISE, written in Egypt in 1981, describing a plan to form intelligence units in various countries and disguise them as educational organizations. A similar format to WISE. These units were designed to collect intelligence information for Iran. The FBI accused John of giving the document to Gad. John called me, upset, and said that now they'd added this to his file.

"Why do they claim it's you this time?" I asked.

"Because they know Gad and I worked together on Sami, that's why."

"But that document is in the public domain, John. Anyone can get it."

When Sami's brother-in-law Mazen al-Najjar was released from prison in 2000 (only to be arrested again and eventually deported), the INS released a large amount of information on Sami. This document that the FBI accused John of sharing illegally was among the documents made public by the INS almost two years before.

The FBI didn't have a clue as to what was out there and what wasn't. And regarding John—to date, the agency hasn't proved any wrongdoing on his part. He's clean, but he's out.

That's the power of the government. To get rid of someone, you don't really have to prove anything. A simple allegation, however unfounded, a mere suggestion of a deviation from protocol—and the blemish in the personal record is there to stay. Forever.

In any U.S. court, the accused is considered innocent until proven guilty. Terrorists and their supporters in America know their rights well, and they scream "freedom of speech" and "human rights" left, right, and center. John Canfield was accused, tried, and sentenced to exile across the Atlantic—yet his only crime was to be a good investigator.

But as far as my relationship with him was concerned, we were back to normal. He and I are still in close contact.

SURE ENOUGH, as I'd told him, John was promoted by Customs in early 2002, a few months after he was investigated. Big-time promotion. At his new level, he became eligible for a position overseas that he was interested in. He applied for it and, being the best man for the job, was chosen over the other candidates.

He called me, happier than at any other time since he'd returned from the infamous trip to Israel. He told me he was going abroad.

I wished him luck. He really deserved that promotion.

"But that's not the only reason I called," he said. "Some of my friends are throwing me a farewell party. You have to come and bring the guys from the office with you."

"Aren't you afraid that the FBI will record in your file that I attended your party?" I asked.

"Yeah, no kidding." Now he really could care less about them.

I then asked him whether he'd heard the news about Sami.

This was shortly after 9-11. Sami's name was all over the news. On September 26, 2001, he was interviewed on Fox News's *The O'Reilly Factor,* thinking, perhaps, that he'd be asked about Muslim rights and discrimination post–9-11. Instead, Bill O'Reilly grilled him on his ties to terrorism, and in particular on his relationships with Ramadan Abdallah Shallah, Tariq Hamdi, and Mazen al-Najjar. Sami denied any ties to terrorism. O'Reilly then said:

"All right. So now what we have here is you saying death to Israel. You're bringing a guy over here [Shallah] who gets paid by the good citizens of Florida and then goes back and becomes one of the lieutenants or generals of the Islamic Jihad, but you don't know nothing about it. Another guy [Tariq Hamdi] sets up an interview with Usama Bin Laden for ABC, and you don't know anything about that. You know, Doctor, it looks to me like there's something wrong down there at the University of South Florida. Am I getting—am I getting the wrong impression here?"

Sami replied: "You're getting completely wrong impression because you can pick and choose and interpret it, you know, different ways. The fact of the matter is we have been involved in intellectual-type activity. We brought dozens of people. All of them are intellectual types. You're going to get the apple—a bad apple or two, but that—if you focus on them, you get one conclusion. The fact of the matter is that we've been investigated by the FBI for many years . . ."

O'Reilly: "Correct."

Sami: "And there has been no wrongdoing whatsoever even suggested."

O'Reilly: "Well, I don't know about that. Your—your brother-in-law is going to be deported right now. I mean, it looks like he's going to get kicked out of the country, correct?"

Sami: "It has nothing to do with this."

After a similar exchange, O'Reilly summarized:

"Yeah. Well, Doctor, you know, with all due respect—I appreciate you coming on the program, but if I was the CIA I'd follow you wherever you went. I'd follow you twenty-four hours—"

Sami: "Well, you don't know me. You don't know me. You do not—"

Sami's interview on TV stirred a huge outcry, following which the university put him on paid leave. On the other hand, the university came under fire from human rights groups, which claimed that whatever opinions Sami expressed were a matter of academic freedom of speech. They said that the FBI couldn't prove that he was a terrorist; ergo, he was an honest man. Because he was tenured, the university had to make a decision, either to take him back or try to get rid of him.

A few months later the University of South Florida filed a lawsuit against Sami; that's what it had to do to be able to fire him on account of his terrorist ties. It contacted the FBI for help. The FBI didn't give any.

An attorney from the Treasury Department came to visit me in the office on some other matter a few days after the lawsuit was filed. She told me that we all needed to celebrate because of that lawsuit.

"Celebrate?" I was astounded. "Celebrate what? That you—that the government, the FBI, did nothing about him for ten years? That the FBI refused to help the university when it asked for help? That the public has to defend itself where the government failed to do its job? This is no reason for celebration. The handling of Sami's case is a disgrace!"

She was just happy that Sami was finally in trouble, and she expected anything but this response.

I wasn't finished. "If the FBI can't put together a case on Sami, it should at least have the decency to release the mountains of information it has on him, so that others—like the university—could do something useful with it."

She was abashed. She knew I was right.

But the most maddening fact about Sami al-Arian and the FBI's handling of the investigation against him became known to me only several months after that.

JOHN CANFIELD'S GOING-AWAY PARTY took place in a large, unexceptional restaurant bar located in a small shopping plaza. Some of the people at the party were familiar to me, but most I'd never seen before. I knew Barry Carmody and Kirk, the two agents who had come with John to our office that very first time. I also knew—at least from phone conversations—some of the task force's translators, who'd worked on Sami's investigation. John introduced me to a few guys and went off to talk with other guests.

At some point in the party, Barry gave a speech. He talked about the early days when he and John first started to work on the Tampa task force, how he'd had the time of his life working with him, and how he'd miss him.

And then he said something I'd heard him, and John, and many others say on numerous occasions, but I'd never really understood what it meant.

Not until a few months later.

He said that in all the years he was with the FBI, he never got used to the way the Bureau operated. "In Sami's investigation," he said, "we always got there second."

There was the time they went to a bank to subpoena Sami's and Shallah's accounts, thinking they'd had a great lead.

"That's easy," the bank manager told them. "Since we were already asked to do it by you guys a few months ago, we have everything ready on file."

Barry described how this came as a very unpleasant surprise to them. Same story when they went to the telephone company and mostly everywhere else they went during their investigation. Whatever they did, whatever they found—other government agents had already been there.

In mid-2002 I was asked to collaborate with a task force in California on an investigation of a man they'd been working on for years. They'd had difficulties building the case against this man, who was involved with Hamas and other terrorist organizations. I went to California to meet this task force. After two days of intensive briefings, the agents revealed to me over dinner something that finally connected all the dots and organized what I'd already guessed about the way the FBI operated. It gave Barry's speech at John's party a whole new meaning.

"We only wish we could reveal to you what we have on this guy," one of the agents told me. "We've got enough incriminating evidence to put the man away for the next twenty years. It's a shame we can't show you that stuff."

"So why don't you use it?" I asked. "Why do you need my help? Why, instead of taking this to court, do you so desperately need my input on him?" Intuitively, I knew what their answer would be.

"Because it's intel information. Unusable."

"Doesn't it make you feel bad to sit on such valuable information and instead of utilizing it to have to ask me to fly here, at the taxpayers' expense, and help you get what you've already got in the first place?"

"It's not us, you see. It's the FBI. They have a certain unit called FISA. Everyone calls it 'the Dark Side.' " FISA was short for Foreign Intelligence Surveillance Act. The Dark Side, I learned later, was a name invented by Barry Carmody. "They get valuable stuff, but it stays with them. All their files are in safekeeping somewhere, but they're not allowed to use them."

"So why do they bother to get this intel in the first place?" It drove me nuts. "They tap, follow, collect, collect, collect—and that's *it?*"

That was exactly what the Dark Side did. It investigated, obtained information, and . . . nothing. Its job was to get the information. Not to do anything else with it. Obtaining was as far as FISA went. But the

Dark Side also never shared its discoveries with anyone else—not even other FBI branches.

So *that* was how the FBI operated. Two FBI guys may have been sitting in adjacent offices, maybe even behind a dividing screen in the same office. They'd been working on the same investigation. One of them was with the Dark Side. He had all the intelligence material, he knew that the other agent was on the case, he knew that they were fighting the same enemy. Yet he'd never tell his fellow agent anything, never even let him know what stuff he had in his files. A terrible shame.

Around that same period I learned something else, more disturbing. The worst revelation I'd ever had on the investigation of Sami al-Arian. It seems that the investigation of Sami and his PIJ comrades didn't start in 1995, after Shallah became PIJ's secretary-general.

FISA worked on Sami for years before the formal investigation started, years before the Tampa task force was formed, years before Shallah went to Syria. The Dark Side had Sami in its sights in the very early 1990s, when Shallah moved to Tampa. The FBI was tipped off by British and Israeli intelligence forces, which suggested keeping a close eye on Shallah and on Sami. So the Dark Side did just that. More than ten years ago, they tapped Shallah's and Sami's phones and put them under surveillance. This was what Barry meant in his speech, then, when he said that someone was always there before them. Someone, no doubt, from the Dark Side.

The Dark Side intercepted and recorded the communication among Sami, Shallah, and the guys in Syria—Fat'hi Shikaki and others. These men were discussing terror attacks the way you'd discuss whether or not you should order fries with your cheeseburger. One time even the FISA agents were shocked; in one of those communications, the men in Florida discussed with PIJ's headquarters in Damascus a certain terrorist attack. Hamas publicly claimed responsibility for the attack. The PIJ operatives were all furious about it. "It is our operation," they said. "How dare they take credit for it?"

Shallah was constantly on the phone with Syria, and his phone bills to that country alone amounted to seven or eight hundred bucks' worth every month. His monthly bills often exceeded $2,000. This was just about how much he was officially earning from WISE.

What did the FBI do about it?

Pretty much—nothing.

The FBI had recorded all these conversations, but it just did nothing. It had smoking guns on Shallah and Sami years before Shallah became PIJ's leader. But as it was intel information, the FBI couldn't use it, and there was nothing it could do to change the situation. This information is probably still sitting in file cabinets in FISA's offices.

But I'll tell you what the FBI *will* do after this book is published. It'll go back and investigate John Canfield. It will accuse him of giving me this information about FISA. Poor John. He had nothing to do with this, and he never mentioned any of it to me. But the FBI will still go after him and give him a hard time. This is what the FBI does best. And John won't be the only one the FBI will investigate as a result of the information I've written in this memoir. My book will be the cause of many inquiries. Because I know that the FBI doesn't accept that there is a great deal of knowledge in the public domain. Besides, it's so much easier to investigate a government agent than it is a terrorist. I sometimes wonder about the size of *my* dossier in the FBI. Definitely much larger than that of Khalil al-Deek or Ishaq al-Farhan or Wa'el Julaidan. I have no doubt about it.

The same must have been the case with al-Deek's training camps in California. The FBI knew—or, perhaps, its Dark Side knew—and the only thing that was done with the information was saving it in a neat file. Likewise with HLF. The Bureau has been following HLF since the early 1990s, but HLF was designated a terrorist group only after 9-11. So was the investigation of Abdalhalim al-Ashqar (the hunger striker, remember?), who was followed around the clock for years, and of his charity, al-Aqsa Educational Fund. These investigations never went anywhere. And now the Dark Side was concentrating its energy and spending its resources on John and me, wasting the taxpayers' money, so that the information could end up in some obscure file in some remote drawer. An "outrage" would be too mild a word for this.

They said that new legislation, introduced in late 2002, would finally change the ability to use intel information. Maybe some of that FISA material would be put to good use at last. Maybe even in Sami's case.

And Sami . . . well, he'd probably be very proud to realize how much time, money, and resources the U.S. government had wasted on him throughout the years; in November 2002, a second FBI delegation went to Israel to obtain information on PIJ. Upon their return, rumor had it, they were finally working on indictments for Sami and his wife.

Even if Sami is eventually indicted, it will be a decade too late, and credit for the indictment will probably go to Jerry from Tampa, although it would not be his to claim.

THE MORE EXPERIENCED I became, the more the government's inability to read the map and find its way through the maze of Islamic terrorism became evident to me. This inability to combat Islamic terrorism is a result of several factors. One is an operational issue. Many investigations and court cases make little or no progress because of the incompetence and recklessness of government agents. I've given many examples, and more are coming in this and the following chapters. These agents have, many times, very little knowledge of Arabic and Islam. They work on these cases using concepts and strategies borrowed from criminal investigations, and they approach these matters in the same way they'd have investigated murders or drug deals.

But in counterterrorism, trying to rely only on intelligence information and facts related to the crime itself would barely be scratching the surface. It is insufficient to fully understand the scope of the crime, to build a robust case in court that would lead to a conviction or, most important, to prevent the next attack. What's needed here is in-depth understanding and knowledge of the reasons, the sources, the resources, the temporal and geographic progression, and the ideas behind the crime.

This is where I come in and where I can be of help. The government failed, big-time, with al-Qaeda, not just because the agencies didn't cooperate with one another and neglected to consider the warning signs, but mostly because they didn't learn al-Qaeda (and its predecessor, Maktab al-Khidamat) thoroughly. However, investigations where the government sought the advice of experts like me, in order to obtain in-depth understanding, frequently met with success.

Finally, there's the fierce competition among agencies. Instead of collaborating with the mutual aim of hunting down terrorists, some agencies are obsessed with prestige and credit. Who gets the gold star for the case is the main driving force. 9-11 is the ultimate, devastating evidence of their failures. As Richard Shelby, top Republican on the Senate Intelligence Committee, bluntly put it, "If a lot of information from the FBI, CIA, NSA and Immigration had been put together at a central place, they may have thwarted the attack of September 11."

Because of stories like the California State attorney who called me for information that the Justice Department wouldn't give her, and Loraine, the INS attorney who'd received almost no help from the FBI in her investigation of Sami, and others I will tell about later, I find it very hard to believe the promises being made nowadays of reforms and collaboration and rearrangement in the major law enforcement agencies. I've heard this tune before.

Among the government agencies I deal with, the FBI is the most notorious for withholding information. The agents of the task force in California, who told me about the Dark Side, told me how they had to struggle with their FBI counterparts. Like many other task forces, theirs, too, had an FBI agent on the team. At every staff meeting, the Customs agents would pull out documents they'd prepared in the course of their research and distribute them to all the members of the team. As would the INS, IRS, and other representatives of government agencies. But when the others would ask the FBI agent for his input, he'd pull out his notebook, open it carefully five inches from his face so that no one would be able to peek in it, check over his shoulders, and say, regarding one fact or another:

"Yes, we are well aware of that, and we certainly have valuable information on that matter."

"So what is it?" the others would ask. "What is it that you know"

"Can't tell. It's classified."

At some point, these agents told me, they got fed up and began hiding information from him in return. They even stopped notifying him of their meetings and arranged them so that he'd be unable to attend. And all this is happening long after 9-11.

Having said all that, I must add that I did work with a number of government agents who wanted to do the right thing. In INS, Customs, Treasury, NSC, even some in the FBI. A good percentage of agents I've worked with certainly have had their hearts in the right place. Whenever I was asked to help, I did my best to teach them what I knew. I saw it as my responsibility to show the interested parties the way.

This, of course, had to be behind the scenes. I couldn't be revealed, nor would I ever get credit for what I did. But that's the name of the game I play.

THE RALLY WAS scheduled to start at eleven A.M., and it was now noon, but I wasn't worried that I'd missed it. At this point in my career, I was experienced enough to know that even an hour late was too early to show up; these things hardly ever started on time. Leisurely and self-assuredly, I woke that morning, dressed, and caught the day's first Acela express train from Penn Station. I knew I just had to be at the White House before noon.

It was a beautiful, sunny Friday, if a bit too chilly for me. Lafayette Park, where the rally was supposed to take place, was nearly empty.

This rally was neither my first in that park nor the last. I've always admired this great symbol of democratic freedom: practically anyone could stand there, within spitting distance of the White House, and express any view or protest. Only in America. This would be unthinkable in such countries as Russia, China, or Saudi Arabia. Anyone who dared congregate at an antigovernment rally in these places would, within minutes, cease to exist.

I knew that Sami al-Arian would be here today. I knew that he would rail against the Secret Evidence Act and condemn its use in the imprisonment of his brother-in-law, Mazen al-Najjar, who was deported from the United States less than a year after 9-11. But at the time of this rally—long before 9-11—his fate was unclear. Sami, the law-abiding professor who is married to Mazen's sister, was asked to testify at his trial. On the stand, Sami took the Fifth Amendment on ninety-nine out of the one hundred-and-two questions he was asked. Why, if this honest professor had nothing to fear, did he hide behind his right against self-incrimination in the overwhelming majority of his answers? I was really looking forward to hearing what Sami would have to say, publicly, on the matter of his brother-in-law.

I took a walk around the park, and when I returned, around twelve-thirty, there was still no rally. Maybe they'd circulated a cancellation notice that I somehow hadn't received? Or maybe they'd shown up on time and finished before I arrived? Then a strange-looking guy, carrying a large TV camera, approached me and asked—in Arabic—whether I knew anything about a rally. It was clear that he wasn't local.

"Yes," I replied in Arabic, "as far as I know, there is one planned for today. But I came late, they may have held it already."

"Not unless they started before ten-thirty, which is when I came here," he said.

Hesitantly he asked, "Do you mind if I asked you a few questions in the meantime?"

He pulled out an ID. He was Egyptian. A reporter for the Egyptian national TV.

"I was commissioned to do a report on Muslims in America at the turn of the millennium," he said. " 'Muslims Facing the Millennium' is what I am going to call it. Could you spare a moment and answer some questions?"

"Why not?" I said.

He asked how I envisioned the new millennium in the United States from a Muslim point of view. He asked what I thought the Muslim community would face in America in the coming years. He asked what I thought of the Jewish problem and how I saw the situation of Jews in America and throughout the world. Then he asked me whether I thought that America could have a Muslim president in the next decade.

It amused me, but with a straight face I told him that I thought the situation of us Muslims in America was bad and that it was going to get worse. That what we really needed to do was unite. I gave him the example of the poor people in Iraq, suffering from hunger and no medications because of the Allied forces' sanctions. "Who," I asked him, "in Egypt or in Saudi Arabia ever worried about them?" I gave other examples, such as Palestine and Kosovo. When he asked about a Muslim as president, I told him that Muslims here in America worried more about their personal well-being and financial situation than the real issues at hand—unity and the struggle for Muslims worldwide. "Let our brothers here stop enjoying the good life America offers them," I said, "and then maybe we'll be able to think about a Muslim president."

As I was getting into making answers for this guy, the situation was growing funnier and funnier. In my struggle to refrain from laughing, tears welled in my eyes. I told the reporter I had to stop. As I left, he was speechless. I walked to a corner in the park and sat on a bench. I called the office and told them that the most hilarious thing had just happened. When they heard my anecdote, they asked whether my face was covered during the interview. Only then did I realize that it was not, and that my mug was going to be shown all over Egypt, and maybe beyond.

Now that wasn't funny at all.

I ran back to the guy. Gave him some stupid excuses, told him that my husband was a government employee and that while I meant every word I said, I couldn't allow my face to be seen on TV without endangering my husband's job.

"Do you mind, then, if you gave me these same answers with a covered face? I just *have* to have that interview with you," he said. "You're unbelievable."

He didn't have a crew; he was the reporter, director, producer, cameraman, and sound technician all at once. So he rewound the tape—I made sure that he erased the evidence—I covered my face, and we started all over again. This time, veiled, with only my eyes peeking out, I couldn't control myself at all. My attempts to suppress the giggles made me sound as if I were mooing. The struggle to finish this interview without laughing caused tears to *squirt* out my eyes now, and the reporter thought that I, very upset, was crying my heart out. Again I asked him to stop. While he was folding up his equipment, he told me that I was one of the most sincere and brave women he'd ever met. He said that if his producers back in Egypt only allowed him to show one bit of all that he'd taped while in America, it would be my interview.

Mata Hari had nothing on me.

The rally did take place, a little while after my interview concluded. The people were all late because of the Friday sermon; they could come only when it was over. As billed, Sami spoke, his brother-in-law's attorney spoke, others spoke. It was tiresome, really. And then, at some point, a high official I'd worked with in the White House came out. I saw him surveying the protesters, and because I knew him well, I knew what he was thinking of them—of us—standing there and claiming that Mazen al-Najjar was a hero.

He was disgusted.

Amused, I videotaped him as he was throwing spiteful looks at us and wondered how he'd react if he recognized me in my current outfit.

By the time the rally was over, I knew that traveling by train, I'd miss the Sabbath dinner. I hailed a cab to the airport. The driver, an Arab, saw my robes and asked me where I'd been. I told him about the rally and explained what the Secret Evidence Act was. When we reached the airport, I asked him how much I owed him. He turned around, and in a very soft voice he said, "I would never dream of taking even one penny from you, Sister. What you people do is sacred, and you are true heroes of Islam. I beg of you to take my fare and donate it to where it's really needed—give it to the *cause.*"

ON THE PLANE, I closed my eyes, as I often do, the minute I was belted in. It was a tiny plane. The pilot, nine other passengers, and me. No aisle seats, only one row, and way too many windows. This little plane looks more like a taxi, I thought. After we survived take-off—

the part of flying I hate most—I replayed the conversation in the cab. What would the guy have said, or done, had he known who I was? Come to think of it, who am I? *What* am I?

My family and I live in a nice neighborhood, our kids go to a good school, they have friends. Leo has colleagues from work, he and I have friends. In short, we know many people. Inevitably, the question arises: What do you do for a living? What *do* I do for a living, really? What can I say to the parent of one of my kids' classmates, when she asks? What do I write on the mortgage application or on the school forms my kids need me fill out? Sure, I can write "terrorist hunter" or maybe "spy." Even if it were safe to do that, can you imagine how insane such a thing would look? Our neighbors know me, they like me, but they don't know who, or what, I am. Even with relatives and close friends, to tell or not to tell—that is the question. Whom can I trust with my secret? And if I did tell them what I did for a living, I couldn't blame any of them for not keeping my secret. By telling them, I myself wouldn't be keeping the secret. How could I expect them to?

The excuses and confabulations were most difficult in the first months after I'd started, because then even *I* wasn't sure what I was doing at work. As time passed, I was more oriented, my goals became clearer, and my fabrications—lies, really—became more professional. I learned whom to trust, what to tell where and when. I had one cover story for my undercover jobs and another for everyday use. But none of this is over, not even now that you're reading this book. What I do concerns national security. When I see or hear of a news item that I created—an investigation, a raid, a deportation, an arrest—how can I say: *I did that?*

I can't, and I don't think I'll ever be able to.

THE SECOND *intifada* in Israel didn't begin spontaneously. In the months preceding it, starting in mid-2000 and escalating in September–October, there was an enormous outbreak of rallies and demonstrations, pro-Palestinian, pro-Jerusalem (a Palestinian Jerusalem, that is), anti-Israeli, and anti-American. Such rallies took place around the globe. American flags were torched at rallies in Russia, Germany,

Britain, France, Malaysia, South Africa, and, goes without saying, in nearly every Arab country. In the United States, all major Muslim organizations arranged and participated in rallies. I practically ran from one rally to another. I wanted to attend as many as possible, and although it was a few short months after Shirley's delivery and I was still breast-feeding her, I frantically jumped from one place to the other trying to cover all these events. Some of the rallies I went to, dressed as a Muslim woman, were extremely emotional and difficult to cope with. The most distressing notion to me was that although the stated issue was the Israeli-Palestinian conflict, the hatred toward the United States was clearly evident and the United States was repeatedly accused of being the reason for all the problems in the Middle East.

On September 16, 2000, I attended a rally for the "Palestinian right of return," in front of the White House. That day parallel rallies took place in Britain and Israel, and all of these gatherings were intensely emotional. At the day-long event in Washington, accusations of genocide, racism, and brutality were leveled at Israel from a number of speakers. One of the moderators suggested that we observe a few moments of silence in memory of "martyrs." The mob around me screamed, "A'yash, A'yash!" Yihya A'yash, nicknamed "the Engineer" for his planning skills, was a terrorist responsible for dozens of murders. He was, as they say, "martyred" when a bobby-trapped cellular phone exploded in his face. Then elderly people went up onstage and told stories of how they were thrown out of their houses in the middle of the night and then cruelly deported into exile. Some of the stories were truly gruesome, and for the first time I was knocked off balance. I cried a great deal, not for show this time, and I cried even more on my way home. At some point I was so upset—my hands shaking, my eyes blinded by tears—that I couldn't even videotape anymore. But I had to have the material, so I asked one of the protesters standing nearby to videotape for me for a while. Overjoyed at being able to help a sister in need, the amateur videographer even climbed on the stage and recorded the speakers, as well as the ecstatic audience, with me in it.

I thought, if I, with my background, responded to the conference so sympathetically, when I certainly knew better, what effect would the speakers' words have on young and hot-tempered Muslims? Whether the stories told to us were true or false, they had a powerful effect.

What kept me on track and reminded me who I was—and who they were, really—were the speeches made by the leaders of the American Muslim community. They brought me back to reality.

Nihad Awad, executive director of the Council on American-Islamic Relations, CAIR, was one of the organizers and the speakers. CAIR portrays itself as a moderate Muslim organization that focuses on human rights and promotes justice. Many terrorist-related news articles in the media have been met with ferocious attacks from CAIR representatives. At the rally, Awad said, "They [the Jews] have been saying 'Next year to Jerusalem,' we say 'Next year to *all* Palestine.' " In other words, eradicating the state of Israel.

At another rally, Nihad Awad called for hatred, not only against Israel, but also against the United States. Awad denounced Israel as an instrument of the American persecution of the Palestinians, declaring that "more than fifty billion dollars have been given to soldiers acting in the name of Israel, but in reality they were acting in the name of the United States. . . . To use my money and the people's money to fund terrorism . . . who is the real terrorist? Isn't it the Israelis? The Israelis have been maiming children, have been killing innocent people, have been bombing cities, no objection by the United States. . . . All these things are happening, are happening in the name of the United States."

The same United States in which Awad lives and prospers.

Other leaders of the Muslim community also had interesting things to say about America during that period of time.

Muzzamile Saddiqi, president of the Islamic Society of North America, said at a rally in front of the White House: "We want to awaken the conscience of America. America has to learn that. Because if you remain on the side of injustice, the wrath of God will come. Please! Please, all Americans, do you remember that, that Allah is watching everyone. God is watching everyone. If you continue doing injustice, and tolerating injustice, the wrath of God will come."

The wrath Saddiqi promised did come, less than a year later, on September 11, 2001. Shortly after the catastrophe, a ceremony for the victims took place in the National Cathedral in Washington. At President Bush's side stood a priest, a rabbi, and an imam, to deliver the prayers. That imam's name was Muzzamile Saddiqi.

What was it, I thought, that provoked this hate toward America? Why did these people, self-proclaimed moderates living in America for decades with their families and enjoying all the freedoms and plenitude of the greatest democracy in history, hold such a grudge against the country? I found it hard to believe that these people wanted to live in a nation they so ragingly attacked in their speeches. Let them try to go back to their countries of origin and say the things they've been saying here, and see how long they'd survive afterward. The tragic stories told at the rallies, the speeches at conferences, and the incitement such as I'd heard in mosques meant only one thing: deep hatred of the United States. The speeches were hate speeches, plain and simple. This easily explains the existence of the American Taliban and American terrorists such as the so-called Buffalo Six, who were indicted for supporting al-Qaeda and training in its camps in Afghanistan. For such individuals, taught and indoctrinated to hate the land that nurtured them, the road from listening to an imam who advocates violence to what happened on 9-11 becomes a very short path.

Shortly after the second *intifada* started, a rally took place in front of the Israeli embassy in Washington. The rally was planned to start at one P.M.; I arrived a half hour later. Only three people were there besides me. By two o'clock it had begun to drizzle, and I decided to fold up my camcorder and equipment and go to the train station. I was drained from many emotional events of the previous few weeks and I was glad the event was not going to take place and that I could go home to my baby. As I was about to leave, buses began arriving. I saw Nihad Awad, Abdalhalim al-Ashqar, and some of the activists from Dar al-Hijra, and eventually some two thousand people had congregated.

Hate speeches and exhortations to violence against Jews were heard throughout the rally, and slogans used by Hamas and PIJ such as "With our blood and soul we will liberate Palestine" were frequently uttered by speakers and the crowd.

One of the speakers sang a song in Arabic, and the crowd sang along.

> Al-Aqsa is calling us,
> Let's all go to jihad,
> And throw stones in the faces of Jews.

I'd participated in unpleasant gatherings before, but this one topped them all. The hate expressed toward Jews—not Israelis only, but Jews in general—was of a ferocity I'd not seen before. It was crystal-clear that if I was uncovered and recognized for the Jew I am, I'd be lynched by the inflamed mob.

One speaker at the rally, Dr. Ayman Sirajuldeen, a member of the Muslim American Society who was introduced as a professor of political science and international law, equated Israel with the regime of the Nazis. "There is no difference between Barak and Sharon and Hitler. All are the same," Sirajuldeen said, referring to Ehud Barak and Ariel Sharon, then Israel's prime minister and head of its Likud Party, respectively. Comparisons of Jews to Nazis, probably the most cynical and sadistic rape of history, were commonplace at many of these rallies.

Sirajuldeen then continued to praise "martyrdom" and led the crowd gathered outside the Israeli embassy in a chant of *"Khaibar, Khaibar."*

I looked around. *"Khaibar, Khaihar?"* Did the journalists gathered here know how chilling this was? Obviously not. In the next day's papers it got written up as "a peaceful pro-Palestinian rally."

A Muslim woman was standing next to me with her three children. She was holding a baby not more than two months old. Her other two children, perhaps three and four years old, looked terribly miserable in the cold and rain and congestion. I pitied them. Throughout the four hours of the rally, the mother kept screaming, "Death to Jews!" and, *"Khaibar, Khaibar!"* at the top of her lungs. Looking at her baby, thinking of my own, sadness overwhelmed me. I saw a four-year-old child wearing a T-shirt emblazoned with a print of Hassan Nasrallah, the leader of Hizballah. The child was chanting along with everyone else.

"*Khaibar, Khaibar*" was chanted at that rally and at many others. It echoed all over the country, as Israeli flags burned in the background, from Florida to Texas, New York to California, and back to Washington, D.C. To an outsider, this chant, *"Khaibar, Khaibar, Ya Yahud, Jaish Muhammad Safayood,"* sounded perhaps like a cheerful freedom song. Many journalists told me that this was what they thought they were hearing. But its meaning is somewhat different: "Khaibar, Khaibar, O Jews, the army of Muhammad is coming for you." This song originates in a tale from the days of the Prophet Muhammad. As part of his campaign to conquer the Arabian peninsula, Muhammad laid siege to the city of Khaibar, which was inhabited by Jews. After losing several battles to the city's powerful army, Muhammad decided to try a new tactic. He sent emissaries to Khaibar's leaders with a message of peace. As soon as a peace treaty was signed and the gates of the city were opened, *Jaish Muhammad,* Muhammad's army, stormed the city and butchered every last one of its inhabitants. "Khaibar, Khaibar" means "Let's trick the Jews into making peace with us, and when they accept our offer, let's go ahead and kill them all."

A freedom song indeed.

Other such songs were sung. At a rally held in front of the Israeli consulate in Miami, they chanted:

"We don't want negotiation, with jihad we'll claim our nation."

"With jihad we'll claim our land, Zionist blood will wet the sand."

One child led a chant: "U.S. taxes paid the bill, Israelis used it all to kill."

The worst incitements, in my view, came from the religious clerics. These imams are the leaders, they've got the power; their word is an edict, their recommendation a decree from Allah.

"Rhetoric is not going to liberate al-Quds [Jerusalem] and al-Aqsa," preached Mohammed al-Asi, the former imam of the Islamic Academy of Potomac, Maryland. "Only carrying arms will do this task. And it's not going to be someone else who is going to carry arms for you and for me. It is you and I who are going to have to carry these arms."

Such words easily find their ways into action.

Most of the rallies didn't make the TV news. One did, however, and in the most unexpected way. Like many others, it was a very emotional event. But after attending lots of rallies, I'd already become inured to the power of the rhetoric. This rally, in Lafayette Park, was planned as an ambitious gathering; groups arrived on buses from New York, New Jersey, Michigan, Illinois. We, the demonstrators, began by marching from Freedom Plaza to Lafayette Park. Protesters sang "Victory comes from Allah, and our model is Hizballah," and "O dear Nasrallah [Hizballah's leader], we are allied with you in liberation."

The rally lasted all afternoon, and by four-thirty the reporters were long gone and the protesters were starting to leave. I too was ready to take off. It was then that Abdurahman al-Amoudi, of the American Muslim Council, AMC, climbed the stage fifteen feet from where I stood with my camcorder and addressed the cheering crowd in English:

"I have been labeled by the media in New York to be a supporter of Hamas. Anybody support Hamas here?"

The crowd cheered in response.

"Anybody is a supporter of Hamas here?"

The crowd cheered again.

"Anybody is a supporter of Hamas here?"

The crowd cheered louder still.

"Hear that, Bill Clinton? We are *all* supporters of Hamas. *Allahu Akhbar!* [Allah is the greatest!]"

More enthusiastic cheers.

"I wish they added that I am also a supporter of Hizballah. . . . Anybody supports Hizballah here?"

The crowd roared in approval.

Even after so many emotional rallies lately, I still couldn't believe my ears. Was this guy for real, to publicly support terrorist organizations such as Hizballah, the terrorist organization that is second only to al-Qaeda in the amount of American blood on its hands? The organization responsible for the murder of hundreds of United States soldiers in Beirut and at the Khobar Towers in Saudi Arabia?

The American Muslim Council was considered by many a moderate Muslim organization. Al-Amoudi had made a name as a Muslim moderate. He was a regular visitor at the White House. And he publicly supported two designated terrorist organizations—right in front of the White House. Have I gone mad, I thought, or is this indeed an abuse of freedom of speech?

In a state of great agitation, I rushed for my train and as soon as I was in my seat I checked my videotape, to make sure that I had got it right. Next I called the *New York Daily News*. A reporter was waiting for me at New York's Penn Station when I got off. I handed over the tape. The paper called al-Amoudi for a response. First, he claimed that he'd spoken only in Arabic and therefore was clearly misunderstood and misinterpreted. The *Daily News* played my tapes for him. After he listened, he told the paper that from that point on he'd speak only through his lawyer.

When the story broke, it spread like wildfire, and my tape was broadcast on the Fox network nationwide. It was election time, and Hilary Clinton, running for the U.S. Senate seat in New York, had received some $50,000 in donations from al-Amoudi's AMC and from other Muslim organizations. Al-Amoudi had been considered a friend by Mrs. Clinton. Her opponent's campaign saw the tape on TV and, without my permission, used it for his campaign. I was horrified to wake up one morning and see that my tape was being aired on TV in this political affair. All I wanted was to expose al-Amoudi.

Clinton returned the money to al-Amoudi and to the other Muslim groups, broke off all her ties with them, and did a 180 in her views of the Palestinian issue. After that incident, George W. Bush also returned $1,000 he had received from al-Amoudi.

Months later, al-Amoudi appeared on a TV show. He acknowledged his statements and said they were "a mistake" and that he believed that Steven Emerson, a former CNN journalist who was writing on the Middle East conflict, was behind all this. Al-Amoudi said that since that incident, he'd felt as if he were going to bed with Mr. Emerson every night and waking up with him every morning.

If it's any consolation to him, I was the one al-Amoudi was repeatedly taking to bed. In his dreams . . .

But I haven't finished with al-Amoudi yet. I'd soon get back on his case in my "555" investigation.

DONNA CHABOT IS DETERMINED, extremely knowledgeable, and, to a large extent, unpredictable. A lot like me, come to think of it. She appreciates the power of the media, unlike other government agents I've encountered, who think that they're above everyone and that the media is nothing but a useless nuisance. Donna is well aware that in our field, public opinion—shaped primarily by the media— plays a critical role. And she knows how important it is to study her subjects in depth.

When Donna first called me, she said she was looking for public information on Ghassan Dahduli, the IAP officer I've written about. She asked me the usual questions, whether I was familiar with Dahduli, whether I had anything on him, where my information came from. She was trying to muster whatever evidence she could because the task force she belonged to was trying to nail him on visa violations. Not that this was his worst offense, not by a long shot, but this was an easy and straightforward way to get rid of a terrorist, not unlike the way IRS violations put Al Capone away for good. The idea was to prove that the visa arranged for Dahduli was invalid. Dahduli was sponsored as a religious cleric, but there was nothing on his résumé even closely resembling religious studies. As Dahduli and his family had been living in the United States since Thomas Edison invented the lightbulb, more or less, visa violation charges were not going to get this guy out of the country so easily. The task force filed for Dahduli's deportation, a judge ruled in favor of the task force, but then Dahduli appealed and requested political asylum. To block the asylum application, the task force now needed to build a much stronger case against Dahduli and to actually prove he was a terrorist.

I listened, and then I asked Donna, "So why did you pick on Dahduli all of a sudden? Is it his recently discovered ties with Wadih al-Hage?" I was already used to the long pauses that occur after I throw a bomb like that into a conversation. I waited.

Finally Donna asked, "How did you know about al-Hage? I thought this was supposed to be classified information!"

Obviously it wasn't.

A few days after she and I spoke on the phone, they knocked on my door and came in. Donna told me she would be coming from Texas, but she didn't say that she'd be bringing a whole delegation. She showed up with an assistant U.S. attorney and two FBI agents. After introductions all around, Donna and her team told me that they were very worried. Dahduli's lawyer had submitted a list of some twenty people willing to testify on his behalf. Not only prominent Muslims, but also Americans, Christians and Jews. The task force didn't have sufficient unclassified evidence to convince a judge that Dahduli was a terrorist; all they had was this minor visa issue. I gathered up some binders and took everyone to our conference room. My office could not accommodate five people for a conference, at least not comfortably. I asked for some cookies and soft drinks for everyone. Then, without further delay, I opened the first binder. I always say that I have a binder for every occasion, but it's the truth. I always do prepare a binder for each appointment. I had prepared a lot of documents and material for the Dahduli case. Material that was worth its weight in gold, as it turned out. And actually, I made four very large binders, two identical sets. In each set, one binder was in English and the other in Arabic. Two for them, two for me. So that we would be on the exact same wavelength when they next called me. I knew they would, because no one could absorb so much information in just one meeting, even if we went for several hours. Which we did.

This task force knew that IAP was a front for Hamas. But they had no idea how to prove it and, moreover, how to tie Dahduli to all of that. I began by throwing a question at them. Not a cheap trick to get their attention: they couldn't have been more attentive. I just wanted to demonstrate where I thought they would get the most criticism from the judge. I asked them how they could go to court claiming that

IAP was a front for Hamas, when IAP was incorporated in the United States in 1981, at least six years before Hamas was formed in the Middle East. They didn't like that question at all. They looked defeated. I smiled, and I told them to cheer up. And then I started to explain how IAP was connected to the Muslim Brotherhood, out of which Hamas has emerged, and how HLF was formed then, in 1987. Then, to demonstrate to them that their prayers were indeed heard, I showed them something that they, or any other government agency, could never have gotten without me.

I opened my binder and asked them to open the corresponding page. I pulled out a small booklet in bright green and white. The booklet was published by the IAP Information Office. It had been printed in the United States, with "the Islamic Association for Palestine" in English, but the booklet was otherwise in Arabic. On its back cover was printed a list of IAP offices in the United States and a post office box for parties interested in obtaining additional copies of the booklet. On the front cover, it said in bold Arabic lettering: "the Hamas Charter."

After my first visit to Dar al-Hijra, I tried my best to go to that mosque each time I was in the Washington, D.C., area. My visits there became more frequent with the years, as my ties with the government strengthened. I worked with several government agencies—and with some nongovernmental organizations studying Islamic terrorism. Besides, more and more rallies were taking place in front of the White House. Thus I sometimes visited the White House from the inside, sometimes from the outside—and sometimes both ways during the same visit to D.C. I always tried to arrange my briefings and conferences for the latter part of the work week, when I could use the opportunity and visit the mosque on Friday. One time, after the sermon, I went to the store in Dar al-Hijra. They already knew me there. I was a regular customer. I even had an account, which allowed me to buy things and pay for them later if I didn't have enough money that day.

While browsing in the store on this occasion, I noticed a publication titled *The Hamas Charter.* I was familiar with the charter, parts of which I'd seen in *Ila-Falastine,* the Hamas publication. My heart missed a beat; my astonishment grew as soon as I saw that the pamphlet was published by the IAP in North America.

But the icing on this cake was that the address the IAP provided for people who wanted additional copies of the pamphlet was Ghassan Dahduli's post office box.

The task force agents who'd been following IAP and Dahduli for a few years would never have found this Arabic IAP publication, this neat booklet wrapped in the whites and greens of the Palestinian flag. When I showed them this document, proving Dahduli's ties to Hamas, the agents couldn't have been any happier.

And then I threw the second bomb of the briefing. I told them how this IAP Information Office had operated in the Islamic Center of Tucson in the late 1980s, right at the primary location of the al-Qaeda cancer in America. As I expected, they knew very little about that center. They looked at me, bowled over, but it was evident that they were becoming happier with every passing minute. Dahduli headed the Islamic Center of Tucson at about the same time that he was in charge of the IAP Information Office. I told them that at that time, Wadih al-Hage was a member of that Islamic Center. They knew everything about al-Hage. They also knew that Dahduli's numbers—his home, his work, all his numbers—had been found in al-Hage's confiscated telephone book, which proved that these two were much more than just acquaintances. Al-Hage's telephone book was one of the reasons this task force was suddenly so interested in Dahduli. But then I told them what they didn't know. I explained to them that al-Hage and Dahduli were associated from the time they both were involved in the center, a crucial factor in Dahduli's case. I also told them about Wa'el Julaidan and his association with the center, and I showed them the documents proving his role in al-Qaeda. I stressed how important the center in Tucson was and told them that it continued to be a recruitment center for mujahideen years after Julaidan had left it. At this point, the agents were much more relaxed. I even saw a hint of a smile on Donna's face.

But I wasn't through yet. I showed them, in the Arabic binder, issues of *Ila-Falastine,* published by Dahduli's Information Office. Because this newspaper stopped publishing in the early 1990s, the government agents had never heard of it. I showed them what *Ila-Falastine* was all about and how *al-Zaytuna* replaced it. That publication they were aware of, though they didn't know of the explosive content in its back issues. Then I showed them some IAP publications in English, the *Palestine Monitor* and the *Muslim World Monitor* that succeeded it. In these *Monitors*, every other page contained news of Hamas and Sheikh Yassin (Hamas's spiritual leader) and terrorism propaganda. Clear-cut. The agents had never heard of those publications, either. Finally, I showed them brochures and leaflets by the IAP and by Dahduli, plus many other pertinent documents. These documents clearly showed the robust ties among Dahduli, IAP, and Hamas. As far as I was concerned, Dahduli was toast. Everything was there in my binders. All of it obtained from public records. Anyone, theoretically, could have found all that information. But the task force hadn't, and I had.

After listening, absorbing, and grasping the value of the material I was handing them, they asked me a question not directly related to Dahduli. They wanted to know which other organizations linked to Hamas should be investigated. They asked me which group or organization was the most dangerous, which one should be the subject of their investigation. Was it Hamas, IAP, HLF, or the Islamic Center of Tucson? I deliberated for a moment, considering whether I should tell them what I really thought. I knew that they'd rather be kicked in the stomach than hear what I was about to say. I decided to tell them what I really thought. I threw the third bomb. I answered, "That's really easy. That would be InfoCom."

Donna and the federal prosecutors literally sprang from their chairs, as if my revelations had administered a physical shock. In a quavering voice, Donna asked me why I'd just named InfoCom. "Because they can easily launder money. They deal with hundreds of Saudi organizations and some in the Gulf states. Large amounts of money flow from Saudi Arabia and the Gulf to their operation here, and that would be difficult to track. Stated as money given for the computer services InfoCom provides, this money is funneled to Hamas and possibly other terrorist organizations. Besides, InfoCom is Abu Marzook's company."

InfoCom was a very profitable computer business, importing and exporting software and hosting Web sites. It operated more than five hundred Internet sites in Saudi Arabia alone, including one that belonged to Bin Laden's construction company. InfoCom was run by the same people who'd operated IAP and HLF, but unlike these two fronts, InfoCom was dealing with really large sums of money. It was founded by Musa Abu Marzook. Remember him? The guy who'd been the head of Hamas's political arm, and on whose account someone from the office of Ishaq al-Farhan, the Jordanian diplomat, explicitly threatened the U.S. embassy in Amman? Oh, I apologize. InfoCom wasn't actually created by Musa. It was Musa's *wife* who established this multimillion-dollar business, by initially investing some $250,000 in it. No wonder she could spare that kind of money; after all, she was a housewife!

After I'd mentioned InfoCom, Donna and her crew looked as though they were in a great hurry to leave my office. They'd heard enough, I thought, and perhaps more than they'd ever hoped for. But they were much, much happier going than they were coming. I'd definitely earned my salary that afternoon.

Donna called me frequently after our meeting. We discussed the documents Dahduli's lawyer filed, and I faxed her documents that proved the opposite. Dahduli's lawyers even sent documents claiming that their client, as well as the IAP, ran some publications that were clearly geared toward Muslims and were promoting Islam. And these publications were—you guessed right—*Ila-Falastine* and *al-Zaytuna*. Boy, were these lawyers in for an unpleasant surprise.

I respected Donna and her team. They were professional and dedicated, and they knew their subject well. They couldn't on their own find the information I'd provided them, but they did have significant knowledge of other relevant facts regarding Hamas and IAP. They also understood the concept of front groups covering for terrorist organizations. Most surprising to me was the cohesiveness of this task force.

Even the FBI agents on that team were gladly sharing information with their teammates, as well as with other government entities—with practically anyone who needed it, in fact. (I hope I'm not getting them in trouble with the FBI for revealing this.) It was evident that they enjoyed working as a team, and therefore I enjoyed working with them.

A few months later, early in September, Donna called me. I could hear that a lot was going on in the background, and she sounded very excited.

"Guess where I'm calling from?" she asked. How could I have known?

"No clue," I told her. "Where?"

"I thought you should have the honor of knowing about this first. I didn't want the reporters to call you and catch you unprepared. Here's where we are. We are raiding InfoCom as we speak!"

I appreciated her gesture. It meant that I'd be ahead of everyone else with the important news about the raid. She was grateful for my help, and this was her way of showing it. Not just with words, but with solid action. She later told me over coffee that on the same day they came to see me, she and her staff met with Treasury Department officials about InfoCom. This was one of the reasons there were so many of them: their other mission on that trip was to plan their strategy regarding InfoCom.

That was why they were so surprised—and impressed—when I named InfoCom as the most dangerous of the lot. IAP, HLF, and Hamas were constantly in the news, but hardly anyone ever mentioned InfoCom.

A year after the raid, InfoCom's officers had been indicted. This was just one in a long string of successes Donna's task force had had. Nowadays, members of that team are invited to conferences and briefings to instruct others about counterterrorism and to provide them with useful leads.

One quiet Saturday afternoon in October, the kids were with Leo, taking their piano lessons, and I was working in the office. The phone rang. That was strange. Who might be calling here on a Saturday? It was Donna. She'd called me at home, and when she couldn't find me there, she tried the office.

"Guess again," she teased me. I could picture her smile all the way from where she was calling in Texas. This time, though, I guessed right.

"It's Dahduli, isn't it?"

"You betcha!"

Now I couldn't suppress *my* smile. "How did you do that?" I asked.

"Actually, I didn't. You did. As we approached the date of his appeal, we held a conference with him. We didn't have to do anything, really. We basically showed him what you gave us on him. Guess what he did?"

I was dying to know.

"He looked at the documents," she said, "and he just withdrew his appeal. Said he wanted out. Gave up without a trial."

Hearing that, I wiped away a tear. They'd been on this guy for almost four years. He was finally getting what he deserved.

"Dahduli and his lawyers just couldn't figure out where we, the government, obtained documents Dahduli had published over a decade ago. They were awed when we easily proved a lie what they tried to present as 'Islamic publications.'

"It was all your work," Donna concluded. "We could never have done this without you."

After a few weeks in detention, Ghassan Dahduli was personally escorted to the airport by Donna, who took the flight with him all the way to Jordan. When they landed in Amman, the Jordanians immediately arrested and imprisoned Dahduli for his ties to terrorism.

THE BIBLE MAKES a clear distinction between false and true prophets. In biblical times science was but in its diapers, kingdoms disappeared as quickly as they were formed, and prophecy was an everyday tool for planning and making military and other state decisions. Until kingdoms fell, and armies were wiped out, and it became clear that some of these disasters were facilitated by the influence of charlatans. So a set of rules came from the wise men to help kings and rulers decide which prophet was true and which was false.

After generations-long deliberations, the conclusion was simple.

Prophets who prophesied good fortune were false.

Those who predicted disaster were true, concluded the wise men; they were the ones who warned of God's wrath and, therefore, must have been guided by divine supervision.

Such is Joseph's gift, my curse. I'd say something, and the exact opposite would soon happen. Usually, it'd be a calamity. Many a time Leo teased me and asked me to say, "We'll never win the lottery." He said that if I uttered those words we'd win it the next day. But I never felt strongly enough to say something like that. What I did say, for instance, feeling a sudden urge to say it, was that Gil was very handsome. The next day Gil fell on his chin and was left with a disfiguring scar. One time I said that Charlie never got sick. The next day he developed a bad ear infection that needed surgery. I said that I was impressed by the tremendous success of a certain apparel store that I liked. They went bankrupt a month later. Such things happened to me a million and one times.

In early September 2001, I was asked by the Customs-Treasury intelligence service to give a briefing on money laundering by Muslim charities in the United States and particularly in Michigan. I usually don't go alone to these meetings. I try to get the younger investigators in the office to come with me so that they'll learn, both from me and from the situation itself, and also so they'll make important contacts. Some of the guys who worked with me used such contacts to find jobs with the government. So I took Sam with me. Very young, just out of college, but very dedicated and unusually bright. We went down to D.C., to Customs headquarters. There we were taken to their war room. Before I began, I looked at a giant screen displayed on one of the walls of the war room. Fancy, high-tech screen, with a map of the United States and twinkling lights all over it.

"What's that?" I asked.

"This is our current intelligence warning on terrorist threats to the United States," I was told. "See these marks—those are potential targets. And see these lights—they can go from green, which means no threat, to yellow, orange, and finally to red, the highest alert."

All the lights were green.

"Why are they all like that?" I asked. "Why are all these lights green?"

"Oh, I think you don't understand." The man was so patronizing. "This is the map of the United States. Continental USA only." Gee, thanks for telling me. "We're not saying that there's no danger anywhere on the globe, we're just saying that things on U.S. soil are pretty safe right now."

"But what about the plan to blow up LAX?" I insisted. "How can you be sure that there is no danger at all?"

"Oh, that. That was a long time ago, almost a year ago, before the millennium. We did have quite a few orange lights lit here at the time. But things have significantly cooled down since then, don't you think?"

I gave them my briefing, in which I explained several methods used by charities to funnel money to terrorism. But I left the war room with a very uneasy feeling.

"Do you think we're perfectly safe?" I asked Sam as we boarded the train.

"Sounds too good to be true, if you ask me. But they're the ones with the intel information."

A few days later I met Leo for lunch. I love it when we can sneak out of work like that and go have lunch together. Feels like almost having an affair—only with your own husband. We went to a Vietnamese place that we like. The screen in the war room kept bothering me. "I keep thinking how these things follow me wherever I go," I told Leo. "I thought when we left Israel that that would be the last I'd hear about terrorism. But look where I am now. Right in the middle of it. The terrorists are there, but so many of their leaders and their headquarters are here. It's frightening."

"Is something wrong? Are you worried about your safety?" he asked.

"No, not really." It was the feeling inspired by the green lights in the war room. And those were the days of the second *intifada,* when dreadful terrorist attacks in Israel occurred daily. But then again, I thought, that was Israel.

"I guess this is different," I said. "I guess it *is* safe here. This is America we're talking about, after all. Terrorist attacks are a Middle Eastern problem. I deal with their fronts and charities here, but not with the people who actually detonate the bombs."

Having a sudden urge, I looked across the table at Leo and concluded: "I think we're safer from terrorism here, on U.S. soil, more than we'd be anywhere else."

When I came back to the office it was late already, a little after three o'clock, on Monday, September 10, 2001.

CHAPTER 10

Birds on Fire

IN A WAY, I was alone in the office. During the summer of 2001, our more experienced researchers, George, Bruce, and Neil, had all left. Bruce went to work for the government; the others went to graduate school. Our crew was small and my research staff was new. The most senior researcher was Sam, who at that point—it was September—had been with us for only two months. During that short time he learned a lot and became my right-hand man. But I was the only terrorism expert there at the time.

Early on that bright, warm, beautiful Tuesday morning, I watched the breaking news on the television set in my office about the plane that had crashed into the World Trade Center. I saw the live coverage of the second plane hitting the second tower. As soon as it did, the words from the FBI report on its interview with Abdel Hakim Murad echoed in my head: "What the subject had in his mind is that he will board any American commercial aircraft, pretending to be an ordinary passenger. Then he will hijack said aircraft, control its cockpit and dive it at the CIA headquarters. There will be no bomb or any explosive. . . . It is simply a suicidal mission."

So Bin Laden's men, Murad's comrades, had finally executed their plan, I thought.

Realizing that something exceptional was happening, the staff began appearing in my office on the third floor. Max, however, was nowhere to be found. He hadn't called in, nor did he respond to the two messages I'd left on his machine.

Like most other Americans in those first hours, we were overwhelmed with confusion and disbelief. I tried to call Leo—we all tried to call our families and affirm that they were safe—but all lines were jammed. In the surreal silence, the staff began to panic. They wanted my instructions—and my reassurance.

And then a phone rang. After forty-five minutes of no incoming calls, the ringing was alarming. The caller was a former CIA agent and a friend of Max's. "I suggest you leave everything and evacuate the office at once," he advised me. "As you know, the reports are conflicting, but it seems like a war has begun. The Pentagon has just been attacked. They're saying that the State Department is under attack, that smoke is rising from the National Mall in Washington, and we know that there are unaccounted-for planes—at least three—still in the air. Looks like doomsday."

"But why," I asked, "would anyone want to attack our office?"

My co-workers overheard the conversation and completely lost it. One even rushed out, and by the time I got him on his cell, he was already twenty blocks away. "We don't know anything yet," Max's friend said. "If I were you, I'd shut all my computers down—we don't know whether they might attempt a cyberattack—and go to a safer place, like your homes."

For a moment I thought that maybe this was what we should do, that I should take everyone to my place, just outside the city, and work from there. But what about the computers, the telephones? No, we had to stay put. Anyway, I knew that the city would be in a transportation lockdown.

I turned to my staff. They were frightened.

"I think we should evacuate," one said as the others nodded.

"You heard the conversation," I told them. "If you'd like to leave you have full permission to do so. If you have family you're worried about, go. I'm staying, and those who want to stay with me are certainly welcome to. People will need us now more than ever before. And we don't really know where's safe and where isn't."

My confidence inspired theirs. They all decided to stay. The guy who'd left came back, too. I sent two of the staffers to Max's place to try to find him. I wanted to see that he was okay, and I thought that he needed to be in the office at this terrible time.

Only later, as the second tower collapsed, Max showed up. The moment he did, I cried out: "That's it. He did it. Bin Laden finally finished off the job he started in 1993!"

Like everyone else in America, none of us at work on 9-11 would ever forget those first hours of terror.

LATER THAT DAY and in the days after the attack, the eerie silence in our office was replaced by a frenzy of ringing phones. The media, naturally, went haywire. We got calls from every journalist we'd ever worked with—the first to call were the television networks. "Was this Bin Laden?" they asked. "Were there trained pilots in al-Qaeda?" Later, government agents whom I'd worked with started to call. They were frantic with security concerns in those first hours and days, but then they too wanted to know whether I thought this was Bin Laden.

Anyone can say now, in retrospect, that he knew it was Bin Laden right from the start. But as journalists and government agents called me after the attack, their first question was, "Did Bin Laden have pilots?" None of them knew.

For years I'd been following al-Qaeda's interest in flight-training schools. I knew that key al-Qaeda players, such as the merry bunch from the Philippines—Murad, Ramzi Youssef, and Khalid Sheikh Mohammed—had taken flying lessons. Murad, who'd disclosed his plan to conduct a suicide mission using a commercial jetliner as a guided missile, took flying lessons in New York, Texas, and Florida. The FBI was well aware, as its interview with Murad indicates, of his plan and of his flight training.

Furthermore, during the embassy bombing trial in Manhattan in early 2000, Bin Laden's people disclosed how al-Qaeda operatives were taking flight lessons in America and the Sudan, learning to pilot both large commercial jets and crop dusters. Some testimonies described how money was allocated by al-Qaeda for members' flight lessons. Most American flight schools offer English lessons for foreigners who want to enroll so that they'll learn the necessary vocabulary for their courses. These schools advertise all over the world.

Bin Laden's interest in training pilots arose in the early 1990s, it seemed, when he needed to be flown from here to there and was forced to hire pilots who weren't al-Qaeda. Essam al-Ridi was one pilot to whom Bin Laden offered a permanent position. Al-Ridi refused the job, because the salary Bin Laden offered him was too low. (Like others who knew Bin Laden, al-Ridi later described him as stingy. He recounted how Bin Laden would ask his operatives for a detailed report on every dime they spent on their missions.) Bin Laden shrewdly realized that by making pilots of those who'd sworn loyalty to him, he'd buy himself security cheaply.

Al-Ridi flew freelance for Bin Laden until he crashed one of his planes, at which point al-Ridi, who survived the accident, fled. In 1994, however, before the accident, al-Ridi was already flying with a co-pilot named Ihab Ali.

Ihab Ali was a cabdriver living in Orlando, Florida. His wife and family lived in Egypt, his homeland, and he often visited them there. Ali was arrested in 1999 as an al-Qaeda member after the FBI found letters to and from him in Wadih al-Hage's Kenya home. In 1994, Ali took flying lessons in Oklahoma.

Not only were the major American media seeking our office's opinion; journalists from around the globe, including Germany, Britain, France, and practically every large city in the United States were calling, too. The vast majority of those calls were getting put through to me. Everyone was interested in the general plot and in Bin

Laden's involvement, but also on their minds was their country's or city's ties to the plot and catastrophe. Over and over I repeated the same facts about the flying and pilots; whenever it was relevant I fed each journalist specific information relating to his or her locality. After we'd talk, I'd have to provide them with material that substantiated my statements. I sent out scores of copies of Ihab Ali's indictment, the addresses he'd been associated with, his ties to such terrorists as al-Hage, and so on. When asked how I was so sure that the attack was Bin Laden's work, I replied that the targets, the method, and the accuracy of execution had al-Qaeda's signature. Combined with Murad's scheme, the flight training, and the fact that the first World Trade Center bombing was al-Qaeda—there was no doubt left in my mind as to who had done this. The latter fact came as a great shock to many of those journalists—and to most government agents as well. Practically none of them had ever heard that there was any connection between al-Qaeda and the World Trade Center bombing in 1993.

On the fourth day after the attack, a federal prosecutor in Manhattan called and asked for information on the first World Trade Center bombing and related material such as the interview with Murad. He asked the FBI for the material, but he got nothing from them. He asked them—no; pleaded with them—to give him leads, any leads, about 9-11 or al-Qaeda. Nearly every government body felt, in the immediate aftermath of 9-11, that it had to combat terrorism. The FBI's attitude, however, didn't change; when a counterterrorism task force spearheaded by the New York Police Department was formed in New York a few months later, they asked for the FBI's help. They got nothing from the FBI, and they too ended up calling me.

I spoke with the federal prosecutor, gave him the information he sought, and then told him about al-Muhajiroun, the Immigrants, a U.K.-based group with a branch in New York. This group, which I'd been following for years, held a rally in front of the United Nations building on April 28, 2001, less than six months before 9-11. Kamran Bokhari, head of the New York office of al-Muhajiroun, said at that rally: "We are only a few here, but we have a billion Muslims behind the jihad. . . . Although you may see a few before you, one day we will liberate all Muslim lands. One day you will see the flag of Islam over the White House! *Allahu Akhbar!*" Bokhari then led his followers in chanting, "Hizballah, Hizballah, Hizballah," and, "We support Bin Laden! Bin Laden! We support Bin Laden! What do we want? Jihad! What do we want? Jihad! Jihad! Jihad!" After that rally I tried to interest the government with my videotapes of these statements, but my recordings were discounted and I was told that Bokhari's statements were well within reasonable limits of freedom of speech. Several months after I'd given the al-Muhajiroun tapes to the prosecutor, documents were released showing that al-Muhajiroun was doing far more than chanting: the group also recruited mujahideen and paid for their training inside the United States. Particularly, for flight training. Furthermore, members of al-Muhajiroun themselves also trained as pilots.

A week after the attack, Sam called me at home one night at eleven P.M. and said that he was reading an article about the hijackers and flight schools in Oklahoma. He said he wanted me to know about it because he'd overheard me saying something on the phone about Oklahoma and flight schools. I checked the article, and then I looked at Ihab Ali's file.

Bingo.

Ihab Ali had taken flying lessons in Norman, Oklahoma, at the Airman Flight School. Muhammad Atta and Marwan al-Shehhi, two of the nineteen hijackers, listed their first address in the United States as that of the school, before they enrolled in schools in Florida. And the so-called twentieth hijacker, Zacarias Moussaoui, also had received flight training in Norman.

After the disaster I agonized countless times over whether it could have been prevented. Whether more could have been done, and what was my part in missing the writing on the wall.

The government certainly had clues. It had the information on Murad's plot. It had Ali, an al-Qaeda member trained in flying, in custody. It knew that the Philippine gang had trained in aviation. It knew that al-Qaeda was vigorously training pilots in America. There was even a report, submitted by FBI agent Kenneth Williams in July 2001, that al-Muhajiroun members were taking flight lessons in Arizona. He also noted that they were paying for their training in cash. The counterterrorism supervisor in Washington, D.C., to whom this memo was sent and who was also involved in Moussaoui's investigation, reportedly never saw Williams's report. Only two weeks before 9-11, Moussaoui was arrested. Above all, the government knew that Bin Laden had declared war on the United States.

In retrospect, what would have been simpler than to instruct flight schools to report to the FBI anyone who'd paid cash for flying lessons and then check out those individuals? Could acting on this knowledge have changed the face of things? I don't know, and I don't think anyone ever will. Nowadays the FBI keeps a close watch even on diving schools, because of information Ramzi Youssef shared with federal agents about his training in scuba diving. But only after 9-11 did the FBI finally acknowledge that the Philippine plot was al-Qaeda.

After 9-11, many blamed the Clinton administration for not taking al-Qaeda seriously, but three years prior to that, after the missile strikes in Afghanistan and Sudan, which didn't even risk American lives, a media firestorm ensued, with many accusations against Clinton that he was trying to provoke a war to deflect public attention from his personal affairs. A loud outcry came from the American Muslim community, of course. "Our country is committing an act of terrorism," Maher Hathout, spokesman of the Islamic Center of Southern California and a prominent American Muslim leader, preached in one of his sermons. "What we did is illegal, immoral, unhuman, unacceptable, stupid, and un-American." He also said that firing the missiles constituted "hate crimes" worse than the embassy bombings themselves, because the missiles, according to Hathout, killed innocent people asleep in their homes.

This pattern of rhetoric did not change after 9-11. Prominent Muslims downplayed the attack itself and focused instead on Muslims' potential suffering at the hands of vengeful Americans. Some of the most respected and mainstream Muslim leaders, even those with strong ties to the White House, condemned the attack—not as being committed by Muslims, but as one orchestrated by Israel. "If we're going to look at suspects," Salaam al-Marayati, executive director of the

Muslim Public Affairs Council, said on 9-11, "we should look to the groups that benefit the most from these kinds of incidents, and I think we should put the state of Israel on the suspect list."

Al-Marayati was not the only Muslim leader to hold such views. Mohammed Gemeaha, who was the imam and spiritual leader of the Islamic Cultural Center in Manhattan, the city's largest and most influential mosque, suggested that Jewish forces were behind the attack. To complete that picture, he later said that Jewish doctors in the United States were poisoning Muslim babies. Shortly thereafter, he left the mosque and went to live in Egypt. If he expressed such views publicly in New York, imagine what rhetoric this man must be spouting in Egypt.

Other leaders even refused to accept the evidence presented about the hijackers. Ghazi Khankan, director of interfaith affairs at the Islamic Center of Long Island and a moderate in the eyes of many, said that Muhammad Atta, the ringleader of the attack, was "alive and living in the United Arab Emirates. His passport was stolen. It is in the Arab press. Yet the FBI insists he was one of the hijackers. Why hasn't the media reported this?"

Even after the release of the videotape in which Bin Laden boasts about the success of the attacks, the view in the Muslim world that Israel launched these attacks remained unchanged. These beliefs, and others more alarming, are still prevalent in certain communities around the world and even in America.

Al-Qaeda, in the view of the Arab world, is fighting for a just Muslim cause. In U.S. senator John Kerry's words, from a June 2002 interview, "If you had an election tomorrow in Saudi Arabia or Egypt, Usama Bin Laden would win. They know it. We know it. The world knows it."

A Gallup poll conducted less than six months after 9-11 showed that most residents of nine Muslim countries, including Pakistan, Kuwait, and Saudi Arabia, resented the United States and described it as "ruthless." The majority of the people surveyed labeled U.S. military action in Afghanistan "morally unjustifiable."

Sixty-one percent said they did not believe Arab groups had carried out 9-11.

IN THE FIRST FOUR DAYS after the attack, my staff and I worked like maniacs. My office became a war room. Max moved in, as did most of my researchers. As I was the only one capable of answering everyone's questions, I worked harder than ever before. I gave new meaning to the term *multitasking.* I was sometimes doing ten, twelve things simultaneously. The phones rang perpetually. I was taking two and three calls at the same time while looking for documents and reading others and giving instructions to my staff to find and get and fax and copy and . . . For four days I didn't sleep, save for a few short naps sitting at my desk. I didn't rest, and I barely got a chance to put some food in my mouth or use the rest room. Everyone who called us wanted to know everything, wanted to get all the related documents, and wanted them right away.

For four days I didn't feel, didn't pause to search my emotions, didn't have time to respond sentimentally to the events. I worked around the clock and was too busy and too tired for secondary issues such as emotions or my family.

On the fourth night, at three A.M., I went to my house for the first time since the catastrophe. On the way home, my head so filled with thoughts that paradoxically it felt almost drained, I finally began to feel again.

No words can ever describe the emotions people have in response to calamities such as 9-11. Growing up the child of a murdered father, becoming a woman in a country where all men—including mine—went to fight wars time and again and where terrorism and grief were an everyday occurrence, I was much more vulnerable than I ever admitted to myself. My emotions were roiling as I approached my home.

When I got there, an unpleasant surprise awaited me.

Knowing how busy I was, Leo hadn't told me that Shirley was sick. She had a severe ear infection and was febrile and in agony, screaming with pain. Leo was awake with her. He'd repeatedly given her Tylenol, but it wasn't doing much good. Meanwhile, the house was in chaos. Leo was trying his best with our four kids, but he was far from capable of handling everything. Definitely not to my standards.

At three-thirty in the morning, after three sleepless nights. I found myself cleaning the kitchen, folding laundry, preparing lunches for the boys for school, putting the house back in order. I wished I could afford a maid, as Mama used to have in the old days in Iraq. But I couldn't.

While I was doing the house chores, my head emptied and suddenly there was plenty of room there for emotion. After four days of acting like a machine, my heart began to take over. Like vultures, memories swooped in and attacked me in my vulnerable state: the Trade Center, the Pentagon, Flight 93 in Pennsylvania, the Yom Kippur War in Israel, numerous terrorist attacks I recalled from my youth, and, finally, my father's execution.

I finished in the kitchen and went upstairs. Shirley had at last calmed down. Leo was still with her. I went into our bedroom, took off my clothes, stood in front of the mirror, and looked. A woman was staring back at me, but she wasn't me. She was old, tired, and defeated. She was the saddest woman I've ever seen.

After the four-day emotional disconnect that had kept me going, my feelings surged and swept over me like a tidal wave. For the first time since the collapse of the Twin Towers, I broke down and wept for a long, long while.

At eight-thirty the following morning I was back in the office again.

ONE DAY, several weeks after 9-11, when I thought that I'd regained my bearings, I stumbled upon a piece from *The New York Times* on the Web. The story, headlined THE YEAR IN PICTURES, had obviously dedicated a significant portion to the tragedy. Attached to a close-up of the burning towers was a short description of the photographed scene. It read, "Occupants of 1 World Trade Center, which was hit first but stood longer, hung from openings as heat intensified. Later, as people inevitably fell, a child escaping from Public School 234 on Chambers Street called, 'Look, Teacher, the birds are on fire!' "

I was wrong. My emotional wounds were still open and bleeding.

WITHIN MOMENTS of the attack on the Trade Center, I realized that we were at war. There was no other name for this but an all-out war. President Bush used the word the next day, and for a while everyone was debating against whom, or what, exactly, this war was. How do you declare war on an organization like al-Qaeda, which has no country? Within a few short weeks a term was coined that would become part of everyday lingo in most of the civilized world: "the war on terrorism."

I had my own dilemma. I'd been drafted into the war on terrorism years before it was declared as such. But who, or what, did *I* have to fight? After 9-11, I knew I had to do something, and I knew that all my previous efforts were nothing compared to what was now needed. What exactly that was I didn't figure out for a few days.

Hamas, PIJ, al-Qaeda, Bin Laden, the 1993 World Trade Center bombing, the U.S. embassies in Kenya and Tanzania, the USS *Cole*— what was the mysterious thread of scarlet, the characteristic sign that was staring me in the eye and I was unable to name? What was the connection of everything I knew to 9-11? What was the name of the enemy against whom I was going to war? Then it struck me. Simple, really, but I knew it had to be the thing I was looking for. I remembered the night I lay in bed in the delivery room, when Shirley was born. There and then, tired, exhilarated because of Shirley, petrified because of Batterjee's book, I got a short glimpse of the face of the monster. In that moment, there were no poisonous tentacles anymore, there was no small game anymore. It was the monster and I, one-on-one, face-to-face.

The revelations were too much; I buried and suppressed them. But immediately after 9-11 I remembered that monster again. With the immense knowledge I'd accumulated on charities and fronts for ter-

rorists, I realized what my part in this war had to be. I knew that I had
to attack terrorism by cutting its power supply, by slashing the umbili-
cal cord that gave it life.

I had to stop the money flow to terrorists.

"JEROME?"

"Yes?" He hurried over and stood, chin up, like a U.S. Marine in
front of his drill sergeant. He was tall, athletic, and shy.

"I know that you came to volunteer for a limited period of time
only," I said, "but we may as well put your time to a better use than we
did in the past few days."

Sam had recommended his friend Jerome to me. Jerome's Wall
Street office had been temporarily closed down by the 9-11 attacks, and
he'd decided to take a break from moneymaking and do some good
instead. He was one of many volunteers who joined us in the days after
the attacks. For a few days, I was too busy to give him anything but
administrative errands. When I thought of a task for him, coming from
the finance world as he did, I suddenly had an inspiration.

I took him to a dark corner in the office where there were two large
boxes. I opened one of them and pulled out a large binder. It said
"SAAR" on the cover. "This is something I began working on a long
time ago," I told him. "I almost feel like it's my baby. I've accumulated
bits and pieces of information on it, sporadically, for a few years, and I
put all of them in these binders. All of it is connected to a certain
address in Herndon, Virginia: 555 Grove Street. And to a certain organization called the SAAR Foundation. For starters, all you need to
understand is that SAAR funds several front groups for terrorist
organizations. You'll learn more about it as you go through the files. I
want you to begin by making a table summarizing all the organizations
you come across in these files."

A couple of hours later Jerome showed up and with great urgency
sought to talk with me. It wasn't like him at all; usually he was all "sor-
rys" and "excuse mes," if he was visible or audible. Now he wanted to
talk, right away.

"I'm sorry to tell you, but SAAR—your baby—was dissolved," he said. "I thought you needed to know this."

This was strange. SAAR dissolved? It had to be a mistake.

"Let me have a look," I said.

In mid-2001, SAAR had filed its 990 for the fiscal year 2000. I'd seen all its previous 990s, but I hadn't had a chance to look at the latest one yet. I should've paid more attention to this baby of mine, I thought as I studied the documents Jerome had brought me. Near the bottom of the current form there indeed was a statement that SAAR had been dissolved in December 2000. It also specified how it sold its stock in Mar-Jac. Mar-Jac was a poultry company selling *halal,* or traditionally slaughtered chickens for Muslims. Mar-Jac, I found out, grossed $240 million in just one year. Sounded like a whole lot of chickens to me. . . . The Mar-Jac stock, which SAAR purchased for $11,964,000, was sold for only $2,650,000. Rough times, tough market. So SAAR had reported a loss of $9,314,000, which meant it paid taxes only on the $2.65 million.

The stock was sold by the dissolving SAAR to a company by the name of Sterling Charitable Gift Fund. Jerome and I looked into this Sterling fund and saw that its address was . . . 555 Grove Street.

Moreover, Sterling's president, Yaqub Mirza, was also SAAR's president. So SAAR went bankrupt, sold nearly $12 million worth of stock to itself at a bargain price of $2.65 million—and laundered more than $9.3 million. Not bad for one day's work.

I continued to look into SAAR's 990 for the year 2000, and to my astonishment, I saw something that I hadn't seen in the corporation's previous tax forms. In 1996, according to item 15 on the form, the company received $120,000 in gifts. In 1997, it received just over $1.1 million. In 1998, according to the 990, the SAAR Foundation, which was dissolved on December 20, 2000, received gifts, grants, and contributions totaling $1,783,545,883. Yes, you read that right. One *billion* seven hundred eighty-three million, five hundred forty-five thousand, eight hundred and eighty-three dollars in gifts to a company that never held a fund-raising event, never published an ad, never sent a letter or e-mail to donors, never appeared on the Internet—never tried to raise money. Not bad for one year's work.

I made sure it wasn't my mistake, that I hadn't missed that piece of information previously. I went back and checked SAAR's 990 for 1998. That astronomical figure was not there.

"Jerome," I told him, "forget any other task I've given you. Concentrate on SAAR alone. I want you to find anything that's available on them. Be twice as thorough everywhere you see that Saudi Arabia is mentioned. We have to know everything about SAAR and 555. We're at war, and our job is to stop the funding of terrorism."

Half an hour later, Jerome had found something. When he looked at Sterling, the company that bought out SAAR, he saw that one of its directors was Cherif Sedky. Sedky got Jerome's attention because of his address, in Saudi Arabia. Sedky used to live and practice law in the United States. He had an office in Washington, D.C., and he served as the registering agent for a large number of the SAAR companies. When Jerome looked at Sedky's other assets, he discovered that he and Khalid Bin Mahfouz were among the owners of a venture called Yeminvest. Bin Mahfouz: Brother-in-law of Usama Bin Laden. Yeminvest: Owner of a port in Yemen.

The port where the USS *Cole* was bombed.

Jerome was horrified. "This *is* war," he said.

THE FIRST TIME I stumbled upon the organizations located at 555 Grove Street was early in my career, when I was studying Sami al-Arian. I first learned that his WISE received most of its money from the Washington-based International Institute of Islamic Thought (IIIT). Then I saw copies of checks and 990s showing that the SAAR Foundation and the Safa Trust also funded Sami's fronts for PIJ. Safa, SAAR, and IIIT all listed their addresses as 555 Grove Street, Herndon, Virginia.

Taha Jaber al-Alwani and Jamal Barzinji, two of the men heading SAAR, Safa, and IIIT, were also active participants in PIJ conferences. On Christmas Eve 1989, at an ICP conference, al-Alwani gave a speech titled "The *Ummah* and the Islamic Movement and the Intellectual

Challenge." These were the days when the end of the war in Afghanistan was imminent and the first *intifada* in Israel was peaking. In his lecture, al-Alwani said:

> There is no doubt that the ideological and organizational crumbling of communism that we are witnessing is due primarily to the Afghan jihad and its effects. This jihad succeeded in achieving a mighty victory in every respect. However, today this jihad is facing an ideological impasse. . . . The *intifada* is going well. Let us ask the Almighty Allah to grant victory to it. . . . However, alongside this jihad we require another kind of jihad, an ideological and cultural jihad in order to reconstruct the Muslim mind and its build so that when victory is achieved we'd be in a position to profit from it and to make use of this achievement for the benefit of the *ummah*.

It wasn't just a coincidence, then, that the organizations headed by Barzinji and al-Alwani funded PIJ's fronts. They were clearly linked to PIJ in more than one way: they shared the same ideology and they were fighting the same war. But at that point I didn't yet understand al-Alwani's words about the "ideological and cultural jihad." Not fully.

Bashir Nafi, one of the four pillars of WISE, was named in a government affidavit as one of the potential successors of Fat'hi Shikaki, the assassinated head of PIJ. After the story of Shallah's nomination as PIJ's secretary-general broke, the INS looked for Nafi in Tampa, where he was supposed to be working for WISE. But they couldn't find him there.

They found him in Virginia instead. His only tie to WISE, they learned, was that WISE was the sponsoring organization on the visa that Sami had arranged for Nafi. Nafi had never worked one single day for WISE.

But he did work for IIIT.

Nafi was deported shortly thereafter and went back to Britain.

IIIT and Sami's PIJ were indeed tightly linked.

I decided to learn about SAAR, Safa, and IIIT, using my favorite method: reading old publications. I plowed through all the Islamic publications I had, searching for articles, ads, bios, anything. I knew that such organizations always publicize themselves, advertise, to make themselves known to their potential readers and donors.

I could find absolutely nothing on SAAR. Not one word.

I tried the Internet. A Google search yielded one single mention of SAAR.

This sole link led me to a Web site called Islam Online. The site specializes in posting various fatwas. Muslims submit questions, prominent scholars and imams answer them. Among these prominent imams are Dar al-Hijra's Muhammad al-Hanooti; Salah Sultan, who at the Chicago IAP conference lectured on how the "children of Zion" cut into the wombs of Muslim mothers; and Sheikh Yousef al-Qaradawi, the prominent cleric who was denied his U.S. visa as a result of my work. I discovered that two prominent Muslims had created that site. One of them was Qaradawi. The other was Abdurahman al-Amoudi, president of the AMC (American Muslim Council), whom I would later catch on tape in Washington's Lafayette Park defiantly declaring his support of terrorist organizations.

Al-Amoudi's résumé was posted on the site.

According to it, he was "the first exclusive endorsing agent for Muslim Chaplains for all branches of the U.S. Armed Forces." How impressive. In addition, the résumé stated, before his work at the AMC, al-Amoudi had served as the executive assistant to the president of . . . the SAAR Foundation.

Since I couldn't find anything else on SAAR, I tried Safa, but I couldn't find a single mention of it.

I obtained a good number of Arabic publications I didn't usually read, including many from Saudi Arabia.

Nothing on SAAR or Safa in those, either.

That was extremely strange. Usually when I'd search for an organization in old newspapers, I'd find enormous amounts of information.

But this time—one big void. That unsettled me. I couldn't figure it out.

I then looked for IIIT. In this case I *was* able to find some links. IIIT, it seemed, was formed in the early 1980s as a think tank; its stated purpose was to educate the public about Islam.

SAAR, Safa, and IIIT were nonprofit organizations. Meaning that, like HLF, IAP, and ICP, they had to live off donations. They did not advertise, nor did they hold fund-raising events—yet they were able to fund other organizations, such as Sami al-Arian's WISE. To check how much money they were handling, I pulled their 990s. What I discovered was unlike anything I'd seen in any of the hundreds of 990s I'd studied.

Safa was giving hundreds of thousands of dollars a year to IIIT.

SAAR was giving millions of dollars a year to Safa.

SAAR was giving to IIIT, too.

SAAR and Safa both invested their money in Mar-Jac, the *halal* chicken factory. Its address was also listed as 555 Grove Street, Herndon, Virginia.

SAAR was also moving millions a year to Humana Charitable Trust, located on the Isle of Man in the British Islands. A location often used for money-laundering operations.

And SAAR was getting millions in gifts.

How did these organizations, a think tank and two charities that weren't making the slightest effort to raise funds, end up with such budgets every year?

REMEMBER THE FIRST TIME I went to Dar al-Hijra and saw Abdalhalim al-Ashqar there? Al-Ashqar, who'd been released from prison around that time following a hunger strike, starred in numerous government documents as the named military leader of Hamas. For years he was under 24/7 surveillance by the FBI. After seeing him at Dar al-Hijra, I looked into the fund he'd incorporated in Mississippi, the al-Aqsa Educational Fund. This charity was described by the FBI, years later, as a Hamas front. As I always do when I research charities such as al-Aqsa, I obtained its IRS forms. In its 1023s—the application for tax-exempt status—I discovered that Muhammad Jaghlit, a member of the board of al-Aqsa, stated his address as 555 Grove Street.

So a member of the board of al-Aqsa, the charity described by the FBI as a Hamas front, was linked to 555. The address that was funding PIJ was now also linked to Hamas.

That was peculiar. After PIJ and Hamas split from their mother organization, the Muslim Brotherhood, they didn't work closely together. In fact, because they were competing for the same target population, there was fierce rivalry between them. Why were they both linked to that address?

The link from 555 to PIJ and Hamas completed the picture for me. I understood the connection, and I reviewed in my mind the important leads that led to an inevitable conclusion.

I knew that Ishaq al-Farhan, the Jordanian diplomat who was deported on account of me, or rather on account of his ties with the Muslim Brotherhood and Hamas, served on IIIT's board of directors. He, of all people, serving on IIIT's board? I knew that IIIT held numerous conferences hosting speakers who were identified with the Muslim Brotherhood. In 1991, for instance, IIIT held a joint conference with the United Association for Studies and Research, in Herndon, Virginia. Among the speakers at this conference were Taha Jaber al-Alwani, Sami al-Arian, Ramadan Abdallah Shallah, Ishaq al-Farhan, Musa Abu Marzook (head of the political bureau of Hamas at the time), and Kamal al-Hilbawi (head of the Muslim Brotherhood in North America).

My conclusion: The reason IIIT was linked to both PIJ and Hamas, the reason Farhan was on its board, the reason IIIT served as the voice of the Muslim Brotherhood even before Hamas and PIJ emerged out of it, and the reason that it sponsored conferences at which members of Hamas and PIJ participated, was that IIIT *was,* for all practical purposes, the Muslim Brotherhood.

Al-Ashqar's conection to 555 gave me another critical clue. Before, because of their funding of Sami's groups, I was concentrating on SAAR, Safa, and IIIT. Now I understood that 555 was more than these organizations. I decided to look into the address itself.

Using a database of public corporate records, one I'd used countless times before, I tried "555 Grove Street, Herndon, Virginia." Typing any address in this database causes a split screen to pop up; on the left appears the name of the company, or companies, listed at that particular address. On the right, the names of the individuals registered as founders and officers of these organizations.

This time, to my astonishment, some 130 names of organizations appeared on the left side of the screen. The list was in alphabetical order. African Muslim Agency, Child Development Foundation, Global Holdings, Grove Street Corporation, and on and on. Farther down the list were IIIT, Mar-Jac, Safa, SAAR, all the way down to something called the York Foundation. Most of the names sounded inconspicuous, as corporate names often are.

Typically, when you click on each organization, the right side of the screen shows the corresponding list of officers of that particular company. With more than a hundred companies, I would've expected hundreds of people's names to pop up. But the names of only a dozen individuals, including Hisham al-Talib, al-Alwani, and Barzinji, all of whom I knew from IIIT, kept appearing in company after company.

If you're having trouble following this, don't feel bad: I was having trouble, too. More than a hundred organizations, twelve individuals, one address, next to no paper trail in any Arabic or English-language publication, virtually no trace on the Internet. And, most important, no evidence of fund-raising. Yet plenty of money flowing freely in all directions.

The stench coming from 555 intensified the deeper I dove.

I continued to study these companies and individuals. This group of twelve men was running the bulk of the Muslim organizations and charities listed at 555, but these men ran still other organizations; this network spanned the United States. Many times the connection worked both ways; the founder of one charity was a board member of another was the president of another. For example, while al-Amoudi was an officer in SAAR, Barzinji, one of the founders of SAAR and IIIT, served on the board of al-Amoudi's AMC.

These one hundred–odd organizations were transferring money among themselves and to and from organizations on the outside of 555 Grove Street. Money was given by organizations at 555 as a gift to

AMC; AMC gave gifts to 555 Grove organizations. 555 Grove charities gave to Dar al-Hijra; Dar al-Hijra donated money back to 555. Some charities, such as HLF, received money from 555 Grove organizations but didn't return the favor. Above all, large sums were flowing constantly to the Isle of Man. Money, I realized, was moving around in circles, the same organizations donating to and investing in one another, and since many of these organizations were tax-exempt, the complex money trail was untraceable.

I wanted to check whether these hundred organizations at 555 Grove were real or just on paper. I began with the telephone directory. A real corporation has to have working phones.

I called 411. You can ask for only three numbers at a time from 411, so I had to call back dozens of times. The vast majority of these companies weren't listed.

SAAR was one of the few that did have a telephone number. I did a reverse search of public records to see which names were attached to that number. The listed number was also that of the Heritage Education Trust, another company headed by SAAR's directors—and listed at 555. Another number I found was for Mar-Jac, the poultry factory. That number was shared with the Safa Trust. And so on. Nothing was making sense.

I realized that I had to see for myself what 555 Grove Street looked like. After all, it could have been a multistory building large enough to accommodate some 130 organizations, and they all might have shared a centralized telephone exchange that created the confusion with the numbers.

George came with me. He was willing to drive, and I was more than happy to avoid flying or having to travel on the train in my Muslim disguise. We reached Herndon, found the address, and looked at the building. It was an office building all right, but it was tiny; it had only three levels, counting the ground floor. The building was made of light brown brick and its windows were tinted so you couldn't see in. The number 555 was proudly displayed on a front-facing window. Across the street was a mosque, the All Dulles Area Muslim Society Center. The ADAMS Center. I decided to go there too and perhaps glean some background information on 555, but first I wanted to visit the address itself.

In the small entrance hall was a board with nameplates. These included a computer company that occupied the lower level, and SAAR.

Not Safa, not IIIT, not Mar-Jac, not any of the other hundred entities claiming residence at 555 Grove Street.

Just SAAR.

What *was* SAAR?

We went to the second level.

Vacant.

On the third floor, at the far end of the hallway, was a glass door with a tiny gold-colored plate reading "SAAR." I knocked on the door.

Silence.

I tried again.

Nothing.

It was the middle of the day, a regular business day, yet there was not one live soul in SAAR.

I decided to go to the mosque across the street to see what I could learn there, and then come back to 555. George stayed in his car. Perhaps the SAAR people were simply out to lunch? Still, I'd expected SAAR, an organization that was funding so many others, to be in a large office with a significant number of employees.

The mosque was equally peculiar; it occupied the third floor of what seemed to be an office building. In the center's office, I approached a bearded man dressed in Pakistani attire. He didn't speak Arabic, so our conversation took place in English. I presented myself as a resident of Pennsylvania, said that I was looking into moving to the Herndon area, and asked for information regarding the community and employment opportunities. The man said that the area was excellent for Muslims, that their community was large and active, and that they even had a Muslim school in their mosque. But he wasn't sure about job openings.

"What about SAAR?" I asked. "I've heard that they are a large business operating in the area."

"Sister," he said, "I wish I could be of more help. But I've never heard of SAAR."

I crossed the street and together with George went to see SAAR again.

This time a man did open the glass door. He wouldn't let us in, wouldn't talk to us. Was very cautious. But behind him, behind the glass door with SAAR's nameplate, I could make out a tiny office with one desk, one telephone, and one computer. I could see that the guy at the door was the only person there.

I now knew for certain that these numerous organizations were a sham. The question remained, what was the need to establish so many organizations in such an intricate network? The tentacles of this network in the United States included companies in North Carolina, Georgia, Utah, Pennsylvania, Maryland, Delaware, Washington, Indiana, Washington, D.C., and, of course, Virginia.

The relationship between IIIT and the Muslim Brotherhood was key to my answering that question. The Muslim Brothers had formed eight decades ago. With time, and owing to constant persecution by the Middle Eastern countries where they operated (and later by the West as well), they developed an impressive cunning and sophistication. Decades before the Western world realized it, the Muslim Brothers perfected techniques using the resources and the financial systems of the West to fund terrorism and promote fundamentalism. One such method was creating a complicated mesh of organizations and charities that would make tracking of their activities impossible. The SAAR network was plotted according to these principles.

But where did the money to SAAR come *from?* What stood behind it? And *what was SAAR,* for crying out loud?

I knew I could solve the mystery. I just needed to find the right clue.

TWO WEEKS LATER, I had to be in the Washington area again for a briefing. I took along two guys from the office, one of whom drove a dark pickup truck, the perfect vehicle for three conspirators with a large load to haul. We brought dark clothes, flashlights, and large black bags. After the day's business, we changed, I tied my hair in a knot, and we drove to 555. We went to the far end of the building's parking lot, where a small structure stood. Four walls and a door, but no ceiling or windows. An identical structure was at the opposite end of the lot, closer to the road and to the building. We decided to start with the one that was more remote.

The small roofless building was where 555's Dumpsters were housed. I'd spotted them the first time I went there, and I decided that since I couldn't find sufficient information on SAAR elsewhere, I'd better take a look in its trash.

We'd researched the garbage pickup schedule and learned that a private hauler came for 555's trash twice a week. The next garbage collection was scheduled for the day after, so the bins would be full when we were there.

We drove up, and to our dismay, some sort of gathering was taking place at the ADAMS Center. Many cars were parked on the street, people kept arriving, and the lights of the third floor were lit. That wasn't good. Although it was dark, somebody might look out from the mosque and notice people going through the Dumpsters across the street! But I wasn't leaving without checking 555's trash. We parked the pickup in front of the trash house to hide our endeavors. One person remained on guard, and two others—in rotation—picked through the garbage. I dove in first.

The stench from SAAR finally got to me, literally. I couldn't tell, of course, what was SAAR's trash, but amid the food remains and other disgusting residue, I found large boxes crammed with papers. I examined them under my flashlight. They were filled with rolls of used computer paper. Not what I was looking for. I continued to look.

You don't even want to know what kinds of revolting items we found there. One thing was certain, though. The people at 555 had a great taste for chicken—*halal,* no doubt. We found hundreds of chicken bones scattered among the papers.

Every few minutes our sentry would call out, urgently, thinking he'd seen someone approaching. One time a few people passed by, and the three of us hid in the bushes behind the trash house. While there, I found an old, dirty, wet, muddied booklet of the International Islamic

Relief Organization, IIRO. I later read in it IIRO's descriptions of its charitable work in Afghanistan and its collaboration with the Saudi Red Crescent.

We tried the other trash house, and after a long while of Dumpster diving, all we could find was an HLF newsletter like the ones I'd been getting in the mail.

I realized that I wouldn't be able to do a thorough job sorting out what was useful there on the spot. I decided to take as much trash as we could with us to examine it in safer and better-lit surroundings.

We began scooping the garbage into the bags we'd brought. I'd fill a bag, push it out of the large container, the guys would load it onto the truck, and then we'd switch.

During one of these cycles the owner of the pickup slipped and fell, headfirst, into the garbage.

We finished loading the pickup and went back to New York.

I can't properly describe the expressions of the tollbooth workers we encountered on our way back to New York. We just prayed we wouldn't get pulled over by a cop. It was late when we got back to the office. While we were hauling the large black bags upstairs, I smiled as I imagined the surprise the next morning of the people who collect 555's garbage. Of course, it would pale in comparison with the surprise of the people in *our* office who arrived in the morning to find a place covered with piles of garbage.

I was dirty and smelly and I probably would've puked if I'd seen myself—so I preferred to finish this job that same night. My researchers and I began going through the trash. Much of the paper was simply used computer paper. Very disappointing. Many of the chicken bones also made the trip to New York. But a few hours into the search, I found some pieces of a letter.

Handwritten, in Arabic. Addressed to a company in Saudi Arabia.

For hours we looked for the missing bits of the letter. We had to go through all the garbage we'd already screened. Shortly before daybreak I was able to put all the pieces together.

It was a draft of a letter sent from Mar-Jac Poultry, Inc., requesting materials and machinery, to a Saudi Arabian company by the name of Watania.

I'd heard that name before. I vaguely remembered it was a large Saudi company. I did a quick search. Watania was indeed a huge conglomerate dealing with chickens, clothes, and a million other things—including publishing concerns, such as the Saudi house that published Batterjee's *The Arab Volunteers in Afghanistan.* Looking at Watania's Web sites—hosted by InfoCom—I found that the company was owned by al-Rajhi. I'd seen that name, al-Rajhi, in some of the companies in 555.

And then, like lightning, it hit me.

SAAR wasn't a what.

It was a who.

SAAR: Sheikh Sulaiman Abdul Aziz al-Rajhi. Or his brother, Saleh Abdul Aziz al-Rajhi.

Two Saudi tycoons, among the richest people on Earth.

This was my missing link, my clue, my Open Sesame to Ali Baba's secret cave. Al-Rajhi was behind it all along, behind SAAR, behind IIIT, behind 555, behind the devious and elusive multibillion-dollar enterprise that funneled money to some of the world's most dangerous terrorist groups. I wasn't sure whether it was Saleh or Sulaiman who gave SAAR its name. Perhaps it was both. It made little difference to me; these two were the main players in the al-Rajhi empire that created 555.

No wonder they didn't publicize SAAR, no wonder they saw no need to raise money from donations. They alone could continue to fund worldwide terrorism for the next millennium.

I'd finally breached 555's wall of deception. First battle won. But I was still far from winning the war.

A CERTAIN ISSUE about SAAR bothered me for some time. SAAR—after I'd discovered what it was, I began calling everything at 555 the SAAR network—was a multibillion-dollar operation that was tightly linked to IIIT and to some hundred other organizations. IIIT was involved with PIJ, Hamas, and the Muslim Brotherhood. Farhan, Sami, Shallah, and Nafi were linked to it. The Saudi billionaires al-Rajhis were funneling money to terrorist organizations through their fronts. These terrorist organizations were Palestinian, a notion that agreed with the Muslim Brotherhood ideology. But it seemed unreasonable that all this monstrous mechanism had been created with only the Middle East in mind.

A year after I'd figured out the connection between 555 and al-Rajhi, the embassy bombings trial began, during which the government released previously classified documents about the investigation. One such document was Wadih al-Hage's phone book. The same book in which Ghassan Dahduli's numbers had been found. I went through the book, parts of which are in Arabic and others in English. Some portions were hardly legible.

Toward the end of the book, I saw the name, with an address in Saudi Arabia.

The name—Saleh Abdul Aziz al-Rajhi. SAAR.

Now why would Usama Bin Laden's personal secretary have the contact information for Saleh al-Rajhi?

A few days later, the government released al-Hage's other phone book. Again, Saleh al-Rajhi's name appeared in it, this time not with the address, but with a telephone number in Saudi Arabia.

During his testimony in that trial, al-Hage disclosed how he started his way with Bin Laden by joining the Afghan mujahideen as a relief worker with the Saudi organization Muslim World League, MWL. I knew that many other al-Qaeda members such as Wa'el Julaidan and Ihab Ali began their jihad with MWL. After I'd heard that al-Hage was also involved with MWL, I checked for the address of its United States office. Naturally, it was 555.

On the twentieth day of the trial, the prosecutor discussed an al-Qaeda cell in the United Kingdom and mentioned a name that sounded awfully familiar to me: Tariq Hamdi. I looked in my ICP binder, and there he was. The last I'd encountered his name, Hamdi was nothing but Sami's secretary. How far he'd gone since then, I thought. Now he was traveling the world and personally delivering satellite phone batteries to Bin Laden. So I studied the distinguished Mr. Hamdi further.

I soon found out that he, too, worked for IIIT. And he listed his address as . . . 555 Grove Street.

Batterjee's book, which in my view is Bin Laden's biography, revealed to me some amazing facts about the al-Qaeda members who were closest to Bin Laden. But that wasn't all I learned from it. On its back cover was BIF's logo and an inscription reading "Lajnat al-Birr al-Islamiya," Islamic Benevolence Foundation, and under that, "World Assembly of Muslim Youth," WAMY. I knew what WAMY was, but I didn't know anything about Lajnat al-Birr al-Islamiya besides the fact that its name was similar to BIF's Arabic name. I searched in old Arabic publications and found a résumé of one Ibrahim Hussain Bahafzallah, stating that he headed the charity Lajnat al-Birr al-Islamiya. Naturally, I looked for possible Bahafzallah links in America. I found that he was the vice president of MWL and two other organizations, all claiming 555 Grove Street as their address.

So there was a strong link between the publishers of the book and 555 Grove. But there was more. On the inside jacket it said that the book was published in 1991, in Jedda, Saudi Arabia, by al-Watania publishing company.

Al-Watania, the same Watania I had found in 555's trash, belonged to al-Rajhi. Its subsidiaries in the United States were Mar-Jac and the other companies listed at 555.

There was no doubt left in my mind. The SAAR network was tied not only to Hamas and PIJ, but also to al-Qaeda.

Al-Qaeda became a part of the 555 story.

Or, in other words, any investigation of mine, be it PIJ, Hamas, or al-Qaeda, turned out to be somehow associated with that address.

Risking a cliché, I found that all roads of terrorist funding and ideology in America lead to 555.

AT THAT POINT in my investigation, two critical questions remained unsolved about the SAAR network. One was how did the men heading the SAAR network, none of whom were Saudi, end up controlling a multibillion-dollar Saudi-funded empire? Many of the directors of the SAAR network live in a fancy neighborhood of Herndon, Virginia, on a street and a court named "Safa." Their group is now believed by the government to be a close-knit and secretive organization.

I found the answer to that in IIIT's corporate records. The records stated the following names of founders and board members:

Taha Jaber al-Alwani, WAMY, Saudi Arabia.

Jamal Barzinji, WAMY, Saudi Arabia.

Oh my God, I thought. IIIT was but a different name for WAMY. WAMY—the World Assembly of Muslim Youth—was for youth. IIIT was WAMY for the youth who came of age. Batterjee, who has been named Bin Laden's financier by the government, headed WAMY in the early 1990s. WAMY published Batterjee's biography of Bin Laden, where the "river of Jihad" is glorified. WAMY published manuals found in the possession of Ahmed Ajaj, one of the conspirators in the 1993 World Trade Center bombing, where the hijacking of buses and murder of civilians were glorified and where poisonous hate statements were made against Americans, Christians, and Jews. WAMY's director in the United States since the day it was founded was Abdallah Bin Laden, Usama's half brother. For these reasons and others, the FBI considers WAMY a suspected terrorist organization. Above all, WAMY was a Saudi organization, a fact over which it took great pride; it even received funding from the government of Saudi Arabia. Barzinji, al-Alwani, al-Talib, and Ahmed Totonji, the four Iraqis who in time would establish the SAAR empire, somehow found their way to Saudi Arabia. The Saudi environment was perfectly conducive to their message and provided them with ample resources with which to promote their views. It was in Saudi Arabia that IIIT was created, and whatever ideas led its founders to do so had to have ripened during their stay there. Something must have taken place in Saudi Arabia, I thought, that put them on the track leading to SAAR.

The most important question, and the most difficult: What was the motive behind creating this gigantic empire in the West? It couldn't have been the funding of jihad only; it was far too big and too complex to serve just that. It had to have yet another purpose.

To understand the motives, to find out what future these four Iraqis had envisioned, I decided to study their pasts.

A chilling picture emerged.

Ahmed Totonji is one of the four Iraqis who are the heart and soul of the SAAR network. Following the tradition I'd described, Totonji went to England for his higher education, as did many affluent young Iraqi men, including my older brother, Ron. While studying petroleum engineering in 1960 in the United Kingdom, Totonji established the Muslim Student Society of the United Kingdom together with other students, most of whom were Iraqis like him. During those years he met his mentor, Hisham al-Talib, whose sister Totonji married. Al-Talib was a close friend of Barzinji's, and both of them were heavily exposed to the al-Ihwan movement—the Muslim Brotherhood. In 1963, Totonji moved to the United States and shortly thereafter created the Muslim Students Association, MSA. He spent seven years on a two-year doctorate thesis so that he could work on community issues for Muslim youth in America. The MSA grew rapidly out of the confines of a mere student organization; Wa'el Julaidan, for instance, headed the Islamic Center of Tucson at the same time that he served as head of the MSA. The MSA, with more than a hundred chapters on American college campuses, raised money for HLF, BIF, and GRF, all of which were designated by the government after 9-11. MSA's Web site, run from the chapter at Ohio State University, published news releases from the Algerian Armed Islamic Group, a terrorist organization according to the State Department. Some MSA publications advertise Muslim Brothers propaganda and its official Web site lists Usama Bin Laden as a "Muslim scholar," with his picture and his first-ever published declaration of war on America in 1996.

Totonji envisioned a worldwide network of MSAs, which was realized as the International Islamic Federation of Student Organizations, IIFSO, in 1966. In 1969, Totonji became the IIFSO's secretary-general. These MSAs were spread worldwide, with the exception of

Arab countries. These regimes were not tolerant of movements that bore Muslim Brotherhood ideology.

Totonji then moved to Saudi Arabia and formed WAMY as the next step beyond the MSA ideology. Some of his colleagues and friends, Iraqi nationals he met in Britain and the United States who shared his enthusiasm about promoting the Muslim cause, moved to Saudi Arabia as well. These men, including Barzinji and al-Alwani, regrouped in Saudi Arabia. The wheels of their scheme were set in motion after they secretly met with Saleh al-Rajhi, whom they described as "a resource for WAMY and a man who served the Muslim *ummah* better than anyone else."

Al-Rajhi's brilliant idea was to use non-Saudis as ambassadors to promote the cause. Non-Saudis would hardly be suspected by anyone of promoting a Saudi agenda. Although most of these Iraqi men who headed the SAAR network had met in the West, they all showed great interest in pan-Muslim issues. Then, when they went to Saudi Arabia, they got hooked up with the Rajhi brothers. All of these men received Saudi citizenship, which is almost unheard of for immigrants to Saudi Arabia. Even Saudi-born children of immigrants rarely get citizenship or any other form of Saudi documentation. These Iraqis received their citizenship swiftly, with the blessing of the Saudi intelligence service.

In 1979 Totonji and his associates attended a conference held by a group of leading Muslims scholars, whom Totonji described in a video interview as the "heads of the Muslim *ummah*." The conference was headed by Sheikh Yousef al-Qaradawi, the man I later managed to block from entering the United States. It took place in Lugano, Switzerland. These scholars discussed the problems of the *ummah,* such as assimilation of Muslims in the West. After careful deliberation, the scholars concluded that they should work on two fronts to improve the situation: establish financial institutions on the one hand and educational institutions on the other.

One of the immediate implications of that resolution was the creation of IIIT as a model for think tanks that would spearhead Muslim education.

But this idea wasn't new to the SAAR people.

In 1973 Barzinji and al-Talib established a religious (and therefore tax-exempt) organization in the United States and called it the North American Islamic Trust, NAIT. Ironically, their imams were censored in the Muslim world, and they could do their work only in the United States, which gave them full freedom of speech.

I knew that NAIT owned some mosques in America. The mosque in Bridgeview, Illinois, was one of them. It was purchased by NAIT in the early 1970s. In a handwritten testimony, Muhammad Salah, the Hamas terrorist cum used-car salesman whom I'd met at the IAP conference in Chicago, explained how the imam of the Bridgeview mosque, a leader of the Muslim Brotherhood in the United States, had recruited him. The mosque in Norman, Oklahoma, the one Zacarias Moussaoui joined shortly after his arrival there, was owned by NAIT. Two of the 9-11 hijackers used the help of members of a mosque in San Diego to set up their network. That mosque belongs to NAIT. Moaataz al-Hallak, imam of the mosque in Arlington, Texas, was linked by the government to Bin Laden and his network. Al-Hallak coordinated the purchase of a private jet for Bin Laden in the early 1990s. The mosque he preached at belonged, of course, to NAIT. Two out of the six men arrested in Buffalo in October 2002 for planning to go to Afghanistan and join al-Qaeda were members of a mosque that belonged to NAIT. When I obtained the articles of incorporation of Dar al-Hijra, I saw that it too was owned by NAIT.

NAIT's articles of incorporation state the organization's mission on the first page: "The purpose of this corporation is to serve the best interests of Islam and of MSA." They also show that Barzinji and al-Talib, the founders of the SAAR network, were the founders of NAIT, MSA, and ISNA, the Islamic Society of North America. ISNA was a subsidiary of NAIT. As was the SAAR Foundation.

It was getting more baffling than ever.

Then I found that NAIT didn't own *some* mosques in America.

NAIT was the entity that owned the largest number of mosques in America—several hundred out of the 1,200 in existence. With the colossal money machine of al-Rajhi backing it, NAIT was able to purchase this overwhelming number. NAIT was able to complete all these acquisitions in less than a decade, easily squashing any opposition. With all these mosques in its control, NAIT began promoting its agenda.

It all fell into place now. NAIT, ISNA, MSA, SAAR, IIIT, ICP, WISE, IAP, Safa, and a hundred other organizations at 555 Grove Street were part of a master plan to promote what al-Alwani had called "ideological and cultural jihad." Only now did I truly understand what he'd meant. The rich Saudi businessmen, the al-Rajhis, used their ambassadors—al-Alwani, Totonji, Barzinji, and al-Talib—to purchase mosques in the United States in order to indoctrinate and radicalize young American Muslims in fundamentalism and jihad.

And thus the al-Rajhis and their naturalized-Saudi, Iraqi-born ambassadors developed a brilliant method of sparking an insidious Muslim revolution. They'd envisioned a Muslim *ummah* some thirty years ago and had shrewdly decided to shape the world without engaging in overt battle or conquest—at least not in the beginning.

The SAAR people understood that they had enough money to buy their way to Muslim world domination.

CHAPTER 11

The Saudi Connection

"AT 12:01 A.M. THIS MORNING, a major thrust of our war on terrorism began with the stroke of a pen. Today, we have launched a strike on the financial foundation of the global terror network."

With these words, uttered in a press conference in the White House's Rose Garden on Monday, September 24, 2001, George W. Bush announced his plan to go after those who fund terrorists. Four days before, on Friday, I'd received a call from a government official. He said he was about to fax me a list of a number of organizations: would I provide information about them? As usual, I didn't even ask what the list was being used for and what would be done with what I gave. My job was to provide information, not to ask questions. Except for one.

"When do you need the material?" The more urgent, the less time I had for research. "How about yesterday?" the official replied sheepishly.

Why do these calls always come on Fridays?

The list I was faxed contained sixty-odd names. Some, like al-Qaeda, Abu-Sayyaf, and Maktab al-Khidamat, I knew very well. Some of the others were less familiar: al-Hamati Sweets Bakeries, al-Nur Honey Center, and al-Shifa Honey Press for Industry and Commerce. Honey wasn't chosen randomly, it seemed; besides channeling some of their profits to al-Qaeda, these businesses helped smuggle weapons and drugs. Their logic in picking the honey trade as a cover for contraband was sickeningly simple. Because of the consistency and smell of honey, U.S. inspectors tended to avoid scrutinizing it.

To be able to make the deadline, I split the list among my researchers. Each team would work on a number of these entities, and I worked with all the teams. One of the names on the list, I noticed at a quick glance, was Rabita Trust. The name bore a striking resemblance to the Muslim World League's Arabic name: Rabita al-Alam al-Islami. I dug up information on Rabita and soon learned that it was indeed a subsidiary of MWL. MWL, the largest Islamic charity in the world, funded by the Saudi government, knowingly funded worldwide jihad. Its address in the United States: 555 Grove Street, Herndon, Virginia. We worked the entire weekend and by Sunday afternoon we'd compiled three large binders of reports and backup material. We discovered that one of Rabita's directors was Wa'el Julaidan. The Wa'el Julaidan I'd tried to interest the White House in years before. The Wa'el Julaidan who, together with Abdallah Azzam and Usama Bin Laden, founded Maktab al-Khidamat and later became al-Qaeda's chief financier. Because Julaidan headed Rabita, it was clear to me that this trust was tightly linked to al-Qaeda. My report on Rabita and Julaidan was six pages long. In it I once again offered proof of Julaidan's activities to the government.

A day after I'd submitted the report, President Bush signed Executive Order 13224, designating a list of entities from around the globe as financiers and supporters of terrorism. Amendments to this executive order, adding several names to the list of designations, followed over the next weeks and months.

To my astonishment and delight, the government used my reports in announcing some of these designations. The results of my research, with the binders of backup material, were presented almost word for word.

I later learned why my work was needed here. The protocol for such designations begins with intelligence information the CIA, FBI, Treasury, and White House receive on potential financiers of terrorism. The information is then evaluated by a team composed of officials from these agencies. A decision is then made whether to designate a certain entity as a financier of terror. This team, however, is unable to determine which parts of the information it has, if any, are in the public domain.

The government will not designate these entities without providing some evidence of their wrongdoing to the American public. That's exactly where I come in. My staff and I are able to provide the information that's available in public records. Using my research, the government can justify its designations to the media without having to publicly reveal intelligence information and jeopardize future investigations.

The first presidential executive order designated several organizations from the list I was given, but not Rabita; I heard that Rabita wasn't in the first group because Pervez Musharraf, Pakistan's president, was on its board of directors. It would have been embarrassing for him to be linked to a charity designated by the United States as a terrorist organization. After Musharraf's involvement with the charity was clarified a few weeks later, however, Rabita was added to the president's list and its assets were frozen.

Rabita's association with MWL piqued my interest. I found it preposterous that an organization designated by the United States as a financier of terrorists was funded by the Saudi government. This meant that the Saudis, our purported allies, were bankrolling jihad.

Rabita, you see, existed solely on funding from its mother organization, the Muslim World League. MWL in turn is financed by the Saudi government. Arafat al-Ashi, the MWL representative in Canada, testifying in a Canadian trial of a suspected terrorist, said, "Let me tell you one thing. The Muslim World League . . . is a fully government-funded organization. In other words, I work for the government of Saudi Arabia."

According to its official newsletter, the *Muslim World News,* MWL supports and funds jihad in Kashmir, Chechnya, Afghanistan, Palestine, the Philippines, Lebanon, Sudan—literally anywhere jihad is taking place.

As I'd advanced in my field, as I studied, one by one, HLF, IAP, WISE, ICP, Maktab al-Khidamat, BIF, GRF . . . all the way to SAAR, what was mind-boggling to me was that under every stone I turned, some connection to Saudi Arabia peeked back at me. From the first days of al-Qaeda and the Afghan war in the late 1970s, one way or another, Saudi money was always part of the picture. Why?

The reason is straightforward, really. Saudi Arabia is a deeply religious country. One of Islam's important creeds is that all belongs to Allah. Wealth, which is abundant in Saudi Arabia, is given to Allah's believers only in trust. To purify that money, to get Allah's blessing for its proper use, believers have to donate a standard portion of that money to good deeds. *Zakat,* "growth," the act of giving alms, is what purifies money in Allah's eyes: "Take from their wealth a portion for charity to clean and sanctify them." And the most worthy cause for such donations, it goes without saying, is jihad.

But why would rich Saudis risk getting involved in remote wars? I wondered. Why should the Saudi government worry about jihad in Kashmir or Bosnia or Chechnya?

The answer to that originates in Wahhabism. Wahhabism is a movement in Islam dating back to the eighteenth century and named after its founder, Abdul Wahhab. It is a fundamentalist movement calling for removal of all innovations from Islam. It seeks to make Muslim nations more Muslim and to make non-Muslim nations Muslim. Its goal, in short, is Muslim world domination. The best places to start such a Wahhabist transformation are where violent conflict between Muslims and infidels is already in progress, such as in Palestine and Kashmir. As the Ottoman empire collapsed after World War I, the Wahhabis found a golden opportunity. They first conquered the two holiest cities to Islam, Mecca and Medina, and then they set up a state.

They called it Saudi Arabia.

For Saudis, then, supporting jihad is equivalent to promoting the growth of Islam. But actually *performing* jihad? As everyone knows, fifteen out of the nineteen 9-11 hijackers were Saudis. How come none of them fit the profile of a so-called suicide martyr? None of them impoverished, none living under occupation, none from a broken home, none uneducated, none desperate. What brought these young men to commit such monstrous acts of ultimate barbarism?

Education. After 9-11, I looked into the Saudi education system, and what I found about it was scary. For example, fourth-graders in Saudi Arabia learn why the sword appears on their flag. "The sword stands for the Jihad for the sake of *Allah*," their textbooks say. Students learn poems like the following, taken from an eighth-grade textbook:

Attention Israel. We are a nation. One day our sword will harvest your head.

By the sword, our country will regain its right and its dignity. . . .

In the sixth grade, one of the new words they learn is *mujahed* and its proper use in various sentences, including the singular and plural forms. Such sentences include "The *mujahidoon* won for the sake of Allah" and "Allah loves the mujahideen." In the seventh grade, in religious studies, Saudi children learn the meaning of Qur'ânic verses. One says, "We have to be careful of the *kufr* [infidels] and we can ask Allah to destroy them in our prayers."

No wonder alarming numbers of Saudi kids absorb this Wahhabi education and start thinking about their future in terms of "What do I want to be when I blow up?"

So *zakat* is the reason money is donated, and Wahhabist education is the reason the donations go toward worldwide jihad. But how does one directly fund jihad? Many of the groups carrying out jihad—Hamas and PIJ among them—have been outlawed in several countries. Bin Laden has waged war against Saudi Arabia itself. How could a good Saudi give *zakat* to him without betraying the Saudi government?

This is the genius of the Islamic charities, as crafted by Abdallah Azzam, bin Laden's mentor and spiritual father. What's more purifying and noble than donating your money to a charity? The charity then forwards the money to a front group masquerading as a think tank or religious or educational institution. Then this front forwards the money to the jihad and the mujahideen. It's a clever scheme that enables easy money laundering and makes tracking of funds nearly impossible. Our government was completely deceived by this strategy for a long time, allowing enormous amounts of Saudi petrodollars to exchange hands uninterrupted.

Now the Saudi government doesn't fund Bin Laden. Not directly. But it does fund, for instance, MWL, which in turn funds jihad—including Bin Laden's jihad. For the Saudis, jihad against any non-Muslim is justified, no matter what, because it is aimed at spreading Wahhabist Islam. But what are all these places—Chechnya, Afghanistan, Bosnia, the Philippines—where the money flows to support jihad? They are al-Qaeda strongholds, where Bin Laden's men play a major role in the jihad. So although money does not go directly from the Saudi government to Bin Laden, it does end up in al-Qaeda's hands. Moreover, the Saudi government openly funds Hamas; the royal family has stated it publicly. And what is Hamas? Its operatives have trained in Bin Laden's camps, and its financiers—such as Yassin Qadi, the wealthy Saudi who was designated by the U.S. government—fund al-Qaeda, too. Hamas's jihad is indistinguishable from that of al-Qaeda.

The United States government still calls the Saudis "our friends and allies." Yet to the Saudis, we are nothing but infidels. The Saudis support jihad; Islamic terrorism, abetted by Wahhabism, originates in Saudi Arabia and is funded by Saudi oil wealth.

And that, to me, is the Saudi connection.

AFTER I SENT to the government my reports on the charities on that first list, I continued to study Rabita carefully. Being particularly interested in terrorist ties on U.S. soil, I searched for possible links between Rabita and American-based organizations. I found that Rabita, unlike its mother organization, MWL, did not have a branch in the United States. So I checked out Rabita's officers. In this world of Islamic charities, as I'd discovered with SAAR, an organization can be nothing more than a name, easily founded and easily dissolved. But if you follow the people behind the organization, you may get to the bottom of things. These people don't come and go as often as the organizations they create. I therefore concentrated my research on two of the three founders and directors of Rabita: Abdallah Omar Nasseef and Abdallah al-Obaid. The third founder was Julaidan; I knew his story all too well. The names Nasseef and al-Obaid weren't new to me, either; I'd read numerous articles about them in *Muslim World News*. Nasseef, who was secretary-general of MWL at the time Julaidan ran the organization's Pakistan branch, had left a deep impression on me. Nasseef was mentioned in nearly every issue of MWL's newsletter. In the majority of his speeches he was quoted stating that MWL had to assist the jihad, which was the only way to liberate Muslim lands such as Afghanistan, Chechnya, Kashmir, and Palestine.

I asked Jerome to try to find out whether Nasseef had any links in the United States.

I was in the middle of an important call when Jerome, wearing an ear-to-ear grin, waved before my eyes a piece of paper showing the results of his search.

A quick look at the paper revealed the whole story to me. Suppressing a shriek, I thumped my fist on my desk and my jaw dropped. Jerome pointed his thumb and index finger like a gun, slowly brought his hand to his lips, and blew away the virtual smoke.

A smoking gun it was. Nasseef was the director of a Saudi organization called Makkah al-Mukarimah, the Holy Mecca. The U.S. address for that organization was 555 Grove Street.

But that wasn't all; Nasseef's personal address was also listed at 555 Grove.

Sam was working on al-Obaid, the other Rabita director. He discovered that al-Obaid, the current secretary-general of MWL (whose office in the United States is at 555 Grove), was also the director of an investment company called Sanabel al-Kheer, Inc. Listed, of course, at 555. Moreover, he was the deputy general manager of al-Watania Poultry, one of al-Rajhi's companies.

So Nasseef and al-Obaid, the former and the current secretaries-general of MWL and directors of Rabita Trust, which was designated for funding al-Qaeda, were closely tied with 555. The tentacles of 555 were reaching everywhere.

As for Julaidan, the director-general of Rabita Trust, only a year after 9-11, the Treasury, using my reports on him, finally designated him as Bin Laden's financier and al-Qaeda's chief logistics officer: "The United States has credible information that Wa'el Hamza Julaidan is an associate of Usama Bin Laden and several of Bin Laden's top lieutenants. Julaidan has directed organizations that have provided financial and logistical support to al-Qaeda. Accordingly, the United States is designating Julaidan under Executive Order 13224 as a person who supports terror."

I'd been trying to interest the government in Julaidan for years. Finally, in 2002, the tables turned. I consider his designation my personal victory.

JOHN CANFIELD PHONED ME one day in late 2001. He was about to leave Tampa for his job overseas and told me that he'd just received a call from a guy on a Customs task force based in Washington. The task force sought John's advice, as an expert on financing of terrorism, on terror-related money-laundering operations.

"They said they wanted me to fly to meet them. I told them that the real expert was much closer to them than I was," he told me. "I've given them your number. I believe the guy who's going to call you is named Mark."

"Do you know this Mark person?" I asked.

"I do," said John. "He's more senior than I am. Although he's never done terrorism before, the guy is a very good agent. He comes from narcs, where his undercover operations made him famous. I heard he disguised himself as a woman in some of his jobs, shaving the hair off his extremities. He was even shot in the shoulder once. Take my word for it: This guy means business."

Less than an hour later Mark called and presented himself as one of the agents of Green Quest. He told me that Green Quest was a newly formed Treasury task force, the stated mission of which was cracking down on money transfers from the United States to terrorist organizations. Could he come to New York and meet with me?

When Mark showed up, I couldn't imagine how this six-foot-tall, broad-shouldered man had ever passed as a woman. The thought amused me. Could I ever pass as a man? Not in a million years.

Mark was eager to learn. I taught him the general principle of front groups for terrorism and how they funnel funds to jihad. I prepared for him a list of topics that I thought were worth looking into. These leads, relating primarily to money-laundering operations, included suspicious activity in Florida, Michigan, and California. As Green Quest is an umbrella unit that supervises and coordinates investigations of local task forces, Mark would take my leads and forward them to the teams in the relevant states. But unlike others who took my leads and forwarded them to "the right people," who did nothing with those leads, Mark immediately proved to me that he was dead serious. He'd forward my leads to the agents on these local task forces; soon after, they'd be calling me to set up a meeting and within a few days we'd all convene. I'd brief them, and they'd investigate, charging full steam ahead. It seemed as though things were finally happening.

A few minutes into my third meeting with Mark, Sam walked in with some documents that had just arrived from Europe.

"I apologize," he said, "but I know you've been waiting for this. I thought you might want to have a look at it."

I looked at the documents—poor copy, hardly legible, and worst of all, in German. But I didn't need to know the language; I could worry about the translation later. The important part of those corporate records from Vaduz, Liechtenstein, was the list of names in them.

I looked at the names. I looked at Mark, and then I looked at the papers again. "Wow, so their empire extends far beyond our borders," I mumbled.

I just kept staring at the names. I realized that I'd been missing what was right under my nose.

"We've been barking up the wrong tree, Mark." My words startled him. "You came to me for leads. We've been chasing these leads around the country. These are all small investigations and we should leave them to the local task forces that are working on them now. The real deal is right in your own backyard, near Washington, D.C. I've got something here in these papers from Vaduz that's complicated and will take me very long to explain, but it would be worth your time, believe me. It's about an address in Herndon, Virginia. It's a lead like you'd never imagined possible. Remember that name and number—555 Grove Street—because from now on this is what you'll be working on. This address is going to change your life and make Green Quest famous."

Mark knew me well at this stage. He believed every word I said.

IN 1976, Hisham al-Talib, Muhammad M. Shamma, and Jamal Barzinji, the founders of the SAAR network, founded a bank in the small kingdom of Liechtenstein, in the city of Vaduz. They named it Nada International after its director, Youssef M. Nada. Nada, an Egyptian-born naturalized Italian citizen in his seventies, a good friend of Iraq's Saddam Hussein, was one of the most prominent leaders of the Muslim Brotherhood. He was imprisoned in Egypt for his involvement in an attempt to assassinate Gamal Abdel-Nasser, the first Egyptian president. After he was set free, he left for Europe, where he established the Muslim Brotherhood's major financial organizations— and those of al-Qaeda. Nada also became director of two banks founded in the Bahamas: Bank al-Taqwa—"fear of Allah"—and Akida Bank Private.

On November 7, 2001, President Bush designated Bank al-Taqwa, its key executives, and its closely affiliated businesses as financial supporters of al-Qaeda and called to freeze al-Taqwa's assets. Akida was designated alongside al-Taqwa. These two banks were later shut down by Bahamian authorities. The president described al-Taqwa as "an association of offshore banks and financial management firms that have helped al-Qaeda shift money around the world. Al-Taqwa . . . raises funds for al-Qaeda. They manage, invest, and distribute those funds. They provide terrorist supporters with Internet service, secure telephone communications, and other ways of sending messages and sharing information. They even arrange for the shipment of weapons. . . . They present themselves as legitimate businesses, but they skim money from every transaction for the benefit of terrorist organizations. They enable the proceeds of crime in one country to be transferred to pay for terrorist acts in another." The president concluded by saying that "by shutting these [al-Taqwa] networks down, we disrupt the murderers' work. Today's action interrupts al-Qaeda's communications. It blocks an important source of funds."

As the Treasury described them, al-Taqwa and Akida were "shell companies" and "not functional banking institutions." Al-Taqwa, a network of companies in Switzerland, Liechtenstein, the Bahamas, and Italy, provided investment advice and cash transfer mechanisms for various radical Islamic groups. Al-Taqwa controlled, at a certain point, $220 million in assets. It had thousands of client investments in accordance with the Shari'a, Islamic law, which forbids charging interest. Among its largest clients were Yousef al-Qaradawi, his wife, his children, and many other members of his family. Other clients of al-Taqwa included several members of the Bin Laden family, including brothers and sisters of Usama. As Akida Bank's director, Nada rather amazingly *employed* one Sulaiman Abdul Aziz al-Rajhi: one of the Saudi brothers behind SAAR.

So al-Rajhi, with his legendary riches, worked for Nada. Yet Nada worked for Barzinji and al-Talib, who in turn worked for al-Rajhi's charity, the SAAR Foundation. Are you good and confused? That's the general idea.

On August 29, 2002, fourteen additional organizations affiliated with al-Taqwa were designated by President Bush, their assets frozen for financially aiding al-Qaeda. These organizations were either owned or run by Nada.

Nada has been designated a "special designated global terrorist" for his financial support of al-Qaeda. He has said he believes he's a victim of guilt by association because he is a member of the Muslim Brotherhood and because some members of the Bin Laden family were his clients. "I have been a member of the Muslim Brotherhood for fifty years," he said. "That is no secret. But it is not a violent organization."

Sure it isn't, Mr. Nada. It's only the mother organization of PIJ, Hamas, al-Qaeda, and many other such groups.

The government designated Nada. Good. Later, his organization, Nada International, was also designated. Better still. But Nada headed only these few financial institutions in Europe and the Bahamas. He wasn't the only man behind the worldwide empire. He was by no means the mastermind behind the plan to dominate the world. The 555 group—the Rajhis and their ambassadors—were those who employed Nada in the first place when they founded Nada International. They were the ones who planned and created a global empire with tentacles reaching everywhere. They created Islamic institutions, such as IIIT, geared toward preaching their kind of Islam. They bought the mammoth number of mosques in America, in which radicalism prevails. They founded financial institutions that finance worldwide terror.

Nada is designated, true. But al-Rajhi, al-Alwani, Barzinji, al-Talib, Totonji, and the other pillars of SAAR are not.

MARK LOOKED at the documents I'd just received from Liechtenstein. They were the evidence that the SAAR group was the founder of Nada International. I understood that the SAAR financial network was spread over much more than just the United States. It was SAAR, its affiliates, and their officers that Green Quest had to go after, I realized. Green Quest, with me as its stealthy guiding beam, had to crack down on 555.

I gave Mark an overview on SAAR, starting from the very beginning. How it funds fronts for PIJ and Hamas. How it's tied to the Muslim Brotherhood. And to MWL. And to al-Qaeda. I showed him the list of the SAAR network's hundred companies and explained how it was divided into organizations, individuals, and addresses. I explained how the same twelve individuals controlled these companies. I showed him the 990s with the $1.8 billion that the SAAR

Foundation received from donations in 1998. Mark was ecstatic from the moment I began telling him about it. But he still needed to get the investigation approved by his superiors at Green Quest.

He called the next morning.

"We've been approved. My bosses think the info you gave us is worth looking into. They wanted our team to meet you and begin working on 555. I wondered whether we can come to see you tomorrow."

"Tomorrow?" I asked Mark. "No, I'll need more time to prepare for such a briefing. I'll need to arrange binders, go over documents—"

"What for?" Mark said. "Just repeat what you told me. No one could be more prepared than you are on this!" There's always *what* to prepare for a convincing presentation. Jerome and I stayed in the office until after midnight to do it.

I was expecting the usual team of two, three investigators, tops. To my surprise, Mark arrived with seven people in tow, all meticulously dressed in suits. There were Green Quest agents, IRS agents, and agents from Customs's Sterling, Virginia, office, which had the jurisdiction over Herndon and 555 Grove Street. Dave Kane, an agent from the Sterling office, a tall, thin man with a kind expression, was among the group. He'd been with Customs for three years, and like Mark, he too had had no experience with counterterrorism until Green Quest, but he would later become pivotal in this investigation. I asked Jerome to join us, we arranged another desk to accommodate the large group, and I began briefing them on 555.

I was impressed. Sending eight people to meet me meant that they were serious. In 1999, I was approached by two agents of the FBI Virginia office who asked for information on Barzinji and other SAAR directors. We met. I worked with them for a few months. The FBI agents investigated and even interviewed some of the 555 people in the presence of their lawyers. Similarly to so many others, this FBI investigation on 555 slowly faded away. To date, nothing happened with it. Maybe this time, I thought, with Green Quest, it would be different. I was highly motivated to give them the SAAR story—and to persuade them that it was very important.

We sat for six hours. I explained that SAAR was a network of think tanks, charities, nonprofit and for-profit companies, some hundred in all, based at 555 Grove Street. I explained who Sulaiman and Saleh al-Rajhi were. I told the agents how I'd first encountered 555 Grove when I looked into Sami al-Arian and PIJ and when I was studying Hamas front groups. With HLF, the al-Aqsa Educational Fund, WISE, ICP, and many other Islamic charities linked to terrorism, I told them, there was always some connection to SAAR.

My briefing, to this point, as I unwrapped the story in a chronological order, was focused on the ties between SAAR and the Palestinian organizations Hamas and PIJ. Interesting by itself, but not Green Quest's top priority, namely al-Qaeda. So I introduced the Tariq Hamdi story to them and elucidated his ties with Sami al-Arian, with IIIT, and with Bin Laden and his satellite phone. This latter story astonished them. Then I pulled out my copies of Wadih al-Hage's telephone books. None of the agents knew who al-Hage was! So I explained to them who he was and what he did. Then I showed them Saleh al-Rajhi's name and numbers in both of al-Hage's books. The agents were speechless as I continued to brief them.

At the end of my presentation I reiterated, "The first thing you need to do is go to Tampa, Florida, as quickly as you can." John Canfield could help them down there, but he was leaving Florida for his next job any day now. "In Tampa you can get all the stuff that I don't have. The FBI there has been working on Sami for long years. They've got documents, videotapes of the SAAR people in ICP conferences, copies of checks given to Sami by SAAR, letters—crucial information for your investigation. You need to go there before Canfield leaves, and he'll be able to lead you through the maze of compiled information and tell you what material you need and where you can find it. Without him it'll take you forever. Then, when you come back, get in touch with the FBI agents who worked on this a couple years ago. They, too, have a good amount of information they gathered on SAAR, which they may share with you."

THE TASK FORCE WENT to Florida, as I'd suggested, and Mark called as soon as they'd returned. I knew better than to ask him what they'd gotten there; I'd been working with the government for years, and the rules were clear to me. I giveth, it taketh away. End of story.

"Remember you told me about a tape where Sami is introduced as PIJ's representative and where he collects money for PIJ?" Mark said. "Can you make a copy of that tape for me?" Naturally, I told him I would. But why would he need the tape from me? They'd just been in Tampa, where this and many other tapes are kept! I guess they didn't have time to copy all the material, I thought.

A few days later Mark called and asked me for copies of FBI and INS affidavits I'd told him about. That was even more bizarre, but I faxed them to him.

Later that day, Dave Kane called me. "You said you had transcripts of Barzinji and al-Alwani in ICP conferences," he said.

"Yes?"

"Could I get them from you?"

"Sure."

"Also, you mentioned having copies of checks from IIIT to Sami. Could you fax me those?"

"Of course," I said, "I'd be more than happy to help you guys. But the copies I have of the checks are of poor quality and are barely legible. The FBI in Tampa must have much clearer copies, and probably many more checks than I do. Why don't you call them and ask them to fax you their copies of the checks?"

"I guess you're right." There was something funny in his voice. "Could you please make copies of those checks, as best you can, and FedEx them to me anyway?"

These requests continued for some time, and I was gradually able to figure out what had happened in Florida. I knew the players; I knew the FBI team in Tampa well. These were the people who'd put me under investigation. These were the people who'd investigated John Canfield and kicked him off Sami's investigation. They'd provided next to no help to Loraine, the INS immigration attorney who'd come to me for help on her investigation after she'd come up dry with the FBI in Tampa. I didn't expect much of that team of people. But I couldn't have dreamed how bad it would be for Green Quest.

The Green Quest agents did meet with Canfield, who told them exactly what they should look for at the FBI facilities and where they'd be able find it. Unfortunately, he didn't have any documents in his possession—he'd had to surrender everything to the FBI when he was dismissed from the case. But he'd continued to play ball with the FBI whenever they called him for information and so he took the Green Quest team to the FBI headquarters in Tampa and introduced them to the investigation's new head, Jerry. The Green Quest agents explained to Jerry what they were doing and asked him for the pertinent information on SAAR and their ties to Sami. They asked him for the material obtained in the raids on Sami's ICP and WISE.

They were told that Sami was under *FBI* investigation. The material the FBI had on Sami was therefore confidential. Green Quest couldn't get any of it.

Remember that we are talking *months* after 9-11.

The Green Quest agents tried to explain that there was no competition between them and the Tampa task force. They only wanted the information relating to their investigation, not general information on Sami. So Jerry asked them to submit a detailed, written report on Green Quest's investigation, explaining exactly which material they needed from the FBI and why they needed it.

That activity took up an entire afternoon of their visit in Tampa.

That was enough to get Marcy Futerman, the head of Green Quest, on the phone to her superior in Customs. Futerman is a soft-spoken, motherly boss, but she's protective of her team. She realized that without some noise, her agents might come back empty-handed. Her boss in Customs called the FBI headquarters in Washington, D.C., and asked for an authorization for Green Quest to examine the material in Tampa. The FBI headquarters authorized the request, called the Tampa office, and instructed them to cooperate with Green Quest.

Mark and his companions submitted their report to Jerry and were finally allowed to enter the evidence rooms. They were given a few boxes, much like the story with Loraine, and told that these were the only boxes that contained relevant material for their investigation. But this wasn't all. They were instructed only to look at the material. They were not allowed to copy, scan, photocopy, or record anything. The only thing they were allowed to do was jot down in their notebooks what they saw. Furthermore, they were supervised by an FBI agent who watched them at all times to make sure they didn't copy or take anything from the boxes—and to listen to their conversation. When they began discussing documents they thought were valuable, as soon as they showed enthusiasm about what they found, they were told by their FBI minder that it was time to take a break; it was time for lunch. The FBI seemed petrified that Green Quest would find in the material something that the Bureau had overlooked, and every effort was made to prevent that from happening.

The trip was a failure in many ways, but Green Quest didn't return to Washington completely empty-handed. They came back with the superb reports that John had given them. What they lacked was evidence, the material that the FBI had yet wouldn't let *them* have. This was the reason that Mark and Dave Kane kept calling me to ask for copies of documents and tapes.

GREEN QUEST IS a supervising and coordinating task force that belongs to Customs. It includes FBI agents and IRS agents, and it works in close collaboration with the Office of Foreign Assets Control, OFAC, which also reports to Customs. Green Quest supervises local offices that lead investigations in their jurisdictions, and sometimes, as in the SAAR investigation, it is involved directly. OFAC assisted Green Quest. So did the FBI guys I was in contact with a couple of years before with regards to SAAR. Unlike their counterparts in Tampa, these FBI agents were cooperative and helpful, at least for a while. They forwarded Green Quest many documents they had. They, like Green Quest, seemed serious to me in the good number of months we worked together on the SAAR investigation; I never really understood why their investigation didn't take off.

For all practical purposes, Mark and Dave were in charge of the SAAR investigation. They were the ones who worked directly with me. Mark represented Green Quest, and Dave represented the Customs office in Sterling. They'd get the material from me, write a report, and show it to a federal prosecutor, who'd weigh in on whether enough was there to merit the going-forward investigation of 555. Mark and Dave were under tremendous pressure from their superiors. Everyone wanted to move as quickly as possible. So Mark and Dave on the government's side, and Sam, Jerome, and I in the office, worked very hard on 555. Mark and Dave practically worked day and night. I devoted most of my time to the investigation and their constant questions, although during this time I was doing a million and one other things as well. I conducted several investigations of my own; I collaborated with federal prosecutors and FBI, Customs, and INS agents from coast to coast. I continued to attend Muslim conferences and rallies. I even found time to search for clues in trash again.

"You mentioned Tariq Hamdi," Mark said to me one day. "How can you prove that he was in fact the one who delivered the phone to Bin Laden?"

I told him it was in the transcripts of the embassy bombing trial. I pulled out the relevant pages and within half an hour faxed them over to him.

He called again. "In the notes I took while you briefed us," he said, "I wrote that Hamdi was also tied to Sami. We couldn't find any mention of Hamdi's name in the documents we were allowed to see in Tampa."

I e-mailed him a picture from the publication of the University of South Florida, the *USF International Affairs Quarterly,* showing Sami and Hamdi sitting with Hassan Turabi, the Sudanese leader who hosted Bin Laden. Hamdi is identified there as a WISE associate. Moreover, WISE, according to research databases, had a P.O. box that was registered to Hamdi. I faxed Mark these documents.

A few minutes later he called again. "So how do you know Hamdi worked for IIIT?"

I told him that Tariq Hamdi was the publisher of IIIT's quarterly publication, *Islamiyat al-Ma'rifah* (*Islamization of Knowledge*). I found the file and faxed Mark the page from the publication with Hamdi's name.

He called again. "Okay, but how do you know he still works for them?"

Good question. I didn't know. But this was a fine time to find out. So I called IIIT—after hours, because I hoped I could get the information without speaking to a representative. The voice mail guided me through a list of choices. I chose the option of contacting the employees of IIIT. I listened to the recording, and sure enough, Hamdi had a voice mail box in the system. He was still working for IIIT, then. Long after it was common knowledge that Hamdi worked for Bin Laden, IIIT still had him on the payroll.

The next day Mark called and asked, "How can you tell that Hamdi was indeed involved in anything else linked to al-Qaeda besides that story with the satellite phone? Maybe this was a onetime gig where he didn't really know what he was doing?"

This too was a legitimate question, albeit a difficult one to answer. After all, the government didn't pursue any charges against Hamdi. He lives happily ever after, and his wife, Wafa Hozien, teaches in the Bethesda–Chevy Chase High School near Washington, D.C. She too was heavily involved in the activities of ICP in Tampa, where she met her husband; she was the managing editor of *Inquiry,* ICP's publication in English, and she served as Sami al-Arian's secretary.

Rumor had it that the FBI assumed that Hamdi had told them all he knew, and that there was no use in dealing with him any further.

But was that indeed the case? I found my file on CDLR. CDLR, the Committee for the Defense of Legitimate Rights, is a London-based Saudi dissident group that is an al-Qaeda front. From that file I pulled out newspaper clips from *al-Zaytuna,* the IAP publication, advertising the opening of a CDLR branch in the United States in the mid-1990s. In these ads two telephone numbers were published. I'd been unable to obtain information on those numbers in the past. As a government agent, however, Mark had access to investigative tools that I didn't. I gave the numbers to him, and two days later he called and told me that I was right: these two numbers did belong to Hamdi. So Hamdi was the CDLR representative in the United States and was thus tied to al-Qaeda in more than one way.

While Mark was cross-examining me on IIIT, Dave was pounding me with the Muslim World League. According to the way Mark and Dave addressed their questions, I understood that they were dividing between them the organizations connected to the SAAR network. They went, systematically, from one category to another. As I'd done years before, they started at the base of the pyramid, the U.S.-based organizations, and slowly made their way toward the pyramid's peak. When they got there, I knew, they'd find the Rajhi brothers. But at that point they were still climbing.

Dave, for instance, asked me how I could tie the designated Rabita Trust to MWL and to 555. I told him that Rabita, according to MWL's Web site, was a subsidiary of MWL. I told him that Rabita's director, Nasseef, listed his address at 555 Grove. I sent him all the corporate records showing the links to the address.

The reason Dave and Mark were unfamiliar with such basic facts as the contents of MWL's Web site was that they couldn't browse the Internet at work. If government agents were to browse sites such as MWL's on their office computers, the traces (signatures) left while visiting them might raise suspicions in those who operate the sites. Amazingly, there was only one computer in each of their offices that could not be traced as a government computer, and the queue for that machine is obviously long. After I taught Mark and Dave how to use the Internet to find documents, browse relevant sites, and figure out who ran these sites, along with the other research tools I often use, they began surfing late at night, at home.

For long months, the investigation continued in that fashion. Green Quest worked nights and weekends, and so did I. They came to my office at least once a week. They needed me, and I was always there for them. Thus between Mark and Dave, Green Quest was studying the ties between SAAR and terrorism. They needed my input for every single step of their investigation because they knew so little at first.

But they were enthusiastic. After 9-11 the government's priorities changed, and many agents were reassigned to counterterrorism. While some agents I'd worked with in the past had resented such reassignment, or even seen it as a demotion, Mark's and Dave's motivation and willingness to learn were sky-high. Working with such a team was an exhilarating experience for me, although it was very labor-intensive. I only had to say a thing once and they'd look into it immediately.

I'd never been involved with an investigation like this before, where the agents would take into consideration practically every word that came out of my mouth. For years I'd been used to hearing that my leads would be "forwarded," "looked into," and "considered"—attitudes that many a time led investigations nowhere. With Green Quest—not just with Mark and Dave and Marcy, but with the whole team—the story was completely different. They took seriously the information I provided and the investigation itself, and they learned religiously everything relating to it.

It had become clear to me that SAAR had been investigated by the government many times. OFAC had information on it, so did the FBI, and other agencies had also noticed that something fishy was going on at 555 Grove Street, Herndon, Virginia. But none of those agencies were able to tie the SAAR network to terrorism. The suspicions were there, but the investigations didn't lead anywhere.

Until I got involved, that is. Using only public records, I studied and researched and spent long nights and weekends delving deeper and deeper, until I put it all together. I made the connection and found the missing link between SAAR and terrorism. When Green Quest, with my guidance, looked deeper and used sources I had no access to, they were able to substantiate my findings. They told me that my information, combined with the backup of the classified information they had, provided solid grounds for investigation. They said that the stuff I couldn't see was better than I'd ever imagined. They too were becoming terrorist hunters.

FROM THE KINDS of questions Dave and Mark were asking me, I realized that they were working on a search warrant. Mark said that they were making significant progress with the investigation but had encountered serious problems when they tried to convince the U.S. attorney that the residences of some of the individuals linked to 555 Grove needed to be searched in addition to 555 itself. I'd explained to Green Quest that searching 555 alone would be insufficient; that examining the individuals involved in the network of companies—who incorporated what and with whom—was critical; and that the government had to investigate these individuals at least as carefully as the material at 555. But it seemed that the U.S. attorney found it highly unusual to search the residences of the directors of the companies, and therefore he requested more evidence before he'd authorize the search warrants.

On my own initiative I called him and asked what exactly was needed. He told me that it was a major problem to convince a judge that these individuals might have material at home that could shed light on the investigation. I said that the individuals were the important players, not the sham operations they had created as a smoke screen. He wasn't convinced and said that no judge would buy that. Then I came up with an idea. "What if," I told him, "I could show you that each of these individuals has incorporated a number of companies at 555, but used their residential addresses as the mailing addresses of these companies?"

"Prepare that list for me," he said, "and I promise you we'll go to their houses."

My staff and I sat for forty-eight hours, pulling out the records of each of those individuals and checking who used his residential address for his companies.

My list was approved by the U.S. attorney.

Then Mark called and said that although the other addresses were approved, the U.S. attorney didn't approve Hamdi's address. I told

Mark that when the battery was delivered to Hamdi, it was sent to his home address. Maybe he had other things sent there, too, that the government might want to know about. Mark called me later. Hamdi's house was now approved for search, too.

IN EARLY MARCH 2002, a government agent named Brandon called me at the office. He said he had a few questions and would like to stop by to discuss them. "What about?" I asked. When agents call me they usually want something specific, some leads or documents relating to a certain investigation. I always prepare material for such meetings, so I asked what I should prepare for him.

"We just want to get your opinion about something."

We? Opinion? This sounded very strange.

He asked to meet me as soon as possible, preferably the next day.

He showed up relatively early the following morning with a woman who presented herself as Anita. I asked them for their IDs and then I invited them in. They asked if we could shut the door to the office. On one of my walls was a huge chart of the SAAR network. On my computer monitor was a new SAAR chart I was working on, at Dave and Mark's request. Brandon and Anita sat down, and I expected the regular pleasant question-and-answer session where they ask for information and I do my best to provide it.

Brandon began. "We are aware of the fact that you are, ahem, very much involved in the investigation in Virginia. As you may have guessed, the day for the raids on these entities is approaching. And this is why we're here."

I certainly knew that they were making progress with the warrant, since I had provided much of the needed information for it. I also knew that the raids were going to be extensive, as I had been asked to provide proof for some of the locations that were to be raided, including the residential addresses I've mentioned.

"Go on?" I became uneasy. I couldn't see where this was leading.

"Well, we have certain concerns," he said. "Regarding the safety of agents in the field."

My throat dried up.

"What do you mean by that, exactly?" I asked in a whisper.

"In other words, we wanted to make sure that *they* won't be waiting for our agents out there."

I regained my composure. "Let me make sure I got it right," I said. "Are you here to ask me whether I called Barzinji, al-Alwani, or Jaghlit to inform them that Green Quest and Customs agents would be coming to raid their homes on such-and-such date? Do you suggest that I told them to wait for these agents with machine guns?"

I was shocked and humiliated as never before in my entire career.

"No, don't misunderstand, we were just worried and wanted to make sure that everything would go smoothly."

"Do you know who you're talking to?" I said, my tone sharp. "I don't know you, and you certainly don't know me or who I am. This is my investigation, my baby, my project—solely—and you accuse me of leaking it? This is all *my* knowledge. It all comes from public records. I can leak any of it as I please. No one can prevent me from leaking it. I could have leaked it anytime, months ago, or years ago. Everything Green Quest has comes from me. Everything. I sat and taught them everything from the beginning, and this is what I get in return?"

Anita tried to undo the damage, saying that they were only the messengers who'd been asked to come here, ask a few questions, and verify that the bad guys would be surprised and not the agents.

"Even a criminal in custody is informed that he is about to be questioned about his alleged crime. You could have at least told me what this was about before you came," I spat.

Now the tables had turned, and they were the ones on the defensive. They really didn't know who they were dealing with. But they never bothered to find out before they showed up in my office.

Brandon tried to change the subject. He looked at the chart on my monitor and asked what it was. I told him that I was putting it together for Green Quest. He asked for a copy. I printed out five copies for him, and then I said: "You see this? This all comes from public documents. And you know what—maybe this is not such a bad idea after all. Maybe I should share this with *The New York Times,* Sunday edition."

They looked horrified.

"Shame on you," I said. "I devoted my life to this cause, and you accuse me of being a double agent. Get out of my office. Right now. Session's over."

They scurried out of there.

I immediately called Marcy Futerman. She was out, and I was told she'd be out the entire week. I asked to speak with her assistant.

"What's going on?" I began firing the second he picked up the phone. "This is how you show your gratitude, sending a team to interview me?"

I didn't know if he or Marcy knew about the little incident, but this was the best way to find out. "Just tell me whether Marcy approved that."

"Marcy was informed about it, yes, but take my word for it, she would never have approved such a thing," he said. He was sincere, and I realized that Marcy was caught between a rock and a hard place. "You know how highly she thinks of you. But you must realize that some things are beyond her. There was nothing she could do to prevent it."

The next thing I did was page Mark. Uncharacteristically, it was hours before he replied. He was distraught. I was trying to tell him that I'd been questioned by some agents I'd never heard of, but he kept repeating that he had the feeling he was being followed.

"I can't seem to shake them. I had this feeling that I was followed throughout the day. I don't know what's happening, but someone's trying to pin something on me."

They're doing it to me too, I said.

"I don't know what they want of me, all I know is that I didn't do anything wrong," he insisted.

I called Dave. He, too, was upset. He, too, was under investigation.

Why do I deserve this? I thought. Every time I'm onto something good, every time an investigation is going well, I end up being investigated instead. It made me sad, and angry, and frustrated. This wasn't the first time I'd been investigated since that business with John Canfield. Not at all. There were other times, which I can't mention here.

But this time it went a step further: this was the first time that I was directly accused of endangering federal agents.

For many days I was gravely agitated. I couldn't focus on anything. I couldn't sleep. I had recurrent nightmares in which I was haunted by these agents who came to question me. I knew my phone was tapped, I knew I was being followed, I knew someone was listening to and recording every word I was saying. . . . Worst of all, I had no one to turn to for help. Whom could I call, the government? Maybe I *was* on the wrong side after all. Maybe, I thought, I should join 555, as these agents had suggested. I'd definitely be much safer in the arms of SAAR than in the government's.

I do what I do because I'm trying to make the United States a little safer, and this is the way the government thanks me.

A COUPLE OF WEEKS LATER, on March 20, 2002, I returned from a meeting out of the office to discover a pile of messages from journalists lying on my desk. I called the top one on the pile.

"So what do you make of these raids in Virginia?" the reporter asked.

"What are you talking about?" I guessed what he was referring to, but I wanted to make sure.

"Early this morning," he told me, "about a hundred and fifty agents from the FBI, police, Customs, and INS raided sixteen locations in Virginia and some poultry factory in Georgia. Haven't you heard? It's all over the news."

So Green Quest and other agents had raided eighteen different locations in Virginia tied to SAAR. It was the largest counterterrorism raid ever in U.S. history. The raids continued the following day. Some one hundred computer companies were subpoenaed as well.

Everyone knew about the raids. Everyone but me. I was the last to find out, and I watched the raids on TV, with feelings as mixed as one could ever have. Content that the raid took place on the one hand, but feeling used and abused on the other. This is how John Canfield must have felt when he was kicked off the PIJ investigation, I thought.

I took comfort in one point I found terribly amusing. I, an ex-Iraqi, was the only one capable of cracking down on the ex-Iraqi SAAR founders and their fiendish plot.

It takes one to catch one.

FOR TWO MONTHS AFTER the raids I didn't hear a word from Green Quest. Then one day Mark suddenly called and asked to see me.

"Why?" I said cynically. "Your investigation is over. You don't need me anymore."

He understood. "Please don't be cross," he said. "I couldn't talk to you. I too was under investigation. I was being followed, my phones were tapped, and I was questioned. I was miserable. They gave me a very hard time. Please don't give me any more grief. I don't deserve it."

What was this, I thought, another rerun of the story with John Canfield? What's wrong with these people who keep investigating the investigators?

"If you don't believe me," he continued, "talk to the U.S. attorney you worked with. He'll tell you. He and everyone else on the team were under investigation."

Mark, I knew, was not a guy to make something like that up. But I was curious, and I called the U.S. attorney to get his take. I didn't press him too much, because the whole thing was—and probably still is— under investigation. But he did verify everything Mark had told me. Practically everyone involved with the SAAR investigation had been under surveillance.

The FBI was among the agencies conducting that investigation.

No wonder! The FBI had long set its sights on this investigation, which became so major and so famous. The Bureau had already been meddling in the SAAR investigation in a manner less than gentlemanly; after the raids, people who had information about the SAAR network called to offer their tips. Unaware of who was in charge of the investigation, some of those people called and gave their tips to the FBI. The FBI, instead of forwarding the tips to the people in charge—Green Quest—kept the leads to themselves and initiated their own probes into those leads, sharing neither with Customs. Moreover, at some point, the two FBI agents in Virginia stopped helping Green Quest abruptly and completely. It was obvious that they'd been instructed to do that. The FBI continues to refuse to give Green Quest documents needed for its investigation. The FBI treats Green Quest worse than it does the enemy; *Zacarias Moussaoui* received from the FBI more documents pertaining to his investigation—including a good number of classified documents—than did Green Quest! And of course the ultimate scandal is that all this is taking place after 9-11.

Now, as I write these lines, the FBI is trying to take over the investigation altogether. Once again, a replay of the story with Sami al-Arian and with John Canfield. The FBI claims that Customs and Green Quest were rightfully the ones to initiate the investigation, when it seemed to be about money laundering. But now that it's become a terrorism-related matter, Customs is incapable, you see, of dealing with it. Isn't that peachy? Judging by what the FBI did with other investigations, if it indeed succeeds in taking over the SAAR probe, we can all kiss this investigation good-bye. How many terrorism-related successes can the FBI take the credit for? Not too many, that's for sure.

Yet the FBI wasn't the worst part in that sticky affair.

The CIA was.

The CIA was investigating me and the SAAR investigators from Green Quest and Customs.

The CIA and the FBI investigated everyone who had anything to do with the SAAR investigation. White vans and SUVs with dark windows appeared near all the homes of the SAAR investigators. All agents, some of whom were very experienced with surveillance, knew they were being followed. So was I. I felt that I was being followed everywhere and watched: at home, in the supermarket, on the way to work . . . and for what?

While undercover, I needed to watch out during the conference, the prayer, the rally. But I could relax as soon as I was out of there. Now— I was being watched 24/7. It's a terrible sensation to know that you have no privacy . . . and no security. That strange clicking of the phones that wasn't there before . . . the oh-so-crudely opened mail at home and in the office . . . and the same man I spied in my neighborhood supermarket, who was also on the train I took to Washington a week ago . . . Life can be miserable when you know that someone's always breathing down your neck.

The Customs agents were questioned. So were their supervisors. So was the U.S. attorney on the SAAR case. One of the questions they were all asked was whether they'd leaked material to me. They all kept saying that this was the most preposterous idea; they all said that before I came none of them had the slightest clue about SAAR and 555. They said that there was nothing of value they could give me that I didn't have already. That it was I who gave them the material, not the other way around. None of the investigated parties has the slightest clue as to the real reason they were being investigated.

Risking criticism for being unfoundedly paranoid, I must convey my theory about the investigation and the CIA's involvement in it. I don't know for certain what's the deal with the CIA investigating the SAAR investigators, but it sure feels as if someone up in that agency doesn't like the idea that the Saudi Arabian boat is rocked. The raids on 555 had taken place already—the CIA couldn't change that—but investigating and giving the people behind the raids a hard time is a most efficient way of making sure the SAAR investigation stops there.

Which, come to think of it, may be the reason the government looks so unfavorably on the lawsuit filed by 9-11 victims' families against several Saudi entities and individuals, accusing them of funding terrorism and seeking damages. Or is it something else? Is the CIA involved with SAAR because the Saudi men heading the network are in fact Iraqi and, as someone reliable had suggested to me, the CIA seeks these people's help in overthrowing Saddam Hussein's regime? Which, by the way, could be the reason the government never did anything to Tariq Hamdi—also an Iraqi—on whom there should have been more than enough material to prove he was a supporter of terrorism.

The CIA clearly has an agenda. I don't think any of us will know what it is, not in the foreseeable future.

But before an agency like that makes an alliance, it better be very careful who it chooses to go to bed with.

If the CIA is indeed trying to make such a deal again, with regard to Iraq or Saudi Arabia, all of us are in for a whole load of trouble. Not just because the SAAR investigation would be sabotaged, but mainly because collaborating with terrorists and their supporters, as history had proven again and again, may seem like a good idea at a some point in time, but in the long run it always ends up being a disaster.

The CIA helped Bin Laden in his war against the Soviets in Afghanistan, and look where it got us.

Epilogue

Spring 2003

"DO YOU REALLY THINK you have to do this?" Leo asked.

I felt I had to. The idea had been building up in me for quite some time. As I became increasingly involved with my career, I learned that outrageous and unbelievable things were happening right under everyone's noses. The more I thought about it, the more I understood that I had no choice but to tell the world about what I'd learned in my life as a terrorist hunter. "I think that people need to know, Leo. Much could be improved if only the problems became public."

The American public is under the impression that the various agencies had learned their lessons from the failure of 9-11 and are working now in close collaboration, supporting one another. Well, they still aren't. Certainly not in the numerous investigations I've been involved with.

"If I write about it, Leo, it could make things happen."

"What about your own safety, then? This is going to make quite a few people angry."

Leo was right. What I'd write would infuriate quite a few people—both the terrorists and certain agencies of the U.S. government. Being a mother and a wife didn't make the decision easier, either. Such a book could endanger my family. I thought about it very carefully. And I realized that there was no choice, really. I had to do it.

Until this book, everything I'd done as a terrorist hunter was incognito. I'd caused some serious damage to many bad guys and bad organizations, but I'd always remained behind the scenes. This enabled me to go undercover when needed. But if I wanted to continue to work, there was no way I could go public with this book, so I had to write it anonymously. Fame and recognition are not what I seek, so this was not a problem.

I needed to find a way to *stay* anonymous after the book was published. I realized that I'd have to go even deeper underground. To continue to do what I do best—hunt terrorists—I'd have to change my address, go into hiding, maybe even move to another country. My life, and my family, could be in jeopardy, and to minimize the risk, our lives would have to be utterly transformed.

As I wrote, I wondered whom I should worry about the most. IAP? HLF? Ghassan Dahduli? Yousef al-Qaradawi, perhaps? Qaradawi is an eminent Muslim cleric with millions upon millions of followers. He's as big with his followers as the pope is in the Catholic world. How many of these followers will want to take revenge on me for blocking their spiritual leader from coming to America? After all, it takes only one fanatic to cause irreparable harm. And how many Saudis and Iraqis involved in SAAR will go berserk to find out that I, an Iraqi-born Jew, and, worse still, a woman, have caused so much damage to them? They certainly don't lack the resources or volunteers to find me and make me pay for what I did.

But will these be my only enemies? What about the FBI, for instance? Or the CIA? Or the State Department? I hardly believe that any of those agencies would choose me for their "Person of the Year" award. I've demonstrated that many things in the government's infrastructure are broken even now, after 9-11, and urgently in need of fixing. While a good number of government agents will thank me for disclosing things about the FBI they wish they could reveal themselves, others will obviously hate me for what I've written. Although I've abstained from discussing events that could hamper ongoing investigations and have done my best not to provide details that will trigger new investigations of agents, I know that the book is going to set off a mass of new inquiries. Anyone who's ever been in touch with me will be investigated. Federal agents, U.S. attorneys, even journalists; I can vouch for that. But will the government be satisfied with that? Or will someone up there decide that I've done enough damage already and need to be dealt with before I do some more?

Leo and the kids had to be part of the decision to write the book. It'd be their sacrifice, too; they'd go through a lot of hardship if I published my story. They'd have to move *again,* give up their current life, hide, and in effect be under house arrest. They will go back with me to the hut in Baghdad in more than one way. I already suffer frequent nightmares about harm coming to them.

Ours is a strange world indeed: we, the good people, have to hide, while terrorists enjoy all the freedoms of the West.

In spite of all that, I knew I was going forward with the book. Because some of the things I've learned in the past few years have to become public if change is ever to occur. I'm a great believer in the power of media and public opinion as catalysts of change. My wish is that the tremendous power of the people will be set into motion as a result of this book. The people need to know that the threat of Islamic fundamentalism is strong and getting stronger, and that the government has to urgently rethink the ways it deals with this threat.

As long as imams preach violence, violence won't be eradicated. These imams live with us; they're our neighbors. They preach in the mosque around the corner. Their followers listen, absorb, and learn. Some of them, albeit not many, will decide to take the next step and turn words into actions.

And as long as we call terrorist supporters "friends and allies," we are headed for disaster. We should never allow such a calamity as the

9-11 attacks to happen again. Countries that sponsor, fund, and educate for jihad should not be allowed to extort any deals from us, either through the ridiculous threat that if a Middle Eastern regime is destabilized a worse one follow in its place or through oil-related blackmail. No regime could be worse than one that pays for jihad.

Our government does take terrorism more seriously than ever before, but it still doesn't go about it the way it should—by studying these organizations as I do. It concentrates its efforts on chasing terrorists, but it still doesn't learn the reasons they became terrorists in the first place.

I'll always do my best to help the government capture, deport, or imprison terrorists. While these are necessary steps in eradicating the problem of terrorism, they will never by themselves lead to a solution. Perhaps this book will help people understand that terrorism needs to be uprooted, not just by trying to stop specific attacks, but also by choking the ideology behind them. Because by the time you catch one terrorist, fifteen others have been trained in his place. Likewise, disregarding terrorists because they're Hamas and not al-Qaeda, or PIJ instead of Hizballah, is a deadly mistake. These organizations carry different names, but they're all one and the same. Wherever terrorism exists, it must be uprooted.

The bottom line is that to win this war, education in countries that sponsor terrorism has to change, and funding for terrorists has to stop. This should be done through application of political and economic pressure. It may take a generation to achieve, but this is the only way terrorism can be eradicated.

Until that happens, government agencies have to rethink the strategy they use to combat terrorism. Not only on paper, but in real life as well. Talking about homeland security won't do the trick by itself. If counterterrorism agents still know nothing about the roots and history of Islam, if they don't know how to search the public domain to find such basic records as IRS 990 tax forms, if they won't even browse the Web to learn about the opposition, if they insist on relying only on intelligence information, which is often inadmissible in court, terrorists will continue to stay ahead of us each and every step. As long as investigations of Saudi businesses and citizens are blocked by government agents, as long as the good guys are being investigated instead of the terrorists, and as long as agencies—namely, the FBI—refuse to share information with others and even sabotage those other U.S. government investigations, this war will not be won by America. If the public understands the gravity of the situation, this story might have a happier outcome.

When Leo and I weighed whether or not I should write this book, I knew that if I let fear or concern for my personal safety keep me from doing it, I'd be sitting in a rocking chair in front of the fireplace with him a few decades from now, and I'd be telling him, "See, Leo, had I written the book, things could've been different."

I'd never have forgiven myself that I didn't. I'd never have been able to look myself in the eye.

MANY TIMES, when undercover in a mosque or, far worse, while being followed and taped by government agents, a thought has troubled me: Why can't I lead a normal life? Why can't I sit lazily in a café like other people, go to the gym, enjoy the things others enjoy? Why do I need these repeated aggravations? Why do I subject myself to learning about outrage after outrage, whether it comes in the form of statements by Muslim leaders or in the U.S. government's bungling of terrorism investigations?

Because I feel that I have to. If I don't, who will?

In fact, others could easily do what I do. Sam and Jerome joined me knowing nothing about terrorism, and now, a little over a year later, they're as good as I am at obtaining information and using it.

Anyone can do it. Will is all that's needed to be a terrorist hunter.

We are at war, whether we want it or not. On 9-11, we were all recruited. We can and we will win this war, because we have progress and freedom and justice on our side. We are the good guys.

It's my honor to be on the front lines of this war. It's the right thing to do, and this is who I am. This is what my father would have wanted me to be.

May we all live in peace.